The Culture of Oklahoma

The Culture of Oklahoma

Edited by
Howard F. Stein
and
Robert F. Hill

Foreword by Fred R. Harris

University of Oklahoma Press : Norman and London

This book is published with the generous assistance of the Wallace C. Thompson Endowment Fund, University of Oklahoma Foundation.

Library of Congress Cataloging-in-Publication Data

The Culture of Oklahoma / edited by Howard F. Stein and
　　Robert F. Hill ; foreword by Fred R. Harris.—1st ed.
　　　　p.　cm.
　　Includes bibliographical references and index.
　　ISBN 0-8061-2498-9 (alk. paper)
　　1. Oklahoma—Civilization.　I. Stein, Howard F.　II. Hill,
Robert F.
F694.5.C84　　1993　　　　　　　　　　　92-50722
976.6—dc20　　　　　　　　　　　　　　　CIP

The paper in this book meets the guidelines for permanence and durability of the Committee on Production Guidelines for Book Longevity of the Council on Library Resources, Inc. ∞

1　2　3　4　5　6　7　8　9　10

Contents

Illustrations

MAPS

TABLES

Foreword

It might have been because, on a senior trip three or four years earlier to Washington, D.C., one young woman got pregnant. Or it might have been that the members of my sister's class, two years ahead of mine, were a little too rowdy and hard to handle on their senior trip to Carlsbad Caverns. Or maybe it was just because our school was perennially hard pressed for money.

Whatever the reason, the senior trip for my 1948 graduating class at Walters High School was restricted to a week-long tour of Oklahoma—in one of the school's own buses! What, some students asked indignantly, was there worth seeing in Oklahoma that we had not already seen? What was there to learn about our state that we did not already know?

A lot, as it turned out. And the senior trip of the WHS class of 1948 wound up being at least as impressive as any before it and, for many of us, a good deal more memorable and worthwhile. Our trip took us east, because we were from the western part of the state, and when we got back home afterwards—back from the oil wells pumping on the state capitol's grounds, from the Five Civilized Tribes center of Muskogee, from Turner Falls and Devil's Den and the Will Rogers Memorial, from the Arkansas River and the Cross Timbers and a lot of places and a lot of different people in between—we knew more, not just about the geography and interesting places of Oklahoma, but about its history and people as well. And we felt more like Oklahomans, somehow.

It was Jean Paul Sartre who wrote of culture that "it is a product of man [and woman]; he projects himself into it; he recognizes himself in it; that critical mirror alone offers him his image." Those of us who took that long-ago senior trip inside Oklahoma began, then, to develop in our heads a self-image of Oklahoma's culture.

It *does* mean something distinct to be an Oklahoman. There is, as this book so richly and interestingly demonstrates, an Oklahoma cultural identity. Despite the fact that when I was growing up in Walters we could cross Red River by car and be in Burkburnett, Texas, in thirty minutes or less, we never once thought of ourselves as Texans. And it was not just the river that separated the two peoples. An imaginary line worked— and still works—just as well. People in Boise City know they are not Texans, either—or Kansans or New Mexicans or Colo-radans. Those who live in Durant never get confused enough to call themselves Texhomans, nor those in Broken Bow, Ar-kansans. From Mickey Mantle's hometown of Commerce you can drive to Joplin in a short while, but none of his old neigh-bors would ever explain that they are from the Show-Me State.

People know they are Oklahomans, even, as I can testify, when they no longer live in the state. Years ago I was in Mo-desto, California, campaigning one Sunday afternoon in bowl-ing alleys and cafes for Representative George Miller's first election to the U. S. House of Representatives. In each place I was immediately able to grab the attention of the otherwise-occupied denizens by calling out the question, "Anybody here from Oklahoma?" Always there was a chorus of immediate responses: "Yeah!" "You bet!" "Damn right!" Talk to many of these people and you found out that although they might have been living in California for twenty years, they still con-sidered themselves Oklahomans.

What is an Oklahoman? That is the subject of this volume of excellent essays. The late Dewey Bartlett, when he was governor of Oklahoma, pushed, with lapel pins and promo-tions, to make "Okie" a term of pride. I thought it was a good idea. But most Oklahomans did not. Many were incensed. "Old John Steinbeck made us look bad," a great number of

Oklahomans have said to me, one way or another, through the years. I do not agree. Steinbeck showed Okies as tough people, with grit, working hard to keep body and soul together in incredibly hard times.

Part of Oklahoma's cultural identity is, indeed, made up of that image that comes out of *The Grapes of Wrath*—and of the real people who lived that way, some who had to leave, most who stayed. But there is more, too, as the editors of this book, Howard F. Stein and Robert F. Hill, and the other writers so ably show. Oklahoma's culture is not simple, one-dimensional. Whose is?

The culture of Oklahoma is part cowboy and part Indian. It is part land rush and part Trail of Tears. It is part oil and part dirt. It is part rolled-up sleeves and part boardroom, part Walters and part Tulsa. Oklahomans are the "just plain folks" that former Governor Johnston Murray's slogan appealed to, as well as all those uncommon people who stand up proudly in dress clothes when they hear Richard Rodgers's "Oklahoma!"

Oklahomans are pioneers. Virtually everyone who first came to the state—and that includes nearly all the original Native Americans, too—came from somewhere else. I think it was that great University of Oklahoma history professor, the late Dr. E. E. Dale, who first showed me that if you were to shrink down an old-time map of America to the size of the Sooner state, Oklahoma Indian tribes would still show up in roughly the same geographic quadrants of the state as they once occupied in the nation before removal. And something similar can be said about so many of the non-Indians who came to the state, too. It is no accident that southeastern Oklahoma is called Little Dixie.

Oklahoma is a kind of composite of America writ small, and if America, as John Kennedy once wrote, is "a nation of immigrants," Oklahoma is a state of internal immigrants. It is indeed "the pioneer state."

Alexander Pope wrote correctly, I think, that "the proper study of mankind is man [and woman]." *The Culture of Oklahoma* is that kind of fundamentally important study. In giving attention to our common cultural identity as Oklahomans, we hold a mirror up to our own faces. We see ourselves in context, and our collective self-image comes more clearly into focus.

FRED R. HARRIS

Albuquerque, New Mexico
1992

Acknowledgments

The editors acknowledge with gratitude the numerous and generous suggestions made by Professor William W. Savage, Jr., in the earliest phase of this book's conception. To Thomas R. Radko, formerly acquisitions editor of the University of Oklahoma Press, and John Drayton, editor of the Press, goes our gratitude for their encouragement and steadfastness of interest in the fruition of this project. Laine McCarthy generously prepared the graphics for a number of figures in this book. The Oklahoma Historical Society of Oklahoma City was repeatedly helpful to us in our historical and bibliographic inquiries. Finally, to Margaret A. Stein go the editors' thanks for both the magnitude as well as the quality of her proofreading and word processing. That this book exists bears testimony to her grasp of details as well as the project's overall scope.

HOWARD F. STEIN
ROBERT F. HILL

Oklahoma City, Oklahoma

Introduction

BY HOWARD F. STEIN AND ROBERT F. HILL

This book describes and interprets Oklahoma as a cultural identity system. It explores the emergence, consolidation, meanings, and consequences of the often ineffable sense of "Oklahomaness," a sense of distinctiveness and uniqueness held by both insiders and outsiders alike. It is a study of images that vie for that sense of group identity and of the significance these images hold for those who invest in them. Contributors from many fields show how, for Oklahoma as for other cultural identity systems, Oklahomaness often comes to be experienced as the measure of life itself. This work considers numerous facets of Oklahoma culture and views of its history and in doing so analyzes insiders' and outsiders' attachment to the notion of Oklahoma culture. An earlier book, *Oklahoma: New Views of the Forty-Sixth State*, edited by Anne Hodges Morgan and H. Wayne Morgan, attempted to "set the history of Oklahoma in regional and national contexts" (1982, ix). The present volume expands upon that effort, showing how people in Oklahoma, in the region, and in the nation continuously shape and reaffirm the Oklahoma identity.

This book examines the ingredients of Oklahoma's cultural distinctiveness and describes in turn how this very cultural identity helps shape the content, form, and selection of these ingredients. In delineating what is distinctively Oklahoma— that is, the boundaries of an identity and the contents within it—this book establishes Oklahoma as a bona fide cultural system. It shows Oklahoma to be not merely a geopolitical organization somehow constituent of real subcultures (for example, ethnic and religious ones; see *Newcomers to a New Land* 1980) and in turn participatory in a real national culture (that of the United States), but also, as a cultural system, a mediator of these both. Its anthropological compass is not limited to traditional anthropological categories of band, chiefdom, tribe, ethnic group, nation-state (although it will encompass them). Rather, this book will show how a state politically contained within a nation-state can evolve and possess its own cultural meaning system, one which simultaneously is shared by, has functions in, and is mirrored in the national image. In 1907, Oklahoma became the forty-sixth state in the Union; this book explores the many facets of the cultural state of mind that underlie Oklahoma's geopolitical existence (see Map I.1).

Using Oklahoma as a case study, the editors and contributors explore the dynamics and history of the sense of Oklahomaness and the consequences of its symbolism and imagery. We contend that whatever else Oklahoma is and does, Oklahoma is, like any other "collective representation" (Durkheim 1912) and "group-fantasy" (deMause 1982), first and foremost a state of mind.

To date, anthropologists, historians, political scientists, and other scholars have written prolifically on the issue of culture with respect to small-scale societies (for example, bands, tribes, and corporations) and large groupings (for example, nation-states and nationality or ethnic groups bounded within empires or nation states). Comparatively little, however, has been written on the cultural identity systems (Spicer 1971), and their boundaries, of more intermediate groups such as states, provinces, counties, cities, and the like (except as they are frequently associated with ethnic entities: for example, the French Canadian province of Québec; the Ibo region in Biafra and Nigeria; or famous cities such as New York, Vienna, Berlin, and Paris). This book begins to fill this void through a study of Oklahoma as an identity system, one with boundaries and distinct iconography (symbols repre-

Map I.1. Oklahoma's situation within the United States.

senting that identity) largely agreed upon within the state, the region, and the nation. Howard F. Stein has lived in Oklahoma since 1978, and Robert F. Hill is a native of Oklahoma, having grown up in Anadarko and Stillwater. Both as editors and contributors, we likewise draw upon our ethnographic experience in this state. As well as being a contribution to the cultural study of a single state within the United States, this study might serve as a model for studying any group identity system and the consequences of that system for group development.

Fifteen years ago, in *The Ethnic Imperative*, we wrote of the late Renaissance, the Age of Exploration, and the Enlightenment image of America as the "last best hope of mankind":

Before America was a nation, it was a land; before it was a land, it was in idea, a dream, and a hope. There was an American Dream more than three centuries before the Revolution embodied it in the ideology of a nation; the nation was created in the image of its vision and ideal. The American Dream was born in the decline of feudalism and the Middle Ages, first in England and western Europe, spreading eastward through the nineteenth century, and is now something of a universal model of liberation and modernization. (Stein and Hill 1977*a*, 50)

The five Oklahoma land rushes beginning with the famous Run of '89, the opportunism of "founding father" David L. Payne and of the expansive railroads, and the enthusiasms—not to say excesses—of the "Boomers" and the "Sooners," are all late-nineteenth-century expressions of another American dream, that of free land (see Lamar, this volume, for discussion of Oklahoma land runs, and Nuckolls, this volume, for discussion of David L. Payne). Thus, when frontier historian Howard R. Lamar (1989) depicts the Oklahoma land rushes as "the most American frontier," he calls attention to the fact that historically, long before Oklahoma became a state (in 1907), it occupied a special mental space in the American imagination—one which Richard Rodgers and Oscar Hammerstein II *could* build on in 1943 because it was culturally there ready for them *to* build upon.

That mental space in national folklore swiftly became realized through a series of land openings. Five land runs and a later lottery form the territorial baseline upon which Oklahomaness was built: (1) the run on April 22, 1889, to the Unassigned Lands; (2) the run on September 22, 1891, to the Iowa, Sac and Fox, and Pottawattomie-Shawnee Reservation; (3) the run on April 19, 1892, to the Cheyenne-Arapaho Reservation; (4) the run on September 16, 1893, to the Cherokee Outlet; (5) the run on May 23, 1895, to the Kickapoo Reservation; and (6) a land lottery on August 16, 1901, to Kiowa-Comanche land. The Panhandle jutting westward from the northwest corner of the state was added by the Organic Act on May 2, 1890.

The crux of our argument, and the major theoretical contribution of this volume, is that Oklahoma is a genuine cultural identity system. It is a culture with boundaries and distinctive features identified both from within and from without. In our view, a culture is where the observer finds it and where the inhabitants claim and construct it (Hill, Fortenberry, and Stein 1990; Stein and Hill 1977*a*, 1977*b*, 1988; Stein 1977, 1980, 1990). Far from being limited to traditional and conventional ethnological categories of band, tribe, chiefdom, ethnic group, and nation state, in contemporary U.S. society cultural identifications and structures can assume such temporary or permanent forms as disability or chronic illness identities, corporate or professional occupational cultures, age-graded (adolescent, geriatric) cultures, religious denominations or cults, ethnic cultures (Euro-American, Vietnamese, the multiplicity of Hispanic groups, Afro-American, and so on), and even the distinctive cultures of sex (male, female) and sexual identification (straight, gay).

An individual might well elect to participate intensively in one of these or two or several for brief or long periods of time, even a lifetime. For example, one could be deeply involved for decades as a member of a wheat-farming family, as a Southern Baptist, and as a member of a male group of hunters for quail and turkey. Another individual might pass rapidly from one identity system to another, trying one then another on for "fit," or alternatively, might well affiliate with different cultural identity systems situationally during a single component or stage of the life cycle. For example, early in adulthood one person might more consciously affiliate with the German or English part of his or her ancestry, but at a later phase, identify with the specifically Cherokee or Choctaw, or more broadly Indian, part of his or her family. Likewise, during a given period of life a person might identify at an annual ethnic festival with being Czech or Bohemian, identify occupationally as a General Motors worker, identify at church with being Roman Catholic, and identify closely with the town with respect to pride in its football team.

Moreover, people are increasingly choosing and changing their conscious identities (Waters 1990; Erikson 1974), with the result that identity is becoming less something one is or has lifelong, fixed by birth, but more something that one makes and remakes by conscious choice throughout life. At the level of theory, what unites this often dizzying array of identities and cultural fragments is Erik H. Erikson's dual-faceted concept of identity: "It is a process 'located' *in the core of the individual* and yet also *in the core of his communal culture,* a process which establishes, in fact, the identity of those two identities" (emphasis in original, 1968, 22).

Now, personal identity is not static; neither is it consistent. It contains a dynamic composite of positive and negative images of the good self—the self consciously and unconsciously aspired to—and the bad self—the self consciously and unconsciously devalued if not repudiated. Erikson writes that "each *positive identity* is also defined by *negative* images. . . . The positive identity, far from being a static constellation of traits or roles, is always in conflict with that past that is to be lived down and with that potential future which is to be prevented" (emphasis in original, 1968, 299, 303). The contributors to this study will thoroughly document that, whatever being Oklahoman *is,* it is inextricably tied to the definition of what Oklahoma *is not,* or tries not to be, or strives to live down.

Like all cultural identity systems, Oklahoma culture abounds in nuances and contradictions, many of which are not supposed to be noticed, let alone acknowledged, by those with cultural probity. The name *Oklahoma,* meaning "Red People," as derived from the Choctaw language (*okla,* "people"; *humma* or *homma,* "red"; Wright 1974, vii), was first

applied to the Indian Territory in the Choctaw-Chickasaw treaty of 1866 signed in Washington, D.C., by the Choctaw and the Chickasaw delegates and federal commissioners. The treaty provided details for the organization of a territorial government in this as yet unorganized region. . . . The organization of the Indian Territory was not completed under the provisions of the treaties of 1866. The name "Oklahoma," however, became popular and was widely known throughout the country, appearing in several bills providing for the organization of the Indian Territory introduced in Congress, none of which was enacted and approved, during a period of nearly twenty years. (Wright 1974: vii)

The naming of the bifurcated territory, following the opening of the 1,880,000 acres of the so-called Unassigned Lands to white homesteading in 1889, as Oklahoma Territory and the "last Indian Territory" is ironic, if not symbolic, because it was the Oklahoma (Red People) Territory that was to be the Euro-American stronghold: it was named for one people and settled by another. Contributors to this volume will delineate and interpret the numerous cultural contradictions in the Oklahoman identity. Throughout this book we establish the definition of what Oklahoma is, both from within and outside Oklahoma, through contrasts and oppositions.

For example, the pursuit of law and morality occur in high tension with the condemnation—and admiration—of the outlaw and of those defiant individualists who defy the law in the name of personal duty or aspirations (such as Colonel Oliver North, popular in Oklahoma, who, within the Ronald Reagan White House, circumvented American law in order to provide considerable military aid to the Nicaraguan Contras). Similarly, many Oklahomans contrast their humility, one-downmanship, and Evangelical Protestant quiet workmanship with Texan bravado, extravagant partying, and overweening bigness. This tension between positive and negative, avowed and disavowed Oklahoma identity is also played out within the state boundaries.

Like a veritable geological fault line that runs long and deep, the rift between rural and urban pervades both Oklahoma history and current culture alike. In the popular imagination—Oklahoman, regional, national, international—Oklahoma is a rural state. The chapters by Pat Bellmon on farming communities and by Arn Henderson on the equation of Oklahoma architecture with sod houses and grain silos and the like confirm how rurality has captured the mythic imagination.

Many Oklahomans, including many inhabitants of Tulsa, do not regard Tulsa as being culturally, even geographically, subsumed inside Oklahoma. Many regard it as part of "back East," a kind of foreign implant from New York or Chicago. Many Oklahomans label its cosmopolitanness, its aura of aristocracy, its cliquishness, as alien to, and violating, the open egalitarianism and "plainness" valued elsewhere in Oklahoma. In terms of identity, Oklahomans often portray Tulsa as external to their ideal cultural system. To put this in a different Oklahoma idiom, if Oklahoma is ideally a rural state, then the presence of Tulsa is too urban to be encompassed within the Oklahoma identity. If, for identity reasons,

Oklahoma *must* be rural, then perceptually, emotionally, it *will* be rural.

Through an exploration of Oklahoma culture and history, this book will demonstrate that the nature of cultural boundaries is far more problematic than many social scientists, and native peoples everywhere, contend. What is a cultural boundary? To begin with, although cultural boundaries might be demarcated by political borders (such as those between states or nations or cities), they are not limited to these. It might better be asked: Where is something located in extensional space? We take boundaries' "thereness" for granted, yet they first and foremost exist in the imagination, built from our experience of our own bodies and those of our early caretakers (Stein and Niederland 1989). Projected outward and subsequently reincorporated, boundaries come to "exist" in reality by the strength of group consensus (literally, "sensing together") on what a group is and where it is located "out there"—where it begins, where it ends, how to recognize it. Most important, whether for Oklahomaness or any other group boundary, is the fact that it is first *imagined*.

Boundaries, together with their cultural contents, are constantly being revised by groups' members. While a geographic boundary is perhaps the most commonly understood type of cultural boundary, a boundary can take literally any symbolic form as long as it serves the mental function of distinguishing "us" from "them." In addition to geopolitical boundaries, clothing styles, musical forms, food preferences, language and dialect, and body posture, to name but a few cultural elements, can all delineate cultural boundaries.

The nature of Oklahomaness is formed, constituted, and continuously revised through a constant interplay between people inside and outside Oklahoma. There is constant interplay between "us" and "them." How Oklahomans perceive and feel about themselves and about those outside Oklahoma interacts with how non-Oklahomans perceive and feel about Oklahoma, which in turn reflects what they perceive and feel about themselves. The geopolitical boundaries of Oklahoma notwithstanding, both inside and outside are essential to the creation and sustenance of Oklahoma's image and boundary. Psychologically, there is a constant interaction between the internalization of others' images and the externalization of Oklahomans' images onto others.

Thus, the Oklahoma identity, which superficially appears to be indigenous to Oklahoma—home grown, as it were—is in fact a reciprocal cultural creation between inside and outside, between Oklahoma and non-Oklahoma. Stated differently, Oklahomaness, like all cultural identities, is a shared fiction or carefully crafted illusion between those who are and those who are not Oklahomans. Just as Jews do not exist apart from Gentiles, Greeks from Turks, Serbs from Croats, New Guinea Mountain Arapesh from Plains Arapesh, Soviets from Americans, and the like (see Stein 1987a, 1987b), so also Oklahomans are bound up in an inner representational system shared with and reciprocally constructed by non-Oklahomans. At the same time, Oklahomans ardently assert their distinctiveness if not uniqueness and superiority. One ubiquitous Oklahoma automobile bumper sticker reads, "It's hard to be humble when you're a Sooner."

This book shows that (1) "Oklahoman" denotes a genuine identity system (Erikson 1968); (2) many people link important themes in their lives to a global sense of being Oklahoman, even to the extent of making Oklahomaness the object of their "primary role identification" (Rohrer and Edmonson 1964); and (3) when taken to the extreme, this identity becomes a narrow, overly invested, constricted one that has the emotionally straitjacketing effect (Devereux 1975) of what De Vos (1978) called "role narcissism," an identity that feels like a highly defended fortress. This book explores this interpretive framework in relation to several cultural content areas, including the concept of "Oklahoma" itself.

In describing, interpreting, and delineating the boundaries of a distinctive sense of Oklahomaness, we wish to avoid what Alfred North Whitehead (1925) once called the fallacy of misplaced concreteness and what Peter Berger and Thomas Luckmann (1966, 106) termed the commonplace error of reification. To commit the fallacy of misplaced concreteness is to ascribe to, displace onto, nature or society what are in fact our own thoughts and feelings. Similarly, in reifying an idea, people fail to recognize that they are the authors of that idea, that it does not exist independently "out there" apart from their own motivated perceptions.

On the one hand, there is no such thing or independent entity (in the Platonic sense) as "Oklahoma." It does not exist in nature. It is a human creation, a symbolic artifact of the interplay of many human imaginations. Yet many people, both within and outside Oklahoma, perceive, believe, and act as if a group called "Oklahoma" is real, just as members of tribes, corporations, and nation-states confer upon themselves emotion-laden meaning and comfort by fancying their group to be real if not immortal.

Cultural identities can be known through the various senses: sight, hearing, taste, smell, and touch. For example, all cultures project outwardly what that culture ought to look like, its visual identity. The other senses likewise have their characteristic "flavors." Oklahoma examples abound: cowboys, wheat farmers, sod houses, and grain silos; flat land and enormous vistas of sky; biscuits and gravy, beef steak, and corn grits; country and western music and bluegrass bands; the scent of freshly cut wheat, alfalfa, and hay and of cow and horse manure; the gritty taste, touch, and smell of wind-blown iron-rich red dirt. These all, in turn, constitute the positively valued portion of Oklahoma's visual and other sensing identities: what Oklahomans project outward as good.

Actual cultural diversity in Oklahoma is often obscured by these sensory identities that act as cultural filters and blinders. Manufacturing looms far larger economically in Oklahoma than does farming. In the state's internal and external myth, Oklahoma remains an agricultural, not an industrial, state. The existence of a wide spectrum of musical styles performed and enjoyed in Oklahoma, or the great variety of architectural types distributed throughout the state, tends to be forgotten, ignored, if not outright suppressed for ideological, political, religious, and other purposes. The visual and other sensory identities that characterize the sense of Oklahomaness refer to what people *ideologically* include within the boundary of their imagination rather than all that is actually present.

There are other anomalies, distortions, and omissions from the Oklahoma cultural landscape—reflected in what is and what is not contained in this book. Native Americans, despite their numerical presence in Oklahoma, are accorded at best a ceremonial presence in Oklahoma's visual identity. For example, Stein has noted and lamented for years, as he has taught physicians, most of whom are white, in their internship and residency, that few of them are interested in learning about Indian culture in urban and rural clinics. Only when the doctors do rotations in designated Indian hospitals (to perform numerous high risk obstetrical procedures to gain numbers of deliveries, among other procedures) are they forced to notice Indian ways and to inquire about Native American culture. Except for such rare contacts, it is as if, for all practical purposes, Indians did not exist in Oklahoma at all. Their day-to-day life, apart from important ceremonial and folkarts functions, is wholly set apart from mainstream white society and imagination. It is their use as a romantic image in the lore and mystique of Oklahoma, rather than their diversity and anonymity (Henderson 1974) that is central to the Oklahoma cultural identity we discuss in this book. Oklahoma African Americans likewise struggle with invisibility (combined with an often painful public exposure) and voicelessness with respect to shaping the official Oklahoma culture. In contrast with Native Americans, African Americans have a history of official segregation and lack the romanticization that at least accords Indians with a partly positive identity.

This book traces the origins of Oklahomaness, factors that make it persist, and consequences of reifying this sense of place. Once the concept of "Oklahoma" and the identity of Oklahomaness seize the imagination, they become frozen in the consciousness. We tend to forget that, like all social categories, that concept was created and its map was projected from the mind onto the globe. Yet, ultimately, it is not permanently there at all. Similarly, based on ethnographic studies of national and ethnic identification in Quebec and Hawaii, Richard Handler and Jocelyn Linnekin question the "primordialist" conceptualization of ethnicity: "There is no essential, bounded tradition; tradition is a model of the past and is inseparable from the interpretation of tradition in the present. . . . The invention of tradition is not restricted to such self-conscious projects [as cultural revivalism or nativism]. Rather, the ongoing reconstruction of tradition is a facet of all social life which is not natural but symbolically constituted" (Handler and Linnekin 1984, 276). Oklahomaness, like ethnicity, undergoes constant revision, updating, and reinvention. Although people in fact might experience their culture(s) as a permanent birthmark, people are constantly changing their identities (see Waters 1990). The crucial theoretical question and fateful issue for Oklahoma identity and all human group identities is: How do our created images come to exercise their powerful if not strangulating hold upon us? (based on Ebel 1989).

An anthropological study into that identity system, this volume is not written wholly by anthropologists. Rather, the selection of contributors from a wide spectrum of disciplines and professions was based upon the individuals' willingness to address the way a particular topic illustrated that elusive Oklahomaness. This volume, like all cultural ethnographic accounts, is not complete: alas, each reader will invariably be disappointed to find a favorite topic omitted. Yet a complete ethnographic record is also a conceit of the imagination and an unattainable fiction. There are, for example, no chapters specifically devoted to Native American tribal groups. This is partly a result of the editors' emphasis in this book on the ideological dimension of Oklahoma culture—that is, as a mind-set, an ideal, rather than as a far more complex reality. The goal of this book is to delineate and decipher the central organizing themes that are played out and continuously reworked in ongoing cultural variations. This book contains eleven chapters, each of which examines a distinctive facet of Oklahoma culture.

In chapter 1, geographer Gary L. Thompson establishes the material baseline, so to speak, of regional geology, geography, meteorology, flora, and fauna out of which the Oklahoma identity was fashioned and onto which it has been projected. In chapter 2, frontier historian Howard R. Lamar considers the various origin myths—interpretations of the founding of Oklahoma—that are popularly viewed as courageous or ignoble beginnings and that serve as the point of reference for cultural and political claims in the present. In chapter 3, historian James M. Smallwood and graduate student Crispin A. Phillips explore the history of blacks in Oklahoma and the pervasiveness of the racial triad black-white-red in the sense of Oklahomaness. In chapter 4, anthropologist Donald N. Brown examines Oklahoma's demography with a keen eye to the interplay among ethnic-national-tribal groups and the distillation of the Oklahoma identity. In chapter 5, anthropologist Robert F. Hill, public health specialists Glenn W. Solomon and Jane K. Tiger, and behavioral epidemiologist J. Dennis Fortenberry examine the complexities of ethnic and other identities among Oklahoma Native Americans through the study of rural adolescents' health behaviors.

In chapter 6, anthropologist Charles W. Nuckolls offers a partly autobiographical account of the folklore—some sacred, some profane—of petroleum exploration and financing and the ubiquity of accidents. In chapter 7, anthropologist J. Neil Henderson investigates the dynamics and meanings of Oklahoma's recurrent economic "booms" and "busts" through the eyes of a community study of Sulphur, Oklahoma, a town in south central Oklahoma known for its mineral springs. Chapter 8, by sports writer Berry W. Tramel, examines the significance of sports—including, but not limited to, collegiate football—in Oklahoma's identity and self-image. In chapter 9, architect Arn Henderson describes themes in the architectural styles of Oklahoma homes and public buildings and interprets the significance of design and space utilization for Oklahoma culture. In chapter 10, journalist Pat Bellmon depicts wheat farming and cattle ranching and their symbolism within and beyond Oklahoma boundaries.

In the concluding chapter, the editors, Howard F. Stein and Robert F. Hill, draw upon themes introduced throughout the book and explore in depth Oklahoma's images, both internal and external, together with their consequences for Oklahoma's culture and history.

The Culture of Oklahoma

CHAPTER 1

Green on Red: Oklahoma Landscapes

GARY L. THOMPSON

*In this chapter, Gary L. Thompson establishes the foundation
upon which the rest of the book is built. In describing Oklahoma geology, topography, weather, and demography, he
quickly establishes that cultural geography is never exclusively
a matter of what is "objectively" out there in reality but is always an interplay between the environment and the symbolic
uses to which people put it. Like an artist, he paints a portrait
of Oklahoma's cultural landscape, one in which east-west and
north-south distinctions play a prominent role.*

Many of those who attended the opening night performance of
the musical *Oklahoma!* in London on April 30, 1945, learned
from the program notes that the play derived its name from a
state of the union. Applause for the play was so enthusiastic
that a stage pistol had to be fired to regain the composure of
the audience. The popularity of the play in Great Britain in
1945 was assured before the opening. It offered a romanticized
view of the heartland of the United States from whence had
come the battalions that had saved the British world. *The
Times* review of the play emphasized that it was "redolent of
the middle western peasantry" (*The Times* 1947, 6; *New York
Times* 1947, 35).

Oklahoma assumed the symbolic dimensions of *Oklahoma!*
with more grace than it had accepted the version of social

conditions in the late 1930s presented by *The Grapes of Wrath* (Steinbeck 1939). The self-image of the state had been assailed by prose and portraits of Dust Bowl migrants streaming to California.

The real stage of Oklahoma, the physical and cultural land-scape, is difficult to characterize through the veils of imagery that have been used to describe the state. Visions of dusty, rural desperation; manic boomtowns; stoic, relocated Indians; outlaws as romantic heroes; land runs; cattle drives; agility in the ballet and the backfield, all elevated to the timeless realm of myth, define Oklahoma in ways that make a straightforward consideration of the natural setting, the environmental systems of the state, difficult.

Scientific views of the natural world often ignore the affective bonding that occurs between humans and their environments even though this crucial relationship influences the emergence of common structures of meaning in the life of a people. The interplay among mind, body, and place, through individual experience, forges systems of belief and behavior. The relationship itself can be as elementally simple as a person or a family coming to terms with a specific place in the environment. Yet the linkages between social behavior and the natural world remain elusive, difficult to identify and set to words.

Fatalism—the belief in the luck of the draw—stalks a ubiquitous presence on the real stage of Oklahoma. An outlook of hardbitten fatalism links many facets of Oklahoma culture: geographic diversity, people who are fortunate to have drawn many kinds of favorable lots (land, oil, gas, rainfall), religious fundamentalism, and the Oklahoma sense of humor. Understanding the Oklahoma experience on its physical environmental stage requires relating the mythic visions that have come to define the state to their geographical roots and realities. The identity of the state rests on the interconnections between people and the land. Both are deeply imbedded in the images that have emerged to define the place called Oklahoma. In a sense, those images and self-images have been cast onto the physical landscape, but the genius of a place begins in the land itself (Map 1.1).

PHYSICAL ENVIRONMENTAL REGIONS OF OKLAHOMA

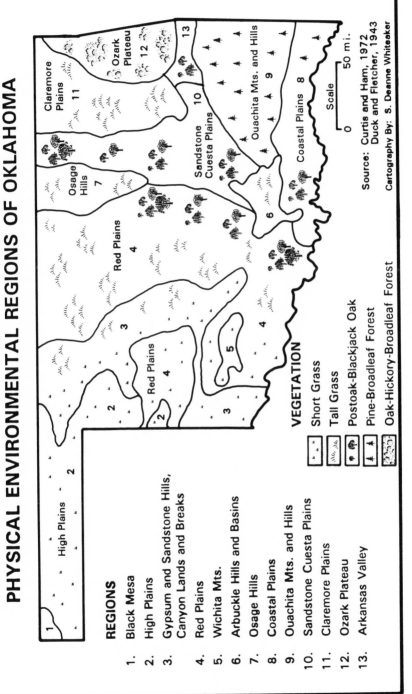

REGIONS

1. Black Mesa
2. High Plains
3. Gypsum and Sandstone Hills, Canyon Lands and Breaks
4. Red Plains
5. Wichita Mts.
6. Arbuckle Hills and Basins
7. Osage Hills
8. Coastal Plains
9. Ouachita Mts. and Hills
10. Sandstone Cuesta Plains
11. Claremore Plains
12. Ozark Plateau
13. Arkansas Valley

VEGETATION

Short Grass
Tall Grass
Postoak-Blackjack Oak
Pine-Broadleaf Forest
Oak-Hickory-Broadleaf Forest

Scale
0   50 mi.

Source: Curtis and Ham, 1972
Duck and Fletcher, 1943

Cartography By: S. Deanne Whiteaker

Map 1.1

"Land, Lots'a Land . . . Where the West Commences"[1]

Oklahoma is a slice of the southern plains. It points a finger toward the west, barely touching the volcanic forelands of the Rocky Mountains in the farthest tip of the Panhandle. Black Mesa, the massive lava flow which marks the western limit of the state, stands in angular contrast to the rounded ridges of the Ouachita Mountains in the far southeast. From west to east, the land falls away, like steps of an expansive staircase, toward the sea. Beds of sedimentary rock eaten away by erosion in the east are still present in the western counties. Between Black Mesa and the eastern uplands, Oklahoma rolls gently, flattens, shows itself through vistas which are modestly dramatic but rarely sublime.

The High Plains spread across the Panhandle like a strip of rolled dough, concealing the porous Ogallala Aquifer, which is saturated with water from rains of the distant past. Forming a resistant cap rock over deeper sediments, the Ogallala is exposed at the Break of the Plains, and the land surface falls away again to a belt of eroded, rough lands known to Oklahomans as the Gypsum Hills. In this broken chain of flat, greyish white mesas, gypsum is interspersed with red sandstone, shale, and thick strata of salt. Badlands topography, known as "breaks," occurs where river valleys such as that of the Canadian are incised into the flat gypsum beds. Vertical-walled canyons cut far into the surrounding uplands, and in some areas, outliers of the Ogallala stand over the Gypsum Hills, forming prominent buttes such as the Antelope Hills.

For its openness, western Oklahoma has remarkably variegated landforms. Where the gypsum is eroded, red sandstone is exposed, particularly in the breaks and canyons off the broad, sandy river valleys, which sweep across the plains in giant, undulating sine curves. The Red, the Washita, the two Canadians, and the Cimarron cut deeply into the land surface. These streams, plus the Arkansas in northeastern Oklahoma, flush great volumes of water and sediment after the spring rains but disappear under their white, sandy channels in the dry heat of late summer.

Along these rivers, fingers of woodland extend upstream into the grasslands. Emergent cottonwoods line the channels, towering above the willows and tamarisks, which also follow each strand. Bermuda grass dominates in the valley floors.

In the higher country above the river valleys, shortgrass covers the earth with a tight sod skin pocked with thousands of shallow depressions, known as buffalo wallows, which collect water during rains. The prairie grass is broken by farms and erosion features which expose the raw, red clay or the thin, greyish gypsum soils underneath. The land has a thorny personality, with flora and fauna designed to puncture, penetrate, and poison: red ants, goatheads, prickly pear cactus, sand burrs, cockleburrs, bull nettles, yucca, patches of tough shinnery oak, wild plum thickets on spots of sand, scrubby mesquite imported from Texas by seeds in cattle dung during the great cattle drives, thistle, milkweed, catclaw, sage, western diamondbacks, horned toads. Barbed wire fences fit the shortgrass country well.

From a thin line of trees in the drier, western reaches of the state, the river bottom forests become more luxuriant as the rivers flow to the east. Black walnut, oak, hickory, hackberry, pecan, grapevines, sumac, and towering feather grasses mature among oxbow lakes and meander scars which provide wetlands for wildlife communities.

East of the scrub-covered broken land of the Gypsum Hills lies the fortunate part of Oklahoma, a diagonal swath of counties from the far southwest to the Kansas border where the most productive agricultural soils lie on flat interfluves between the river valleys. This is wheat country, though in the southwest cotton is an important crop. Sand hills, knobs of granite, and deep sandstone canyons interrupt the swelling, open landscapes of the south, but the northern reaches of the wheat country are quite flat and the soils quite dark. The landscapes of north central Oklahoma are more akin to those of the Midwest—to those of Kansas or Iowa. Parts of fortunate Oklahoma produce wheat, meat, oil, and natural gas in the same fields.

The Cross Timbers—"Those Everlasting Hills"

At about the location of the State Capitol complex in Oklahoma City, porous sandstone begins to dominate the surface of central Oklahoma, signifying the edge of the Cross Timbers forest belt, best described as a dense thicket of dwarf oak which sprawls across the red hills of central Oklahoma from Kansas to Texas. Dominated by blackjack and post oak in the uplands, valleys have groves of taller oaks—red, black, and white—plus groves of pecan, hickory, and walnut trees of considerable height (Oklahoma Board of Agriculture 1959). In summer, the Cross Timbers form a verdant, dark green blanket against the ferrous red soil, the stereotypical Oklahoma landscape pined for by Woody Guthrie when he sang of "those Oklahoma hills where I was born." The soils vary from highly erodible sand to clays that resemble brick in color and consistency. This large area of central and eastern Oklahoma was farmed for a few years after statehood, but the soils failed, and the region largely returned to scrub oak or grazing land. Many of the early oil fields of the state were in the Cross Timbers, supporting boomtowns for the first half of the century and leaving a legacy of environmental disruption in some areas.

The topography of the Cross Timbers is gently rolling except for a number of distinctive north-south ridges, cuestas of tilted sedimentary rock, which parallel each other into Kansas. These ridges maintain a suggestion of angularity similar to that of the western mesas, although they are covered by dense oak forest.

Limestone appears in the Osage Hills and continues across northeastern Oklahoma, rising onto the Ozark Plateau, which is bounded by the rugged Cookson Hills at its southern margin. The Ozark country, with its clear streams and thickly forested hills, continues into Missouri and Arkansas. Following the straight edge of the Kansas border five hundred miles across northern Oklahoma leads from a distinctly eastern forest environment in the Ozarks to a distinctly western landscape of arid, high mesas in the area where Oklahoma, Colorado and New Mexico meet.

The Southern Mountains

Across the southern counties of Oklahoma a linear zone of crustal instability in the surface of the earth connects three distinctly different ranges of low mountains: the Ouachitas, the Arbuckles, and the Wichitas. Each range presents a unique variety of topography and a unique set of resource management problems for human settlement, and each has developed its own patterns of economic pursuits and cultural landscapes. The three ranges are all related to a geologic episode which occurred in the area of the earth's crust that now underlies south central Oklahoma and northern Texas. A spot of increased pressure from the interior of the earth developed into a welt on the surface, causing fractures or fault lines to radiate in several directions. One fault zone extended to the west across southern Oklahoma and the Texas Panhandle into the southern Rocky Mountain region. Along this line huge amounts of magma issued forth from the interior, forming the internal granitic cores of the Wichita and Arbuckle systems.

Deep trenches, such as the Anadarko and Ardmore basins, opened and subsequently filled with marine sediments to depths greater than 35,000 feet. Later movement of the crust folded and distorted the beds of limestone and sandstone, causing rock to pitch at severe angles, particularly in the Arbuckles, where the geological history of North America is displayed in the upturned beds. The Arbuckles hardly qualify as mountains; rather, they are a range of low hills and granite outcrops in the south central region of the state. Of softer visage than the Wichitas, their crystal streams and cedar-spotted slopes also contrast sharply with the red plains country, the Cross Timbers, to the north.

The granite peaks of the Wichitas stretch seventy-five miles through southwestern Oklahoma. Standing above the flat plains country, the Wichitas give a surreal suggestion of a blue, mountainous horizon on a hot day. Massive granite slabs strewn with boulders defy the monotony of their surroundings and suggest primordial events. To the Kiowas they are sacred, and to the U.S. Army they are solid targets for artillery rounds from Fort Sill, a major military post.

The Ouachitas, a larger system that dominates the southeast, is comprised of parallel bands of yellow sandstone ridges which arc to the southwest, forming a span of isolated nooks and valleys covered with short-leafed and loblolly pine forest. The Ouachitas have little more than forest grazing to offer agricultural interests but are more favorable for lumbering. The remote arcadian settings of the Ouachitas have been devastated in recent years by clear cutting, but the range remains one of the least known and most isolated regions of the southern plains.

None of the mountain systems nor the Ozark Plateau reach the elevations of the High Plains in the Panhandle (4,500 feet), yet the local relief is quite rugged in all the upland regions. The northwest-southeast descent across the state is complete along the Arkansas border, where elevations fall to about 400 feet above sea level in the valleys of the Arkansas and Red rivers. The Ouachitas are separated from the Ozark Plateau by the great valley of the Arkansas River, a center of human settlement in pre-Columbian times and in the early phases of the formation of Oklahoma.

Harvesting the Bounty of Nature

Attitudes toward the land in Oklahoma are in part connected to the methods of divestment used by the federal government. The demand for new settlement areas in the southern plains became intense in the 1880s, and the federal government finally succumbed to the argument that unused portions of Indian Territory should be opened. Under the reservation system, tribes relocated from the East were given the right to decide on questions of land tenure; the title was to remain in trust with the government. The tribes held the land in common and leased unused lands to white ranchers and farmers (Baum 1940, 50–68).

The land runs used to settle several areas, including the Unassigned Lands in 1889 and the Cherokee Strip in 1893, were chaotic and caused bitter personal and legal disputes. The lottery method of distributing land in two later openings was more orderly and equable, but both systems developed the idea of a contest which led to the award of a valuable prize: a quarter-section of land, which had to be improved or "proved up" within seven years.

These methods encouraged the view that landownership was a way to economic security, a quick answer to a problem instead of an opportunity with limits and inherent difficulties. The error with the divestment policy was that much of the land was marginal, poor, or worthless for agriculture. In western Oklahoma, no attempt was made to consider the potential productivity of the land available for homesteading. A geometric grid resembling a giant bingo card was superimposed, and each square, except for school land, was available to be claimed.

Most of the families who took claims in the Gypsum Hills were destined to experience hardships and failure, while those with land in the more fortunate counties had an opportunity for success if the rains came and farm prices held at reasonable levels. In retrospect, only a few counties were well suited to agriculture over the long term, and even there, erratic rainfall made it chancy for the region to compete well with the more reliable farmlands of the Corn Belt states.

In the east, where land was allotted to the Indian population, the settlement experience was quite different from that of Oklahoma Territory. The federal government resisted opening Indian lands until it became clear that settlers could not be prevented from entering the reservations, taking leases, intermarrying, and wheedling their way to land rights.

In the Chickasaw Nation, for example, white settlers far outnumbered Indians by 1890, creating a tense situation of imbalanced tenancy. The Chickasaw tribal government appealed for federal assistance in controlling the immigration of settlers, but federal force was insufficient in the face of the large numbers of people involved (Gibson 1973, 251–67).

The land allotments were meticulously planned and executed by the Dawes Commission (Harris 1929). Each quarter-section tract in Indian Territory was classified into one of ten categories according to its productive potential, and the recipients chose parcels based on the quality of the land rather

than the quantity (Brown 1937, 223). Eighty acres of bot-
tomland or black prairie land was considered equivalent to
2,080 acres of rough mountain land in the Choctaw Nation,
for example (Brown 1937, 293–94). Land was selected in units
as small as 20 acres, although 40 acres was common, and
each person on the tribal roles could own a number of parcels
scattered over a wide area. The General Land Office maps
used to enter allotment claims show a pattern of extreme
fragmentation of ownership throughout eastern Oklahoma
compared to the more orderly pattern of quarter-section farms
in western Oklahoma. The allotments were very unstable.
Land was assembled by purchase, court-ordered guardian-
ships, and other means by those whites who were able to mar-
shal their resources and use the legal system (Debo 1940,
92–125). Landownership changed rapidly, and large numbers
of white settlers remained as tenants without title to any land.

By 1920, Oklahoma, with 15 percent less land area, had a
larger rural population than Kansas (U.S. Department of
Commerce, Bureau of the Census 1920). The average density
of population of Kansas in that year was 21.5 per square mile,
while Oklahoma's had climbed to 29.0 people per square
mile (Morris, Goins, and McReynolds 1986; Socolofsky and
Self 1988, 1; Andriot 1983, 270). The clamor for land had
populated Oklahoma to a rural density that could not be
sustained. The resource base for agriculture in Oklahoma
was far less promising than that in Kansas. The eastern uplands of Oklahoma were clearly unsuited to cultivation, and
the Cross Timbers, stretching across the midsection of the
state, proved to have thin, highly erodible soils which failed
quickly under the plow after only a few crops of cotton and
corn. In the west, the belt of the Gypsum Hills was a marginal area, at best, for farming, and the rough lands were
impossible. After settlement, much cropland was abandoned.
By 1987 the state of Kansas retained over one half its total
land area (60 percent) in cropland, while total cropland in
Oklahoma fell to one-third (33 percent) of its area, most of it
located in the fortunate prairie strip immediately to the west
of the Cross Timbers (U.S. Department of Commerce, Bureau of the Census 1987b).

Oil: A Second Chance

The initial hope that free land would mean financial security did not materialize for many families who settled in the state. The hope was rekindled by the widespread discoveries of oil, particularly throughout the Cross Timbers belt from Osage County to the Red River. The great oil fields—the Glenn Pool, Cushing, Seminole, Allen, Healdton, Burbank, and scores of smaller producing areas—held forth the possibility of wealth far beyond that of a small family farm. Neither investment nor labor nor management was required. The oil dollars flowed from the simple fact of ownership. For those few who realized substantial oil wealth, the only task was to enjoy the financial windfall, a perplexing challenge for some. As the oil and gas development spread to western counties, significant numbers of landholders and heirs of landholders came to depend on royalties and lease payments. Oil came closer to being a miracle cure for impecuniousness than did agriculture. It set the equation land equals wealth ever more firmly in the Oklahoma mind.

"Where a treasure is springing out of the earth in a measureless flow."[2]

From these peculiar circumstances—a frenzied claiming of land, the failure of much farmland to provide sustenance, and the spread of oil and gas production—comes a basic Oklahoma attitude, a strong faith that land provides for those who are fortunate enough to have drawn a favorable lot. Harvesting the bounty of nature is the way to survival and prosperity. Well-being in a material sense flows from God, through nature, out of the earth. This fatalistic view, drawn from experience, emphasizes winning or losing, the luck of the draw. It is deeply embedded in the Oklahoma psyche.

Many rural Oklahomans have felt a very limited degree of control over their own economic destinies, with scant faith placed in human ingenuity, innovation, or management. During the course of the twentieth century such matters have

seemed largely beyond human control. The emphasis on ac-
cepting fate as divinely ordained is strongly reinforced by
many of the religious institutions of the state. Fundamental
frontierism or frontier fundamentalism leads back to the acceptance of one's lot in life.

Optimism and enthusiasm in the early days of settlement
gradually changed to tenacity, pragmatism, and resilience in
the face of economic eddies and erratic weather. Rather than
a spirit of grim determination, Oklahoma developed a sense
of humor which played on the lightness of living and the
ironies of hope versus reality. The penchant for humor rather
than despair in the Oklahoma personality has been well represented through folk minstrel figures Woody Guthrie and
Roger Miller and the biting observations of Will Rogers.

East is East and West is West[3]

Social and cultural differences in Oklahoma may be seen
within a geographical matrix of four quadrants: northwest,
northeast, southwest, and southeast. The question of differences between eastern and western Oklahoma is incomplete
without an accompanying question about differences between
the northern and southern parts of the state.

Resources vary significantly between eastern and western
Oklahoma. The east is characterized by hills and valleys
in the Ozark Plateau and Ouachita range, higher rainfall
amounts, a heavy forest cover, and poor soils. The west, with
some eroded badlands topography and an erratic rainfall, is
generally flat, with fertile soils, grasslands, and significant
areas of irrigated agriculture. To what degree do differences
in these resources account for the social disparities between
east and west? Many eastern counties have traditionally ranked
high in the incidence of poverty. The characteristics that are
used to define poverty—low family incomes, low educational achievement, high unemployment, high rates of welfare dependency, and others—are clustered in the southeast
and the northeast. Most western counties have the opposite
characteristics. To ascribe these patterns to resource differ-

ences is too simple, for the historical development of the two halves of the state must be considered.

"Territory Folks Should Stick Together"[4]

In many ways, Oklahoma continues to exhibit the marked differences that existed between Oklahoma and Indian territories, from which the state was formed. The western half, populated with such enthusiasm by land runs and lotteries, suffered great stress from droughts in the 1930s and 1950s and from the shift away from mixed farming to commercial wheat production before World War II. The Great Plains model for competitive agriculture became based on large, mechanized farms. The fertile flatlands of western Oklahoma provided no exception.

The most stressful social result of the change to large-scale wheat farming was the depopulation of many counties. From a dispersed, rural population which blanketed the prairies in 1930, western Oklahoma became a sparsely settled region with most inhabitants, including farmers, clustered in the surviving towns and cities by 1970. The expansive prairies of the western part of the state, once studded with farmhouses, emptied steadily during the years of drought, low commodity prices, and adaptation to the new technologies. The spread of oil and gas production, extensive in the west, slowed but did not stop the rural depopulation. Today, counties west of Interstate 35 are lightly populated but reasonably prosperous, the Panhandle counties being even more sparsely populated but even more prosperous because of the development there of irrigation and intensive natural gas production. Social stress continues to reduce the rural population, particularly in the southwest, where marginal, droughty lands have not shared in oil and gas production.

Western Oklahoma has benefited economically from the presence of large defense installations. Emigration of young people has continued, leaving old-aged populations in some counties. Deaths outnumber births in some areas, a rare occurrence in any inhabited region.

The settlement of the western Oklahoma plains may be seen as a wave of people which washed out onto the grasslands and then receded, leaving only a few to share the vast realm. Wealth flows from western Oklahoma counties to the east in the form of tax monies, but with little political clout, the thinly populated west can seldom resist tax levies to spread equal state services and transfer payments to poorer regions.

Eastern Oklahoma underwent a much different settlement experience compared to the western region. Relocated Indian tribes organized an infrastructure of towns, roads, and schools before white settlement began to overwhelm the various reservations. Allotment parceled the land among those on tribal roles, but the land was levered away from Indian ownership in a variety of ways, most of them unscrupulous. The Dawes Commission, which allotted lands to Indian ownership, was tediously careful in its efforts to provide fair treatment to those on tribal rolls, but at the end of federal oversight, the land was wrested from Indian control ruthlessly and efficiently (see Debo 1940, 203–29).

Several circumstances combined to create a social dilemma in many parts of Indian Territory. First, the land itself was remarkably unpromising for agriculture. The large Ouachita Mountain region in the Choctaw Nation offered only a few valley floors for farm development. The large swath of Cross Timbers, which comprised most of the balance of the territory, appeared to have agricultural potential, but the soils there were exhausted after a few crops of cotton, and the problems of gully erosion made the region one of the most abused soil regions in the country by 1930. The social drama that developed in the Cross Timbers in the early years of the century was in part a result of oversettlement of poor soils and in part because of extraordinarily high rates of farm tenancy. Landownership passed from Indians to large landholders quickly, leaving the region filled with landless tenants who attempted to farm small, rented parcels. The rural poverty which resulted was of such a character that it almost defied comparison to life elsewhere in the United States (Scales and Goble 1982, 66–67).

The situation for many landless families became difficult, then impossible. Social unrest accompanied the failure of tenant farms and led to mass demonstrations, rabid populism, and radical socialism in the years before World War I. Farm tenancy rates became extremely high, over 80 percent for new farmers in some counties, and the vote for Socialist party candidates in 1914 elections corresponds well with the patterns of farm tenancy (see Scales and Goble 1982, 64–69; Jones 1972).

The rural social situation deteriorated in eastern counties earlier than in the western ones, where farms were larger, soils were better, and more farmers held title to their land. The desperate situation in the east, with high tenancy rates combined with poor soils, occurred before the automobile became commonplace, making mobility and migration more difficult. The rural poor of many eastern counties tended to stay on the land and tolerate lives of resignation with whatever resources were available. In the remote valleys of the Ouachita range and the Ozark Plateau, the rural economy reverted to an Appalachian, subsistence model for many families, Indian, white, and black, who began to depend heavily on fishing, hunting, and small-plot farming for food; on the forest for wood; and, as the century progressed, on state welfare assistance, food stamps, and medical and other state benefits. Welfare dependency rates in some counties remained as high as 35 percent of the total population in the 1970s before falling in the 1980s (Thompson 1972).

The pronounced differences in the experience of the rural populations of eastern and western Oklahoma can be clearly related to disparities in soil resources and the peculiarities of initial white settlement. Both east and west suffered great stress in adapting to the land, but in different ways. The east retains a legacy of rural poverty, largely absent in the west. Each side of the state maintains a strong perception of its own regional identity. In a sense, Indian Territory and Oklahoma Territory still exist in the minds of many Oklahomans, although half the population is now clustered in the two large metropolitan regions.

The Canadian River Split

While the idea of an Oklahoma divided into east and west persists, the reality of regional cultural differences may be more clearly found between north and south. The Canadian River divides the state in terms of political and religious affinities, and some measures of economic well-being suggest that the north-south differences are stronger than the more common perception of east versus west. Anglo settlers in the northern counties came principally from the Midwest: Kansas, Iowa, Illinois. Their political party affiliation was heavily Republican and remains so today. The midwestern character of the region is clearly seen in the Victorian architecture and Methodist churches of the pin-neat towns along the Kansas border.

Settlers in southern Oklahoma trace their families to the upland south, many by way of Arkansas or Texas. Their Appalachian roots were clear in the original farmsteads. Smokehouses, chicken coops, dog runs, guinea fowl, sheds, and shacks surrounded T-shaped houses with double front doors and a paucity of paint. South of the Canadian, Oklahoma today remains heavily Democratic in party registration and Baptist in church affiliation.

"High-Steppin' Strutters": The Country and Western Style[5]

Horses have always been popular in Oklahoma, and their appeal seems to grow instead of diminish. Texas has more horses, but Oklahoma, a much smaller state, comes in second (U.S. Department of Commerce, Bureau of the Census 1987a). Clearly, the horse, and the associated western life-style, is a primary symbol in the self-identity of the state. The horse has been adopted to signify origins, attitudes, and a style of life across rural Oklahoma and, to a lesser extent, in the urban centers. Westernness is a thin but potent veneer that lies like a mantle across the social landscape of the state.

The arching paradigm of westernness, which includes dress, music, speech, humor, diet, leisure activities, gender roles, and personal demeanor, is occupation-related, a remnant of the folk culture of the older, rural generations, an effort to preserve the simple cowboy ethos spread across the stage of the musical *Oklahoma!* The western style is largely absent in the affluent northern suburbs of Oklahoma City, southern Tulsa, and Norman, but it remains alive and healthy in the smaller cities in the state, where it is practiced with enthusiasm.

Despite the musical exhortation that "the farmer and the cowman should be friends,"[6] those who earn their livelihoods from cattle retain a distinct identity. Farming involves a different and more intensive use of the land, even though many farmers blend stock raising into their operations. The pasturing of beef cattle on winter wheat is the primary example of such a mixed operation. Farmers label themselves beef growers or stockmen, rarely cattlemen. To a certain extent, farmers still wear khaki trousers or overalls, work shoes, and baseball caps or straw hats with little flair. Cattlemen dress according to the western style.

There was little room for ranching in the areas of homesteading, and cattlemen were confined to the untillable, rough lands of the Panhandle and the Gypsum Hills in the west. In those areas a few ranches persist, but two large grassland areas of Indian Territory, the Arbuckles and the Osage Hills, have been more important as style setting regions. Both areas are dry limestone hills with tallgrass prairie, excellent cattle country. Both areas saw large tracts of grassland assembled after allotment, and both became known as ranch country.

Powerful images of the American West emanated from these two prairie regions. Celluloid cowboys had roots in both areas: Tom Mix in the Osage Hills and Gene Autry in the Arbuckles. Roy Rogers and Dale Evans were married in an Arbuckle ranch house. Pawnee Bill operated his Wild West show out of the Osage country. Both areas were filled with large working ranches, but oil discoveries changed their economies. Affluent oil men began to picture themselves as gentlemen ranchers, stewards of the land, and purchased large tracts in the Osage Hills and the Arbuckles, creating a new Oklahoma stereotype. Many of them continue to live in affluent westernness on their home spreads, while others maintain a ranch in addition to a mansion in Oklahoma City, Tulsa, Dallas, or Houston. This tradition, urban wealth invested in personal ranches, changed the economics of ranching, for large subsidies were needed to underwrite these ranching life-styles.

Cattle graze the forests and prairies of the southeast, providing a flow of calves to central Oklahoma, where farmers and ranchers fatten them as stocker-feeders and then ship them west to the feedlots of the High Plains to be finished and slaughtered. Eastern Oklahoma cattlemen also project a collective western persona similar to that of the Osage Hills, the Arbuckles, or the western ranches.

The cattle industry of the state is still present in most regions and continues to encourage the western life-style with its equine and bovine symbolism. With the passage of time, the general paradigm of westernness has become appropriated by many farmers and urbanites. It provides a highly visible, symbolic style which can lead to erroneous conclusions about the way most Oklahomans live.

Still, the cowboy life-style reflects an affinity for the land. Underlying the superficialities of the style is a common bond, an association of those who yearn for the free life of the mythic cowboy and who feel rooted in the open prairies and hills of the state, or at least the idea of those places. For most, modernism has erased all but a few consciously selected symbolic vestiges of the romantic cowboy mystique.

A. L. Kroeber's lengthy essay on the role of style in civilization suggests the importance of acting out an identity defined within a particular subset of the population and of the rewards which flow from belonging to a distinct group. "A style," he says, "is a strand in a culture or civilization: a coherent, self-consistent way of expressing certain behavior or performing certain kinds of acts" (Kroeber 1957, 150). He suggests that variations of style in decoration, dress, and food are the most sensitive indicators of culture in civilization, but difficult to measure (Kroeber 1957, 155–56). With respect to dress, Kroeber notes that the factors which govern style of dress are utility, erotic allure, social standing, and novelty (Kroeber 1957, 7).

Such forms of regional identity—postmodern tribalism,

perhaps—can be of great importance to the individual personality, which seeks to define itself with an integrated set of symbols, behaviors, and baubles. Compared with other options for the expression of style, westernness, in the context of Oklahoma, seems benign, with positive benefits for many who view themselves as cowhands. The outward manifestations—hats, boots, string ties, big buckles, horses and horse trailers, stylized dancing, ruddy complexions—present opportunities for sharp-edged, class-based putdowns, which cowboys and cowgirls shed without as much as a sidelong glance. Most are aware of the incongruities between these symbols and the lives they lead, but they are also aware that their style of living has a degree of authenticity in the history of their place and the manners of their region. The cowboy style tends toward egalitarianism rather than exclusivity, and it precludes the stigma of poverty and the pejorative label "poor white."

The cowboy-western style endemic to Oklahoma, but not pervasive, is significant as an indication of social-cultural confrontation. It represents a difference on the folk–urban continuum, and it points to a conflict in the collective mind of the state. The cowboy ethos, linked to occupation and, hence, social class, values tradition and clings tenaciously to a distinctive style which sets a significant portion of the population apart from the larger majority, who choose to follow the mainstream life-styles of the American Midwest. Two ethics intermingle in Oklahoma. One reaches to the north, embracing urban life, a social hierarchy based on wealth, and the European arts and humanities, and the other reaches to the south towards tradition, community, and values of taciturn acceptance of fate, independence blended with equality.

The cowboy image is perpetuated by the mass marketing of western clothing stores, country-and-western music, and various levels of government, which seize upon the imagery to attract tourists and to remind the citizenry of its western heritage. Westernness is most apparent at small town rodeos, weekly cattle sales, and local restaurants. The fringes of the metropolitan areas have advantages to keepers of horses, western taverns, and dance halls, which are most active on week-ends. Country-and-western radio stations have faded with the rural population.

In the context of the upper-income groups of the state, western style is seen as inimical to modernism, but a fondness for the image exists even among those who would personally like to shed the legacy of rural roots. Horse racing is popular, as are English riding and polo among those who are well heeled, if not well booted, but the equestrian symbols of social exclusivity struggle to survive in Oklahoma.

"When the Wind Comes Right Behind the Rain"[7]

Oklahomans are proud of their weather. Many see it as uniquely able to wreak havoc and inspire chagrin. There is a certain martyrdom in the face of stifling summer heat, particularly if record temperatures are set, but the tornado captures the central focus of attention in Oklahoma. Weather is a common concern in all rural areas, but in Oklahoma it serves as a spectator sport.

The tornado season begins in March, sometimes with early spring storms but more commonly with media announcements about how to cope with twisters. As the season progresses, through April and May, the media tension builds. Oklahoma City television stations begin their annual competition to capture tornado conscious viewers. It is a short season, eight weeks or so, and it ends rather abruptly with the onset of summer heat in June. In some seasons the tornadoes never appear, but in most years they are sufficiently active to keep video crews in helicopters racing from one overturned mobile home to the next.

Occasionally there is massive destruction, with injuries and deaths. While a storm is in progress, local channels track the development and movement of various cells, lightning strikes, and wind velocities with elaborate instrumentation and visual displays for home viewers. During storm season, each evening of television can include a lengthy subplot of thunderstorm development and movement climaxed by the arrival of an authentic storm. Programs are interrupted, bits of information are fed across the bottom of the screen, and weather crews are seen in states of high excitement bending over radar displays, answering phone calls, and issuing live coverage from mobile cameras. The drama of watching thunderstorms develop on a video screen is heightened by an anticipation of the sublime event.

The settlers who ventured onto the plains for land found themselves facing the conditions of daily weather more directly than they had in the closer environments of the eastern forest. The horizons of their world became immense. In the prairies, swails and rises of the land extended the horizon to twenty or more miles. After rural electrification came in the 1930s, the plains became studded with the lights of farmsteads, and distant towns sparkled in brilliant chains through the clear night air. In such a setting, a storm became a dramatic event which unfolded more slowly and with more tension and expectation than in a closer world defined by tree lines and ridge tops.

Thunderstorms most often approach Oklahoma from the northwest. A wall of grey clouds building and billowing may indicate cooler air approaching from the northern plains. The front bulldozes across the plains, shoving the warm, humid air upwards, where the dynamics of expanding gas release energy by condensation, electrical discharge, and furious winds. Individual storm cells move along the edge of the front from southwest to northeast, while the entire system pushes to the south.

Settlers soon learned that storms came from the northwest at first, then, as the line approached, from the southwest. "Going to the cellar" in rural Oklahoma meant a dash to the "dugout," a large, covered pit in the red earth where a family could huddle together during a severe thunderstorm. The cumulus towers, illuminated by lightning for hours before their arrival, eventually arrived, jolting the family out into the winds of the gust front. Entombed for the duration with a kerosene lantern, the family talked quietly while the world outside moaned with gasps of wind and shuddered from the impact of thunder on the earth. Most storm cellars had wooden benches along the walls and tiers of unpainted shelves for home-canned vegetables. It was common for neighbors to appear unannounced to share the cellar, particularly if the storm came during visiting hours.

In this fashion, storms came to be an important event in Oklahoma life. On most occasions the experience developed as an exhilarating communion between people and nature, but damage and death were common enough to nurture fear. Tales of tornado destruction circulated commonly. The city of Woodward, in northwestern Oklahoma, still carries the legacy of a tornado that occurred on April 7, 1947 (Flora 1953, 137). The 101 deaths there struck the population of the state with unusual emotional force, in part because of the immediacy of radio reports, which brought the public directly into the shocked aftermath, the cleanup, the grief. The image of the tornado was emerging as an extraordinarily newsworthy event.

Weather news and forecasts assumed an eminent role in the early television newscasts of the 1950s. The memories of prairie thunderstorms imprinted on the Oklahoma mind were recalled by folksy television weather personalities. The fascination with tornadoes in Oklahoma grew into pride, and they were adopted as an unofficial mascot of the state. Perhaps the anomie of suburban life calls forth a yearning for a storm, particularly one packaged and presented with appropriate dramatic tension.

Oklahomans identify their state strongly with tornadoes, and many believe that they live squarely in "tornado alley," which runs from Texas to Iowa. The view is correct in that tornadoes are spawned from the admixture of cool northern and sultry southern air (Kessler and White 1983). The validity of Oklahoma's claim to the tornado as an important state symbol was difficult to judge until Theodore Fujita, a University of Chicago meteorologist, produced detailed maps of tornado occurrences over a seventy-year period (Fujita 1987; see Map 1.2). His research shows that tornadoes do occur most commonly between Texas and Iowa in May, giving credence to the perception of tornado alley. Before and after May, tornadoes occur most frequently in other areas of the country. Central Oklahoma and northern Alabama have the

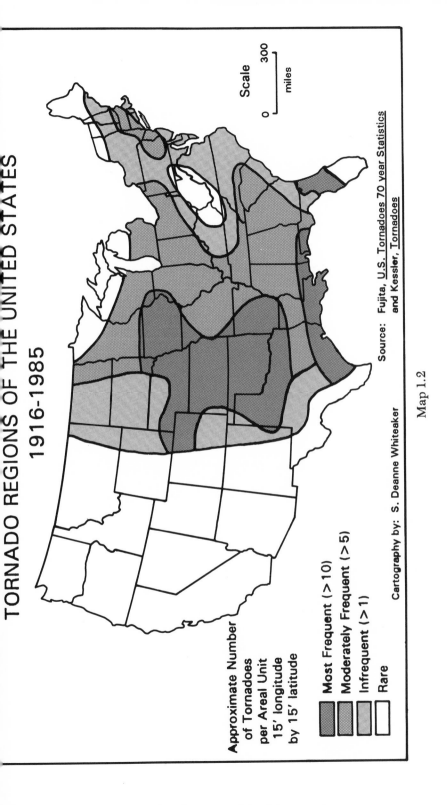

TORNADO REGIONS OF THE UNITED STATES
1916-1985

Approximate Number of Tornadoes per Areal Unit 15' longitude by 15' latitude

Most Frequent (>10)

Moderately Frequent (>5)

Infrequent (>1)

Rare

Scale

0   300

miles

Source: Fujita, U.S. Tornadoes 70 year Statistics
and Kessler, Tornadoes

Cartography by: S. Deanne Whiteaker

Map 1.2

highest probability of receiving super tornadoes with wind speeds above three hundred miles per hour, the most destructive category of storm, an extremely rare occurrence (Fujita 1987, 120). It is clear that Oklahoma does have an abundance of tornadoes, but, as Fujita points out, every agricultural region in the world receives this type storm (Fujita 1987, ii). It is hardly unique to the state. The fondness for seeing Oklahoma at the epicenter of tornadic activity verges perhaps on mild obsession. It fits the general claim to physical endurance in the face of hardship and calamity. Steinbeck (1939) suggests in *The Grapes of Wrath* that the people will endure.[8] The tornado image supports the archetypical notion of uncontrollable power dropping at random on homes and families. Similarities to the outlaw image are clear. Unshackled by society, tornadoes and outlaws spin violence in their paths.

With the tornado firmly entrenched in the state's view of itself, there is small wonder that meteorological research wins popular support. The National Severe Storms Laboratory was located in Norman in 1964 and has reinforced interest in the tornado through a variety of investigations. Development of a significant program of research into the dynamics of mesoscale storms at the University of Oklahoma has also received similar support. The image of young, vital research students stalking the wild tornado for the sake of science has attracted "tornado groupies" who hope for an existential confrontation with the raw fury of a funnel cloud.

A Gathering of Flavors

The notion of Oklahoma as a meeting place of east and west, north and south is useful in characterizing the physical environments and cultural patterns of the state, but it tends to suggest a lack of clear identity. In a transition zone, the defining circumstances occur in other places. The ecological systems of the state represent adaptations to temperature and precipitation regimes, landforms, and altitudes. Available moisture causes flora and fauna in the east to be more like that of the eastern hardwood forest. In the west, xeric conditions are accompanied by flora and fauna more characteristic of the southwestern states. As an ecotonal transition zone, Oklahoma contains species of arid-lands vegetation that can flourish in relatively humid environments plus drought-resistant forms of vegetation found in the eastern hardwood forest. The margins of the ecotonal systems meet in the southern plains, where physical circumstances demand a certain hardiness and durability.

Similarly, the patterns of human culture converge in Oklahoma. Wilbur Zelinsky identified only two places in the United States where three major culture regions abut: (1) southwestern Pennsylvania, where the Middle West, the Midlands, and the South converge, and (2) Oklahoma, where the Middle West and the South give way to the West (Zelinsky 1973, 118). Because of the clear convergence of the three major culture regions in Oklahoma and the presence of Indian cultures, Zelinsky lists Oklahoma as a region of uncertain affiliation on his cultural map of the United States (Zelinsky 1973, 119). In such a scheme, Oklahoma again faces the characterization as a transition, a periphery, to more distant realms where the archetypical cultural systems exist in high forms of purity.

In environmental or cultural terms, Oklahoma does not easily classify. The convergence and coalescence of traits has marked Oklahoma as a place with Appalachian/Ozarkian reticence, the expansive, open humor of the West, and the manners and softness of demeanor from the South. Resignation and tenacity have come from working a hard land while continuing to endure. A strong sense of community and continuity underpins the basis of the Oklahoma vision, which is a blending of regional ideas about independent families living on the land in a nexus of kith and kin, a dislike of social fetters but an affinity for moralistic taboos, beliefs in nature as the great provider and in the corrupting influence of cities, fatalism, guilt, physical prowess as superior to the intellect, sudden wealth, a perception of panacea rising up out of the land, and an inclination toward pathos concerning death and life. The flavor blends ethnic and individual experience and remains heavily seasoned by the parsimonious character of the land.

Notes

1. From "Don't Fence Me In," by Cole Porter, 1944.

2. From the song "Oklahoma, Sweet Land of My Dreams," by Jennie Harris Oliver and Oscar Lehrer. Music and lyrics are preserved in the Bizzell Memorial Libraries, University of Oklahoma.

3. From "The Ballad of East and West," (Kipling 1945); also adapted in the song "Buttons and Bows" from the movie *Fancy Pants*.

4. From the song "The Farmer and the Cowman Should Be Friends" in the musical *Oklahoma!* with music by Richard Rodgers, book and lyrics by Oscar Hammerstein II, Williamson Music Co., 1943.

5. "When I drive them high-steppin' strutters . . ." is from "Surrey with the Fringe on Top" in the musical *Oklahoma!*

6. From the song with the same name in the musical *Oklahoma!*

7. From the song "Oklahoma" in the musical *Oklahoma!*

8. In Steinbeck's words: "We'll figger sompin out" (Steinbeck 1939, 618).

CHAPTER 2

The Creation of Oklahoma: New Meanings for the Oklahoma Land Run

HOWARD R. LAMAR

With prodigious scholarship and a capacity to evoke, not only describe, history, Howard R. Lamar discusses two profoundly contrasting and competing images of the origin of Oklahoma: the Land Run of 1889 and the Trail of Tears. Every group, every culture, possesses—and often rewrites—an "origin myth" that recounts the nobility or ignominy that is the source of the group's existence, an account from which the future ostensibly flows. Lamar shares with his readers the complexity of historical interpretation, indeed changing modes and canons for interpretation itself. His chapter is an important piece of methodology which the reader might use to understand how whole peoples (ethnic, national, corporate, religious) construe how they came to be and likewise how communities of scholars construct worlds of social science and humanities. Finally, Lamar not only describes and interprets Oklahoma history; his is also an ethically courageous statement about the distortions, the profound hurt, that our fondest myths of history can inflict upon history. When peoples exclude one another from their origins, their subsequent histories suffer from it.

In 1987 the Oklahoma Humanities Foundation invited me to prepare a public address to be given two years later on the occasion of the centennial of the famous Oklahoma Land

Run of 1889 (Lamar 1989).[1] Research for that talk not only reacquainted me with the history of Oklahoma settlement, but also rekindled my interest in western territorial history and left me with a determination to learn still more about the remarkable social and political developments that occurred in Oklahoma's territorial period, 1890–1907.

Shortly after my talk in the spring of 1989, a dozen young historians of the American West held a conference at Yale University which they entitled the Future of the Western Past.[2] The participants were concerned with two questions: Can there be a coherent history of the West in the twentieth century? and What models or approaches seem most promising both for writing this new twentieth-century history and in reinterpreting the old classical frontier periods in the light of this new scholarship? In the essay for this volume I have tried to apply some of the new approaches and methodologies advocated by the twelve historians at the Yale conference to the experiences of the 1889 Oklahoma Land Run.

However, it was evident from the first that the new western scholars would insist on recording or noting the Native American experiences as well as the white ones as an integral part of the story. That assumption led me to look first at the origin or creation myth that has grown up around the first land run and then to look at the origin or creation myth of the Cherokees, who were the first of the Five Civilized Tribes to settle in Oklahoma, although the bulk of the Cherokee Nation did not come until 1838. In the saga of Removal and the Trail of Tears is an Oklahoma creation myth which, although nationally well known, takes on even larger symbolic meaning in American history than has been previously recognized. It is, in fact, an American frontier experience that bears some resemblance to the way Pilgrims sought exile at Plymouth in 1620 and the story of the Mormon expulsion from Illinois and their subsequent trek to Utah. The story of the Trail of Tears is also similar to that of other tribes, northern and southern, who were expelled from the lands east of the Mississippi. By looking at two creation myths rather than one perhaps we can not only develop a better perspective on the state's history but also help explain Oklahoma's unique and even radical attitudes when the territory sought statehood early in this century.

The 1989 Future of the Western Past Conference was not inspired just by the search for new ways to write the history of the American West, but also by the scores of centennials and bicentennials, both national and western, that have taken place or will occur in the last quarter of this century. Among them is the hundredth anniversary in 1993 of Frederick Jackson Turner's famous address, "The Significance of the Frontier in American History" (1893), which was itself given at the Chicago World's Fair, the theme of which was the four hundredth anniversary of Columbus's discovery of America. These anniversaries have forced us to think in new terms about some very important specific historical events and their mythic significance. Indeed, the very way we have celebrated them reveals much about our own new perspectives and approaches, whether as members of the general public or as historians. It seems safe to say, for example, that the bicentennial of the American Revolution was celebrated in 1976 and thereafter with very little emphasis on the word *revolution*, for we are now a much more conservative-minded, unrevolutionary society in the United States.

One of the several centennials we celebrated in 1989 related to the American territorial system which was created by the Northwest Ordinance of 1787. In 1889, on February 22, President Grover Cleveland signed what was called the Omnibus Bill, which admitted four states into the Union at once: North and South Dakota, Montana, and Washington. All of the "Omnibus States" have now celebrated their centennials with conferences, publications, parades, and frontier days parties.[3]

But undoubtedly the most colorful of the current centennial celebrations that year occurred in Guthrie, Oklahoma, on April 22, 1989, to honor the first Oklahoma Land Rush or Run in which fifty thousand American Sooners and Boomers occupied most of central Oklahoma in just one day. The 1889 run was reenacted at Guthrie and televised for the nation to see.

The Oklahoma Land Run of 1889—or, as many called it,

"the Harrison Horse Race"—captured the attention of the American public as few things ever have. The country followed it as we did the first moon trip of the astronauts. Newspapers throughout the country covered the April 22, 1889, event. Among many others, the *New York Herald Tribune* sent a reporter named Harry Hill (1889) to cover events not just for a few days but for a month. Hill chose to enter with the Boomers camped at Arkansas City, Kansas, to report, as he put it, "the details of one of the most remarkable episodes of settlement in American history. . . . No more picturesque and dramatic scene has ever been beheld in the settlement of this continent" (Hill 1889, 25). He quickly figured out that cattlemen and the Indians hated the Sooners and Boomers and were hostile to the opening. And while recognizing the key roles of the professional land speculators and the six railroads in the opening, he was most impressed with the Boomers themselves. Nor could he get over the variety of types. While at Arkansas City on the Kansas–Indian Territory border, he encountered a former clerk from a Nebraska drugstore with his father. The latter was a lawyer who already had his "shingle painted and prepared ready to hang out the minute he had located his claim" (Hill 1889, 25). Another Boomer turned out to be a physician who had studied at Heidelberg in his youth, had drifted out to California, had gone to the Cape of Good Hope, and had returned to America ten years later only to find himself then an Oklahoma Boomer.

One land rush participant had been an officer in the Austrian army, and still another had once been exiled to Siberia. These were the adventurers. Hill found that Anglo-Americans were the predominant group. Next came Germans, Irish, and a few Scandinavians. He saw almost no blacks, but we know from other sources that there were black homesteaders in the rush. We also have stories of white hostility to them. By and large the 1889 and 1893 land run participants appear to have had midwestern origins and saw this event as another stage in the national settlement of the American West.

The Arkansas City homesteaders possessed a huge arsenal of weapons and much whiskey, and while waiting they played checkers or baseball. There was a circus in town, or one could attend a boxing match. The desperate "last chance" element was epitomized by a man who had written the following in basic English on his covered wagon:

Chinch-bugged in Illinois
Baldnobbed in Mizzouri
Sicloned in Nebraska
Prohibited in Kansas
Oklimony or Bust. (Hill 1889, 27)

The example is well known, but it tells us once again that this and many other immigrants were from north of the Mason-Dixon Line.

The Boomers were told to leave Arkansas City on April 19 in order to reach the starting line by April 22. That was easier said than done, for there were rains and thunderstorms, and the streams were swollen. At the Salt Fork River the U.S. Army, aided by Indians, tried to raft people across, but the pace was so slow that the soldiers resorted to putting heavy planks on the Santa Fe railroad bridge over the river to let the wagons roll across.

Finally, on April 22 some fifty or sixty thousand people had assembled at the starting line waiting for the sign to start—a blast of the bugle by someone in the Fifth Cavalry. The Santa Fe Railroad had already built a line as far as future Guthrie and had its train at the starting line. Indeed, that railroad was to carry fifteen trainloads of people to Guthrie that day. Our reporter could not get over the variety of people: farmers, merchants, professional men, and speculators, among them the Wild West show owner, Pawnee Bill. Most were law-abiding, but one man stole a pair of mules from a Caldwell, Kansas, farmer along with the farmer's wife. The sheriff found the man and the mules in Arkansas City and compelled him to give up the mules but not the wife, for the farmer said he did not care for her and let the Boomer keep her. Opined the reporter: "It was the severest punishment that he could have inflicted on him for stealing the mules" (Hill 1889, 27).

In the last moments before the rush began, a group of miners from Pennsylvania appeared. Their leader told the reporter "that they were tired of working as miners and were going to work in 'God's sunlight' as farmers." To add further to the variety, a group of lumberjacks from Michigan arrived, saying they had deserted their log rafts to come to Oklahoma (Hill 1889, 30–31). Again, even these random examples suggest that Oklahoma had a midwestern, even Yankee, beginning.

The rush itself was like nothing anyone had ever seen or heard before. One observer compared it to thousands of cattle on the run. In the noise and confusion accidents occurred as wagons and horses careened into each other. We probably have an image of clouds of dust, but the 1889 run was on a damp and misty day. By contrast, dust and prairie fires characterized the Cherokee Strip run in 1893, when one hundred thousand persons participated, for the land was suffering from drought that year (see Fig. 2.1). The trains had orders not to go faster than the fastest horsemen, but the passengers frantically urged the engineers to put on speed and kept shouting "on to Guthrie" out of the windows. People spilled from horses, children fell out of wagons, and bicycles collapsed. The reporter compared the whole thing to the 1849 California Gold Rush and to the 1850s occupation of the Pennsylvania oil fields. The event so impressed the *New York Herald Tribune* that on April 24 it carried a descriptive editorial written in a tone of awe.[4]

After that the reporter wandered from Guthrie to Kingfisher and to Oklahoma City to pick up stories. Perhaps a cowboy, Evan G. Barnard, who had herded cattle in Indian Territory before the rush but had decided to join the rush, best described the swiftness of the change that had come to the land in a single day. He found a claim; then he and his pals fought off claim jumpers, and especially one who said to him, "Why don't we split, you take 80 acres and I'll take 80." Barnard said he would take the whole 160 or six feet. The would-be jumper left. That night, recalled Barnard, "lights flickered all over the country from the campfires of the settlers. It was a great change for the cowpunchers to see the great cattle country transferred in a day from a region with thousands of cattle to one with thousands of people moving about. We wondered what they would do to make a living" (quoted in Morgan and Strickland 1981, 86–90; see also Barnard 1936).

Fig. 2.1. "The Start," land opening of September 16, 1893. Photograph by A. A. Forbes. The photographer was also a cowboy in western Oklahoma during the 1880s. His idea was to take as many photos as possible and then sell them to identified participants. The plates were then sold to local photographers for additional commerce. This picture was taken just south of Arkansas City on the line. (Courtesy of Archives and Manuscripts Division of the Oklahoma Historical Society, photo number 1964.)

Homesteaders had to find the cornerstones the U.S. surveyors had put in the ground in order to register their claim properly at the land office. And one had to stand in line to register. In stark contrast, Guthrie was touted as having been built in an afternoon—far faster than Rome. Even so, its ten to fifteen thousand inhabitants were soon short of food. A meal was soon selling for five dollars, and water was ten cents a glass. But such problems did not slow urban developers. A few days after the rush, Guthrie elected a mayor. Three candidates, all claiming to be conservatives and antisaloon men, ran. It was a mark of the broad Americanness of the rush that one candidate was from Dakota Territory, one from Oregon, and one from Kansas. Because there were no ballot boxes, people lined up behind their candidate, and the candidate with the longest line won. On April 27, a dark horse from Kansas City, C. P. Dyer, was elected mayor (Hill 1889, 43). Given the fact that Kansas City had been a major promoter of both railroads and settlement in the Indian Territory and in Oklahoma, the choice should have not seemed too surprising.

By now our *Herald Tribune* reporter was getting tired of sleeping in tents, eating crude fare, and watching acts of violence, for revolvers and guns were in evidence everywhere. His descriptions of Oklahoma City and Kingfisher were not that complimentary. Still, he kept his sense of humor, and in the style of both Mark Twain and Brete Harte he left us some good stories. For example, one Sunday near Guthrie he found a minister preaching out of doors from the following text:

I am a deputy of the Receiver of the Land Office of Heaven. That office is open for business to-day, as it is every day. I am here to urge you to make your filings right now. You need stand in no long line in the land office of our Father. Your claims are already staked, driven not with human hands. . . . All you have got to do is file your declaration and get a homestead in Zion. You are looking for townsites: Ho for the New Jerusalem—a city not of tents, but of everlasting mansions. . . . Be a boomer of the Lord's. (Hill 1889, 46–47)

The reporter was amazed that the crowd took it seriously, and even more so when a cowboy came forward and confessed his sins and dedicated himself to Christ.

Later, in Oklahoma City, Hill told of a family named Lewis who were short of cash, a crisis made more pressing because the mother had just given birth to a baby—possibly the first to be born in Oklahoma since the rush. To raise money for the needy family, the Boomers held an auction to name the child, the highest bidder having the right to choose the name. One Boomer who had plunked down fifty-eight dollars won and chose to name the baby Oklahoma Lewis (Hill 1889, 47). Both the language of the preacher and the sentimental efforts to help a family could have occurred in California or on any American frontier. Had Brete Harte been there, he would have made a story out of it. The story also illustrates what historian John Thompson calls the trait of "neighborliness" in Oklahoma (1986, 51).

Given our hundred-year perspective, let us note in passing how some of the findings of the historians at the Future of the Western Past Conference, from the point of view of their particular fields, might cause us to rewrite or reinterpret the history and mythology of Oklahoma beginnings and, indeed, the history of the West.

One of the speakers at the conference was William Cronon, an environmental historian, who urged that future historians relate environmental history to human history and not have separate chapters on the environment alone (1989, 14–17). Cronon also noted that the environment has a will and a pattern of its own which we must study and understand if we are to write accurate history. By using such an approach the historian would not be surprised by the eruption of Mount Saint Helens in 1982 or the 1988 fires in Yellowstone or the recurrent drought years on the Great Plains (Cronon 1989, 14). In that connection we now know that Oklahoma was subject to periodic droughts of which its pioneers in 1889 had no knowledge. The 1893 land rushers actually came in a drought year but tried to take no notice of it. In short, as John Thompson has noted in his perceptive study of Oklahoma's beginnings, Sooners and Boomers came to the territory in 1889 assuming that its lands were good for farming, that rainfall was adequate for raising corn and wheat, and that there was enough land for all (Cronon 1986, 3–68).

In future histories, says Cronon, we must be aware of the cultural assumptions of the pioneers and also must make distinctions between settlers who find and use the resources of nature, such as furs, bison meat, or minerals, and other settlers who farm and store. In short, we must analyze patterns of relationships with nature that inform us and make our histories more intelligent and meaningful. As an example of just how neglectful we have been on this front, even with environmental crusades, Cronon notes that the most recent study of bison depopulation on the Great Plains is over twenty-five years old. There are other needless gaps in our knowledge as well. In an impressive list of what has yet to be done in terms of the environmental history of the West, Cronon makes an eloquent plea for "environmental histories of occupational disease, urban populations, toxic wastes, working-class neighborhoods, and environmental studies of western cities" (Cronon 1989, 17).

These assertions may not seem relevant to frontier Oklahoma, but they are. Not only was the soil and rainfall insufficient to support more eastern agricultural crops, but midwestern settlers also were as interested in townsites and cities as in agriculture—and often in both for speculative reasons rather than reasons of settlement. These speculative instincts and the way early cities developed in Oklahoma—and especially Guthrie and Oklahoma City—meant that an urban experience was as much a part of Oklahoma's beginnings as anything else. Given the facts, the Oklahoma myth that it began as a rural farming homesteader's paradise needs considerable revision.

If one applies this line of approach to the history of the Oklahoma land rush, a fascinating if often grim story emerges. A buffalo-Indian culture was intruded upon by the arrival of the farming Five Civilized Tribes in the 1830s. On the whole those nations adapted rather well, for the land and climate of eastern Oklahoma was very much like that which they had left in Tennessee, Georgia, Alabama, and Mississippi (Thompson 1986, 28–29). But in central Oklahoma, after the buffalo were killed off, Texas cattlemen moved in their herds in the 1870s and 1880s only to be succeeded by white, grain-raising farmers in 1889 and after. These dramatic ecological changes in just two regions of present-day Oklahoma in less than a hundred years' time, if reported by an environmental historian, would suggest that the glorious land run was a prelude to an ecological tragedy that led to the famous Dust Bowl of the 1930s.

The older histories of westward expansion often picture the Indians as always in retreat, often passive, with their various cultures on the way to extinction. This was certainly the assumption of the 1889 Oklahoma Boomers, who were further persuaded of this pattern by the fact that the Dawes Severalty Act of 1887 promised to open up still more Indian lands to white settlement while forcing Native Americans themselves to turn into homesteading farmers. At first it appears that this was indeed to be the case with the Five Civilized Tribes, for in contrast to the Sooners' and Boomers' long tradition of successful frontier expansion and conquest, the tribes exemplified a series of defeats (Foreman 1932; King and Evans 1978; Satz 1985; Wilkins 1986; Woodward 1963).

Having been removed from their traditional homelands in the American Southeast, soon after they arrived in Oklahoma they were further constrained by the parceling out of some of their western lands to plains and other tribes. Then they were defeated yet again when some of the tribes—or portions of them—declared for the Confederacy. The outcome was that still more lands were lost. The final defeats came when the Dawes Act forced them to adopt severalty and the Curtis Act of 1898 deprived them of their rights to govern themselves as independent nations.

But to look at only the string of defeats suffered by the Cherokees from the time of Removal and the Trail of Tears to 1900 is not always useful. The fact is that the Cherokees produced leaders like John Ross who kept the nation going even though it was bitterly divided by internal factions. In the midst of the tumultuous debate over removal, the Cherokees learned Sequoyah's syllabary and thus became literate; they wrote a constitution and became a "nation." Thus, to be beleaguered does not necessarily mean to be defeated.

It can be argued that the Cherokees and the others of the

Five Civilized Tribes arrived in future Oklahoma possessed of a strong spirit, acutely aware of white ways and political power through bitter experience, guided by strong leaders, and at the same time engaged in feuds and violence. The Removal, while high tragedy, an incredible example of injustice, and characterized by great suffering, became a symbol of persistence, not extinction. The Trail of Tears thus became a unifying factor, a symbol of the tribe's common past, somewhat as the Mormons saw their own trek to Utah in 1847.[5]

As John Thompson and many other Oklahoma historians have pointed out, however, southern and eastern Oklahoma—Indian Territory—was invaded after the Civil War by Southerners, who themselves had experienced military, political, and psychological defeat when the Confederacy fell in 1865. But that group, somewhat like the Indian tribes with whom they soon became associated and whose assets and holdings they soon appropriated, or at least tried to appropriate, also made a comeback of sort. That is, they continued to pursue their southern rural life-style, developed a passion for acquiring land, and tried to resurrect an older plantation economy. They even seemed content to perpetuate a class society of haves and have nots (Thompson 1986, 22–24, 41).

To the outsider, by most definitions, the origin myths of both Indians and Southern whites were associated with defeat. But the fact was that both were surviving. Social historians see deprivation as a mark of failure, but deprivation not only is relative, but also has its own culture, which can be far richer than outsiders could ever know.

In an essay written for the Future of the Western Past Conference entitled "Directions for Native American History," George A. Miles, a student of Indian history, reminds us that culture is flexible and innovative and that Native Americans can no longer be seen as foils for or mere antagonists of whites but must be recognized as a people capable of independent action based on motives that arise principally from the complex demands of their own lives and culture (1989, 1–15). Miles asserts that we must get rid of the idea that until whites came along, Indian history was apolitical and that discord came only with Europeans. Rather, Europeans and Indians jointly made this world, and so a history of interchange instead of confrontation is what we should write about. We must find out what new institutions Native Americans and Europeans developed to mediate their interaction. Then, says Miles, "we can develop an historiographic tradition in which Native Americans appear as integral parts of American history rather than as esoteric curiosities of a preliminary sideshow" (Miles 1989, 15).

The different responses of various Indian groups to the Oklahoma land rushes dramatically illustrate Miles's point. The Indians protested white land takeovers not with violence and war but through a complex system of accommodations and resistance—the latter often characterized by delegations to Congress, petitions, and the hiring of lawyers (see Prucha 1979). At the same time, other Indians urged acceptance of the new order and accommodation of the whites.

To illustrate my point, I note that one of the first promoters of the sale of Oklahoma Indian lands to whites was Elias Boudinot, Jr., a Native American who was himself a lawyer for a railroad. In 1871, Boudinot had proposed the sale and allotment of lands similar to the way they were eventually disposed of in 1889 and after. Other Indian leaders disagreed and spoke eloquently of defending their last homeland. They hated Boudinot, and at one point in the early 1880s he and Kansas City railroad promoters were ordered out of Muskogee, but he and others persisted (Gibson 1981, 157–59). Coal mines were already operating in the Choctaw Nation during the 1880s, and most tribes were leasing lands to Texas and Kansas cattlemen for grazing long before 1889 (McReynolds 1964, 266–69).

After whites came in large numbers to eastern Oklahoma and during the land rushes in central and western Oklahoma which continued to 1905, Indians alternately resisted and accommodated. In 1889, for example, the Chickasaws petitioned Congress to defeat a severalty bill, which they dubbed a "land shark bill." Certain Cherokee and Creek leaders signed it as well. Yet only ten years later, Pleasant Porter, newly elected principal chief of the Creeks, delivered his first annual address to the Creek Council. The message was mostly about laws, education, land fraud, and the prospect of severalty. Porter had long been an advocate of continued independence for the Indian nations, but on this occasion he said, in effect, let us accept the new American system imposed upon us and seek opportunities under it. Porter urged his hearers, to use present-day slang, to get in on the act.

Porter also gave the council a most important message in a remarkable peroration:

The vitality of our race still persists. We have not lived for naught. We are the original discoverers of this continent and the conquerors of it from the animal kingdom, and on it first taught the arts of peace and war, and first planted the institutions of virtue, truth and liberty. The European Nations found us here and were made aware that it was possible for them to exist and subsist here. We have given the European People our thought forces, the best blood of our ancestors having been intermingled with [that of] their best statesmen and living citizens. We have made ourselves an indestructible element in their national history. (Porter 1900; see especially pp. 13, 20)

What Chief Porter was saying was truly significant. In 1900 Americans were busy reading Indians, as a declining race and population, out of their history. In a single strong statement Porter put them back in, saying that the Indians would survive and, indeed, persist, for "we are an indestructible element in their national history." Chief Porter was also saying what American social and ethnohistorians have come to realize in recent years, and that is the fact that Indian-white intermarriage has been much greater over the entire United States than was previously believed (see Peterson and Brown 1985; Van Kirk 1980). Chief Porter was also a prophet, for only in the past thirty or forty years have Indian history and American history come to be merged, and that because of the emphasis on social and minority history, a theme that was prominent throughout the Future of the Western Past Conference. And finally it is to be noted that Chief Porter expressed himself in terms of historical concepts that Euroamericans think are not Native American.

Oklahoma's own image of itself presents a fascinating story

of contrasts: victory, defeat, and contradictory political traditions ranging from populism and socialism to Democratic and Republican loyalties to conservative capitalism. The paradoxes exist at other levels as well: Oklahoma is both very religious and very secular; its peoples are midwestern, Southern, Indian, and black. It has a rural, town, nonindustrial tradition that is hard to reconcile with its big-business oil industry history.[6]

One clue about the source of these seemingly contradictory characteristics can be found in the photographs of Oklahoma over the past 150 years. In a probing essay entitled "Views and Reviews: Western Art and Western History," Martha Sandweiss, former curator of photography of the Amon Carter Museum, suggests that the art and material culture of the West, despite many photographic accounts, remains virtually untapped by historians (1989, 3–5). In a series of dramatic examples, she noted how the pictures of the United States Geological Survey photographers were used not just to report, but also to shape images in the public mind, and she observes in one case that in a single decade a photograph of an Indian was first interpreted as threatening and then, in later printing, was used to show how nonthreatening Indians were. She urges historians to use visual artifacts with a full appreciation of both their cultural and manipulative qualities. The promotion materials for the Oklahoma land runs provide vivid examples of the manipulative qualities of illustrations.

This essay began with the premise that anniversaries and centennials were occasions for new interpretations of the past based on a larger, broader perspective achieved in part by the passing of time. It ends with a dual plea, first to take a hard analytical look at Oklahoma's origins in the light of new scholarship. Some of that scholarship will inevitably be critical and revisionist. If it is honest, it will have to explore the darker side of Oklahoma history with its violence, both racial and criminal; its sometimes unthinking boom-or-bust economy; and its sometimes ill use of the land. Long before any revisionist historians appeared there was a self-critical theme in Oklahoma historiography, and it is not likely to go away now.[7] Almost inevitably the heroes of one era become the villains of another.

But there is another equally important task at hand, and this is the second plea: it is to seek to understand the nature of the society in which we live today. To do this we must seek a meaningful past to explain the present and even to propose a meaningful future. This means we must ask new questions, must wonder if there is a newer set of origin myths that are more pertinent. We should ask, for example, how the rise of the oil industry changed not only the economy of Oklahoma, but also its image, its meaning to the rest of America, and even how it created a different view of the world itself. In the same way we must ask how our new views and tolerance of ethnicity, and our new awareness of the environment, might reorient all our earlier understandings of Oklahoma origins. With these things in mind, what is meaningful for us today in the land runs of 1889 and 1893 and after?

The Oklahoma Land Rush of 1889 will always be a wonderfully engrossing story of the hardships of those who came and either succeeded or failed. It was and will always be a central part of the history of American pioneering. We will never tire of hearing about it or the Cherokee Outlet saga of 1893, with its hundred thousand Boomers rushing from all sides into an area the size of Massachusetts, again all in a day. But what is its message for today? While we live with the uncomfortable knowledge that we took the lands we had promised various Indian tribes they could keep in perpetuity, there is another message as well, and that is to rediscover what "free land" meant to earlier generations of Americans.

They believed that free or cheap land gave everyone a chance, so it was a democratic concept. Jefferson believed that if one developed the land and became a farmer, the process produced a self-sufficient citizen who was independent and therefore not dependent on government. Such a person, thought Jefferson, was the most reliable citizen one could wish for. In earlier times, owning land also meant that you could vote. Further, it was an investment, a form of collateral. It even gave the owner social status. In some ways the existence of so-called free land on the western frontiers implied that all these things could be realized by the homesteader. But there is another western image that is antithetical: that the West was a moving frontier, that it had a mobile population, that it was full of drifters. Indeed, many historians argue that western individualism prevented the rise of true community (see Hine 1980). But in 1889 Oklahoma was not a vague frontier but a place. Orrin Burright, one of the '89 Boomers, said that Oklahoma was peculiar among the states and territories because of the general sentiment of "homes" in the minds of most people (Burright 1973, 221). British historian John Hawgood has written that Oklahoma was the country's last great natural farming frontier, and because of that it was "opened up with an almost supersonic boom" (1967, 368). For the Sooners and the Boomers, whether they stayed or not, the claim was a symbol of freedom.

Oklahoma then was a dramatic articulation of a traditional American dream. The vividness of that dream was so strong that those living in tents or wagons or dugouts saw beyond to something better. The Oklahoma historian Edwin C. McReynolds has said that Oklahomans seemed very optimistic, and John Hawgood could not get over the fact that Oklahoma had ten times as much population when it became a state as California had when it was admitted—and California had gold.

It is no wonder then, that the people of this country had such a craze for land. It meant security and independence; it meant that as a voter you could get the government to protect your property. The Land Rush of 1889 was the last expression of faith in an American tradition as old as the first colonizers of Virginia rebelling against company-owned plantations in favor of individual ownership. In New England it took the form of one congregation hiving off to found a new town in an area where more land existed. It was the tradition that the Scotch-Irish pursued when they ruthlessly settled western Pennsylvania and the Shenandoah, saying, "God sent us to preempt America."

But most important, the occupation of the land was achieved by ordinary citizens. That made them causal agents in history, not victims or pawns of rulers. Thus, for all of its dark sides—the greed, the selfishness, the dispossession of Native Americans, or the abuse of the land through bad farming or tenanting—the land rush was history being made by ordinary people, and that is fundamental to the operation of a true democracy.

My personal hope is that we can once again pay attention to the older democratic meaning of land and try to apply that meaning to our problems today. We should be able to find ways to use existing lands and other natural resources to benefit all, not just our generation. We must listen to the serious conservationists, try to control mindless urban sprawl, and seek to understand the mysteries of our environment. Somehow we should find a way to make land, opportunity, and democracy synonymous again as the three seemed to be in 1889, but with an eye toward environmental harmony rather than temporary mastery and exploitation. Then it would be a centennial with a profound message and worthy of celebration in a state that historians once called "the most American frontier" but could then proudly call "the most American state."

Oklahoma entered the Union in 1907 after a contradictory decade of impressively rapid growth combined with severe disappointments because of drought, poor prices for crops, and depression. A combination of economic and political frustrations led its citizens to embrace populism in the 1890s and to consider socialism after 1900. In a national era dominated by the Republican party, Oklahoma turned to the Democrats in a further show of rebellion.[8] Its Indian population was equally unhappy and frustrated by the Dawes Severalty Act, the Curtis Act, and the rampant abuse and corruption that affected their lives, and in scores of ways they, too, resisted and persisted through legal and political stratagems. The Oklahoma land runs, which set all of these things in motion, have many positive and negative meanings, but certainly one of them is that they illustrate the power of the free-land, homestead syndrome in American society and culture along with all of the many problems it has caused, as well as achievements it has inspired.

Notes

1. Portions of the address have been adapted for this essay.

2. The Future of the Western Past Conference was held at Yale University, New Haven, Conn., April 26–29, 1989. Those presenting papers were William Cronon, Sarah Deutsch, Ann Fabian, John Mack Faragher, Jay Gitlin, Patricia Nelson Limerick, Michael McGerr, George Miles, Clyde Milner, Katherine Morrissey, Michael Quinn, and Martha Sandweiss. Their papers are published in a volume edited by William Cronon, George Miles, and Jay Gitlin (1992).

3. See especially articles in *South Dakota History* 19 (1989): 1–596; and "The Centennial West," a series of articles about Washington, Montana, North Dakota, South Dakota, Idaho, and Wyoming in *Montana: The Magazine of Western History* 37, 38, 39, 40 (Autumn 1987 to Fall 1990).

4. Editorial in *New York Herald Tribune*, April 24, 1889 (reproduced in Hill 1889, 39).

5. Thompson (1986, 28–30) notes successive adaptations. Thomas F. O'Dea (1957) stresses the sense of Mormon unity brought on by suffering and exile.

6. The contradictory qualities of Oklahoma's culture are a major theme of Thompson (1986). See especially pp. xi–xii, 216–26.

7. Angie Debo's writings (1985), for example, have always been critical of Sooners, speculators, political corruption, and mistreatment of Native Americans. Excellent recent critical political histories are by Thompson (1986); Robert Worth Miller (1987); and Danny Goble (1980).

8. The story of social and political protest by both Indians and whites during the 1890s and the first two decades of this century is well treated by Miller (1987), Thompson (1986), and Goble (1980).

CHAPTER 3

Black Oklahomans and the Question of "Oklahomaness": The People Who Weren't Invited to Share the Dream

JAMES M. SMALLWOOD AND CRISPIN A. PHILLIPS

Racial classification of people according to color—black, red, white, yellow, brown—is among the most durable principles of social structure throughout American history. This is no less true of Oklahoma history during territorial days as well as after statehood. Not only did blacks have to struggle against white racism in Oklahoma, but they also had to overcome control by some Native American groups which had brought black slaves with them from the southeastern United States during their forced removal. What makes race relations even more unusual in Oklahoma is the fact that Oklahoma very nearly became an all-black sanctuary and state. Furthermore, Oklahoma is distinctive in that race relations have long been triadic—black, white, and red—instead of exclusively black and white.

Nowhere does the struggle over the question, Whose dream is the Oklahoma dream? become more clear than in this chapter by James M. Smallwood and Crispin A. Phillips that describes blacks' experience in Oklahoma. Theirs is an experience inseparable from Oklahomaness itself. Race relations between blacks and whites, and racism, have a particular, if not unique, coloring in Oklahoma history. Not only did blacks participate in the Oklahoma land runs, but also Oklahoma, the state with the worst race riot in American history (in Tulsa in 1921), is the state into which whites might not have been admitted at all but for a fluke of history. This chapter about blacks in Oklahoma is about the collision between different dreams of what Oklahomaness is all about.

How do many black Oklahomans define themselves? First, by color: they were and are varying shades of black and brown, and those colors never washed white just as the Indian red did not wash white. Second, African-Americans everywhere share a common heritage, a common history as an oppressed colonial people who endured two and one-half centuries of slavery and another hundred years of third-class citizenship and who were segregated and discriminated against politically, economically, and socially. Long ago now, the noted civil rights leader W. E. B. DuBois commented on the "two-ness" of Afro-Americans: "[One feels] his two-ness—an American, a Negro; two souls, two thoughts, two unreconciled strivings; two warring ideas in one dark body" (DuBois 1903, 3–4). What DuBois wrote about "two-ness" can also be applied at a more local level of geographic identification: African American and Oklahoman.

Given the historical and still ongoing racism and rabid ethnocentrism, then, Oklahomaness for most white Oklahomans excludes black Oklahomans, who in turn claim their own "we-ness" based on color, on similar goals and aspirations, and on their unique history. However, even a brief perusal of Oklahoma's history proves that, indeed, African Americans should have been incorporated into the Oklahoma "we-ness," from the beginning, for they have been a part of the state's growth, its progress—its heritage—since the sixteenth century (Aldrich 1973; Washington 1948).

Blacks and Early Oklahoma History

People of African descent first came to Oklahoma with early European explorers long before white Americans would claim

Oklahoma as their own. Blacks accompanied the Spanish conquistador Francisco Vásquez de Coronado, who marched northward from Mexico City in 1540 and scouted parts of Arizona, New Mexico, Texas, Oklahoma, and Kansas while looking for legendary cities of gold. Several African slaves labored hard for the expedition, tending stock, cooking meals, and serving as advance scouts. Later, Spanish frontiersmen who passed through Oklahoma included African laborers among their retinue (Hodge 1907, 333; Bolton 1921, 174–75). Likewise, blacks accompanied early French explorers, such as Bernard de la Harpe, a pathfinder and trader, who in 1719 traveled through eastern Oklahoma (Lewis 1924, 253–68).

The first African Americans to come into Oklahoma in significant numbers came as slaves. When the Five Civilized Tribes (Cherokees, Creeks, Choctaws, Chickasaws, and Seminoles) were forced to move from their eastern homes into Oklahoma, they brought their slaves with them. On the eve of the Civil War, approximately 8,000 bondspeople tilled fields for Indian masters. The census of 1860 divulged that the Cherokees held the biggest number of slaves, 2,504, and that the small Seminole tribe held the least, approximately 1,000, although that number is open to dispute (U.S. Department of Commerce, Bureau of the Census 1864, 982).

Slavery among the Indians was not totally unlike that practiced by whites in the southern United States. Although few holdings in Indian Territory could have been termed plantations, still the slaves labored for their masters. Most served as field hands, raising such vegetables as corn and sweet potatoes and working the cotton fields. Some, particularly women, toiled as domestic workers (Rawick 1972). The harshness of the institution of slavery seems not to have varied greatly from southern patterns, although the treatment of the chattels did vary from tribe to tribe. Because the Choctaws (who held 2,297 slaves in 1860) were so heavily involved in agriculture that the tribe's economic vitality depended on docile, hard-working bondspeople, their slave codes were harsh. They forbade cohabitation or intermarriage between Indian and slave. They forbade slaves from owning property. Bondsmen could not carry weapons unless they had written permission from their owners. Because northern abolitionist sentiment spread from the 1830s to the 1860s, the Choctaw codes also forbade the teaching of slaves to read or write. They could not sing or gather in groups without their owner's permission. Further, no person with Negro blood could hold office in the Choctaw government. The Choctaw punishment for slaves who broke any of the codes was severe, including whippings, maimings, and other forms of torture (Jeltz 1948, 31–32).

Like the Choctaws, the Cherokees exhibited a typical southern white's prejudice against blacks, and this attitude was manifest in the Cherokees' sometimes brutal treatment of bondsmen (Johnston 1929, 34–35). Creeks and Seminoles, however, appeared to have a different view of the slave, a view which acknowledged their humanity, although sometimes Creeks and Seminoles differed among themselves about ownership of runaway slaves. The lot of these bondspeople, some of whom were allowed to establish their own villages, was better. There was frequent intermarriage of slaves with Creeks and Seminoles, and the offspring were accepted into the tribes (see Fig. 3.1). Apparently, Chickasaws also allowed slaves more leeway than did the Choctaws or the Cherokees (Abel 1915, 23; Jeltz 1948, 30; Forman 1948, 171; Littlefield 1977, 1978).

From the 1830s to the 1860s, slavery flourished in Indian Territory: slave labor built for the Indians what historian Arrell Gibson called the "Golden Era." But the Civil War brought slaves their freedom. The Civilized Tribes recognized that freedom when, in 1866, they signed treaties with the U.S. government wherein the Indians agreed to grant former slaves citizenship in the nations. Later, freedpeople were to be eligible for annuities and allotments. However, the Indians consistently resisted the claims of freedmen, most of whom received neither annuities nor land allotments. Therefore, the lot of freedmen in Indian Territory continued to be precarious and difficult (Halliburton 1977; Rawick 1973; Tolson 1972, 32–40).

Fig. 3.1. Multiracial composition of school children in the Seminole
Nation. School of Mrs. Antoinette Snow Constant, a missionary to
the Seminoles in 1890. (Courtesy of Archives and Manuscripts Division of the Oklahoma Historical Society, photo number 1459.)

The Black Dream of Oklahoma

By the above-mentioned treaties, the U.S. government forced
the Indians to cede the area known as the Oklahoma District
or Unassigned Lands (in central Oklahoma). For some time
forces both within and without the government wanted to
use this land to colonize blacks. Some radical Republicans of
the post–Civil War era considered such a plan, as did many of
the old prewar abolitionists and humanitarians. However,
such dreams never came true (Chapman 1948, 150–54). White

and Indian hatred for African Americans was too strong; moreover, many whites intended to see the Unassigned Lands delivered into white hands.

The famed Boomer era in Oklahoma began in earnest in the 1870s when such leaders as David Payne and William Couch began lobbying long and hard for white settlement. Ultimately their appeals and the appeals of hundreds of others were successful: President Benjamin Harrison issued a proclamation declaring that the Unassigned Lands would be open for settlement on April 22, 1889 (*United States Statutes at Large* 1889).

Still, some African Americans refused to give up their Oklahoma dream. Alongside whites, some made the Oklahoma Land Run of '89; De' Leslaine R. Davis and Peter Flinn, for example, waited on horseback north of the Canadian River with approximately fifty thousand other Boomers. Once the run was on, both men succeeded in laying claim to land near El Reno in Canadian County (*Norman Transcript* 1890; Buchanan and Dale 1924, 206). Other African Americans also claimed land, and along with white settlers they then went about the task of building temporary dugouts where families made do until they could finish permanent homes (Fig. 9.3). Men, women, and children next cleared fields, most of which were overgrown with blackjack (scrubby oak), and planted such crops as turnips, peas, corn, and melons. Many blacks, like their white counterparts, gave up in that first year and deserted Oklahoma. But many hardy African American souls came to stay—to fulfill their dream—and did whatever was necessary to survive (Forman 1948).

By July, enterprising African Americans began forming companies to help other blacks migrate to the new lands. For example, W. L. Eagleson, a black politician from Kansas, began a propaganda campaign to entice settlers. Soon entire small colonies of blacks were settling near such communities as Guthrie and Kingfisher (*Norman Transcript* 1895). United States census data reflect that by 1890 there were 3,008 African Americans in the original seven-county Oklahoma District: 1,643 men and 1,365 women (by contrast, the 1990 census counted 101,053). Kingfisher, Logan, and Oklahoma counties had the predominant number of black settlers after the run. By comparison, the 1890 census revealed that a total of 18,831 African Americans lived in Oklahoma Territory, with about one-third being concentrated in Logan County. Approximately 37,000 blacks lived in Indian Territory in 1900 (U.S. Department of Commerce, Bureau of the Census 1892, 503, 638–39; 1902, 553; 1990, 46–54).

Racism and the Thwarted Dream

From the inception of their movement into Oklahoma, African Americans were subject to the racism of the times. Indeed, after Reconstruction, the overall position of African Americans, nationwide, declined constantly, a trend not reversed until the modern civil rights movement. From 1889 to 1907, blacks in Oklahoma Territory found the same discrimination that they had faced elsewhere. White Oklahomans became ever more fearful of blacks, because many African American promoters still had the dream of turning Oklahoma Territory into a black state. Consequently, Democrats repeatedly charged Republicans with trying to colonize blacks, and violence periodically flared in many areas.

For example, a white mob ran African Americans out of Lexington in 1892. One year later, all blacks had left Blackwell, while poor whites hounded those in Ponca City (*Oklahoma Guide* 1901; *Oklahoma Eagle* 1893). Masked raiders also attacked blacks in Lincoln County, forcing them to leave. In Indian Territory, too, frequent racial trouble flared. Riots against blacks and other violence continued unabated throughout the era of the twin territories (*Indian Chieftain* 1896; *El Reno News* 1896; *Kingfisher Free Press* 1896).

Those whites and reds who drove African Americans away anticipated their modern-day counterparts. For example, well before World War II, whites in little Durant, in the area of Oklahoma known as Little Dixie, were driving African Americans out at gunpoint, forcing them to move south to establish their own all-black community; such had always been the white "answer" to the question of race relations. A perusal of the 1990 census showed that of 675 towns in the state, 312 had no black residents; further, nine of the state's seventy-seven counties had five or fewer black residents (U.S. Department of Commerce, Bureau of the Census 1990, 45–56). Such figures suggest that many racially isolated white Oklahomans are seldom exposed to African American society and culture and thereby lose a valuable learning experience that might lead to understanding.

African Americans who were discriminated against and terrorized by the white and red communities could only turn inward and survive as best they could. One answer to survival —the one blacks in latter-day Durant were forced to accept— seemed to lie in the creation of all-black towns. Langston was one such town. Founded on October 22, 1890, by Edwin P. McCabe, a noted separatist leader, Langston soon developed several thriving business establishments and a newspaper, the *Langston City Herald*, which McCabe used to stimulate interest in the separatist movement. Moreover, the legislature helped ensure Langston's permanence when it located the Colored Agricultural and Normal University there in 1897. However, as late as 1907 the town's population stood at only 274 (Crockett 1979, 25–26; Tolson 1972, 95; Patterson 1979; Bittle and Geis 1964). Yet the town survived; by 1990 it had a population of 1,429 blacks and twenty-seven whites (U.S. Department of Commerce, Bureau of the Census 1990, 46–54).

Langston was not the oldest black town in Oklahoma Territory. Organized in August 1889, Lincoln City was located north of Kingfisher in north central Oklahoma. Early on, it boasted a population of approximately three hundred (Rock 1890, 182–83). Altogether, African Americans founded four towns and one colony in Oklahoma Territory and twenty-five towns in Indian Territory, with Boley being most famous. Located some seventy-five miles east of Guthrie, Boley quickly attracted settlers. By 1907 its population stood at 824 and it boasted several businesses and a free school. However, as Norman Crockett (1979) shows, most African American towns failed, many having no solid economic base; those which survived existed only as small, isolated communities (see also Tolson 1972, 90–105).

Not only did those who advocated separatist colonies or towns in Oklahoma fail to attain their dream, but they also found themselves shut out of the power structure politically, socially, and economically. In the early territorial years after 1889 several African Americans held office under Republican administrations, but their numbers remained small. Ultimately both major parties assumed a "lily white" policy. Whites joined to drive blacks from office and to inflict upon the black community a spate of Jim Crow, segregationist, legislation. (Many scholars believe that the name Jim Crow evolved from black minstrel shows. Jim Crow was a character in one of the minstrel songs, and over time the two words "Jim Crow" became synonymous with segregation, meaning separation of the races.)

Such legislation in Oklahoma had its beginnings in the 1890s. Segregationist principles emerged early in a drive for separate schools. Bitter infighting occurred in the territorial assembly in 1890 before delegates chose "local option"; that is, citizens of each county would vote to decide the issue. Of course dominant whites in each county voted for separate schools, and as mentioned above, the university at Langston was created solely for the "colored." Thus, racial segregation in education came quickly to the territory (*Legislative Journal of Oklahoma Territory* 1890, 703–704).

In 1896 the U.S. Supreme Court entered the momentous struggle over segregation when it issued the *Plessy v. Ferguson* decision, which delivered the "separate but equal" doctrine. In effect the court ruled that all forms of segregation were legal as long as blacks had "separate but equal" facilities. Jim Crowism thus gained legal sanction, and it became the rule in Oklahoma. Beginning in February 1897, the territorial assembly passed the first of its restricted laws: it prohibited intermarriage between the races. Furthermore, it repealed the local-option school law and mandated school segregation throughout the territory in school districts that had eight or more black children (Oklahoma 1908, 212, 266).

Meanwhile, in both Oklahoma and Indian territories, African Americans continued to lobby for their rights. Some formed the Negro Protective League in Muskogee in August

1905. The league fought Jim Crow legislation and tried to ensure that blacks would be treated justly at the statehood convention. Democrats, however, came out solidly for restrictive legislation, and they secured a landslide victory in both the territories when voters elected convention delegates. Then at the convention they began a persistent clamor to "put the nigger in his place" (*Muskogee Cimeter* 1905; *Oklahoma Guide* 1900; Tolson 1972, 137).

Segregationists ran afoul of a problem, however. President Theodore Roosevelt leaked word that he would not accept a constitution based completely on Jim Crow principles. His position, plus continued black protests, persuaded Democrats to modify their views. The final constitution, which Roosevelt approved, contained only a few restrictive acts: schools remained segregated, and the legislature was given the right to determine the franchise question later (Oklahoma 1907).

Democrats, who because of Roosevelt's pressure had been hesitant to push segregation at the statehood convention, threw caution to the winds when the state's first legislature met. Governor Charles Haskell recommended and the legislature passed a Jim Crow law regarding public transportation which provided separate coaches and waiting rooms for black Oklahomans and fines for disobeying the law. Some 540 railroad depots in the state had to be renovated to fit the new requirement, and new coaches also had to be added to the lines (*Purcell Register* 1907). The black community met the coach law with unqualified opposition. In local meetings blacks condemned the law. In Muskogee and other areas African Americans first refused to obey the law, but the authorities strictly enforced the statute (*Daily Oklahoman* 1908; *Kingfisher Weekly Star and Free Press* 1908).

Meanwhile, the first Oklahoma legislature enacted other restrictive laws. It passed a stronger miscegenation law which prohibited intermarriage, making violations felonies with penalties including a fine of up to five hundred dollars and a jail term of up to five years. Furthermore, the new law made it a felony for ministers to perform interracial wedding ceremonies (Oklahoma 1908, 556).

Democrats increasingly became more and more concerned

about black participation in state politics, because blacks
helped elect Republicans. The Democratic legislature took
final action in 1910 when it sent the so-called Taylor resolution to a vote of the people. That resolution provided that any
potential voter had to read or write a section of the state
constitution unless he had antecedents who could vote as of
January 1, 1866 (the Grandfather Clause). The Oklahoma
electorate passed the measure and effectively disfranchised
blacks (Oklahoma 1910, 284–85).

African American leaders in Oklahoma decided to fight
for their political and civil rights in court. A series of legal
cases tested both the discriminatory voter act and the Jim Crow
public transportation law. The latter legal struggle ended in
November 1914 when the U.S. Supreme Court upheld the
segregated coach law. Although blacks were probably disgusted with that ruling, in 1915 they were likely elated when
the court ruled Oklahoma's famous Grandfather Clause unconstitutional (*McCabe* v. *Atchinson T & S.F.R. Co.*, 235
U.S. 151; *Guinn and Beal* v. *United States*, 238 U.S. 347; see
Mangum Weekly Star 1915).

For a time Oklahoma's Democratic legislators continued to
look for new ways to limit the African American vote but
failed. Nevertheless, blacks' position in society continued to
decline. By law, custom, and tradition, black Oklahomans
were segregated in all aspects of life. Perhaps the height of
this folly was best illustrated by a 1915 Oklahoma law, the
first of its kind in the nation, that created segregated telephone booths (Franklin 1980, 17).

Continued Deterioration of Race Relations

Race relations continued to grow worse in Oklahoma even
after whites had created their own totally segregated society.
Nowhere was trouble more serious than in Tulsa in 1921. On
May 31, police arrested a black man for allegedly attacking a
white orphan girl, but what the man actually did or did not

do is still open to dispute. Nevertheless, rumors flew that a mob intended to lynch the African American. Upon hearing of the threats, approximately fifty stalwart blacks, some apparently belonging to the African Blood Brotherhood, which stressed racial pride and solidarity, went to the jail to protect the incarcerated man.

The anticipated white mob assembled, and policemen threw up a cordon to keep the races apart, but a gunshot rang out. Blacks, chased by the unruly mob, retreated back to what whites called "Little Africa," where shots sounded throughout the night. Then when daylight approached on June 1, the whites went on a rampage, attacking "Little Africa" with a vengeance, setting fires to homes and shooting at black men, women, and children. African Americans gave battle, and the riot continued through the day. The authorities finally restored order, but some nine whites and sixty-eight blacks lay dead (these were known dead; the actual count may have been higher); two hundred African Americans and one hundred whites received injuries or wounds; thirty city blocks were destroyed; and homes where fifteen thousand blacks had lived were reduced to ashes. One report, blaming whites, called the Tulsa riot "one of the most horrible scenes of race hatred in America" (Halliburton 1975, *The New York Times* 1921; Teall 1971, 205–206).

If optimists hoped that race relations would improve after sober reflection about the Tulsa riot, they were disappointed, for the 1920s would see the rise of the Oklahoma Ku Klux Klan. Reborn in Georgia in 1915, the Klan reached Oklahoma by the 1920s and quickly acquired a membership that reached into the thousands. In fact, led by Clay Jewett, it allegedly controlled the state legislature for a time. In 1923 the Klan organized more than twenty-five hundred whipping parties that roamed the state. On one night alone, fiery crosses blazed in more than two hundred places simultaneously, thereby showing the power of the Klan (*New York Times* 1923). Excesses continued to occur in the state through the 1920s, but by 1930 the Klan's excesses had led to its downfall as sober, responsible whites finally turned against the organization.

Black Oklahomans: From the Depression to World War II

During the 1930s the struggle against discrimination took second place to the Great Depression. Destitution quickly settled on Oklahoma's black community. Unemployment was high as African Americans became the "last hired and first fired." Rural black sharecroppers found themselves turned off the land or forced off by hard times as Oklahoma became part of the dust bowl. Increasingly, African Americans moved to Oklahoma's urban centers. There, however, they found little opportunity until 1933, when the New Deal came to the state.

Under Franklin D. Roosevelt the federal government moved to relieve suffering with a spate of legislation. From 1933 to 1938, continuing programs helped the dispossessed, and black Oklahomans participated in those programs although they were still discriminatory. For example, at least four thousand black families benefitted from the WPA alone (Dale and Wandell 1950, 359–61).

Meanwhile, in the 1930s African Americans continued their fight against discrimination and managed one notable victory in court. In 1933, Oklahoma City passed a segregated housing ordinance which prohibited blacks from occupying a lot in a block where a white majority prevailed. Ultimately a U. S. circuit court ruled the ordinance unconstitutional and void. Later, in 1938, another battle was won when Muskogee blacks stopped a local school bond issue because the money would have been used exclusively for white schools (*Allen* v. *Oklahoma City et al*, no. 26152, *Oklahoma Reports; Black Dispatch* 1938).

The Civil Rights Movement in Oklahoma

Black Oklahomans watched while the U. S. Supreme Court stepped to the forefront of the civil rights movement. In a series of decisions in the 1940s the court ruled against the white primary, a device the Democratic party used to ban the black vote in the Democratic primaries; the court also ruled against restrictive real estate covenants and further ruled that black passengers in interstate commerce could make their journeys without obeying segregationist laws in states through which their public carrier passed (*Smith* v. *Allwright*, 321 U.S. 649; *Morgan* v. *Virginia*, 328 U.S. 373; *Shelley* v. *Kraemer*, 334 U.S. 1).

However, in cases involving education, justice made its greatest gains. In 1938 the court forced the University of Missouri law school to accept a black student because it was the only way the student could get a law education inside the state (*Gaines* v. *University of Missouri*, 304 U.S. 337). In 1948 the court ordered the University of Texas to accept a black law student even though the state of Texas had a black law school (one "created out of thin air" and located in some rented rooms in a building in downtown Houston). The court ruled that the new black law "school" was inferior to that in Austin (*Sweatt* v. *Painter*, 339 U.S. 629). In the same year the court told Oklahoma to afford a law education for Ada Lois Sipuel just as it would for any other student (*Sipuel* v. *University of Oklahoma et al.*, 332 U.S. 631). Then in 1950 the court decreed that the University of Oklahoma must stop segregating G. W. McLaurin in his classes and on the campus (*McLaurin* v. *Oklahoma State Regents for Higher Education*, 339 U.S. 637; Cross 1975; Swain 1978).

Of course, the most significant and most famous case against segregation was *Brown* v. *Board of Education of Topeka, Kansas* (347 U.S. 483), wherein the Supreme Court ruled that schools segregated by race were inherently unequal. The court knew that its ruling was potentially revolutionary. If the unequal doctrine could be applied to education, it could also be applied to all other aspects of public life. Everywhere in the South, including Oklahoma, resistance flared. In the fall of 1954 all of Oklahoma's public schools opened with the same old segregated pattern. Only the state colleges and the parochial schools integrated. But in 1955 the court issued a second decision calling for a "reasonable start toward full compliance" (*Brown et al.* v. *Board of Education et al.*, 349 U.S. 294). Nevertheless, integration in Oklahoma came slowly. The two biggest districts, Oklahoma City and Tulsa, would not become fully integrated until the early 1970s. Meanwhile, constant racial strife continued. Many state legislators introduced bills to slow school integration, while black teachers suffered discrimination in pay and in some cases lost their jobs if they were activists (Tolson 1972, 176–89).

After the *Brown* decision, the fight against discrimination focused upon new issues, beginning in 1955 with the Montgomery, Alabama, bus boycott, by which activists ultimately won their fight to desegregate buses. Then it was on to new geographic areas and other issues as protests and sit-ins became commonplace. In Oklahoma, teacher Clara Luper spearheaded the early protests. A member of the Oklahoma City chapter of the National Association for the Advancement of Colored People (NAACP), she led many early sit-in protests in the mid-1950s, integrating establishments throughout the state. In 1958, for example, Luper's NAACP Youth Council struck at downtown Oklahoma City stores, particularly with a sit-in at Katz Drug Store. Well-dressed young black people between six and sixteen years of age sat down at the drugstore's food counter and asked for food to eat there instead of to take out, as blacks were customarily required to do. Some whites became angry at the sit-in, but after days of protest the store changed its policy. Later, Luper and her young charges took buses to Lawton, Enid, and Tulsa to repeat their sit-in protests (Franklin 1980, 56; Luper 1979).

Luper's early work encouraged others. Soon other Oklahoma City leaders organized a boycott of all downtown stores, banks, and businesses, and some courageous whites joined in. For example, Father Robert McDole, assistant pastor at the Corpus Christi Catholic Church, and Reverend John Herdbrink, chaplain at Oklahoma City University, joined the movement in time to participate in a demonstration in the Cravens Building, home of a popular cafeteria. Then some white students at the University of Oklahoma became active; they criticized Oklahoma City officials because discrimination and segregation "served only to catapult your city's continuation of social inequality in the nation's spotlight" (*Black Dispatch* 1960; *Oklahoma City Times* 1960).

By March 1961, some success could be seen. Three major

downtown Oklahoma City restaurants were desegregated: the luncheonette in the John A. Brown store, the lunch counter at the H. L. Green store, and the Forum Cafeteria. Further, Harvey P. Everest, chairman of the governor's Committee on Human Relations, ceaselessly worked to improve race relations. Soon, several more stores and hotels integrated, including the Sheraton chain, and throughout the state conditions improved. For example, restaurants in Okmulgee and Henryetta integrated, as did a major hotel in Tulsa. In Tulsa officials also started desegregating municipal recreational facilities (*Daily Oklahoman* 1961a).

Yet much remained to be done. In Oklahoma City, for example, demonstrators picketed the segregated Central YMCA. Sit-in demonstrators remained in one cafe for nine hours. Protests also brought integration to various amusement parks. Blacks in other locales began following Oklahoma City's example. Soon, smaller towns like Wewoka were opening their drugstore counters and restaurants to blacks. Such state progress was noticed by the national NAACP (*Black Dispatch* 1963).

Progress continued. For example, Oklahoma City's manager, Robert Tinstron, moved to end discrimination in hiring, assigning, and promoting city employees. Such action took place throughout the state as whites slowly accepted integration (*New York Times* 1963; *Daily Oklahoman* 1963). Later, the legislature created and adequately funded the Oklahoma Human Rights Commission, with noted black leader William Y. Rose as its director; it was charged to remove all friction and eliminate all discrimination and segregation in state government operations and to work to repeal all discriminatory laws (*Daily Oklahoman* 1965).

By the time the commission was beginning its work, the historic Civil Rights Act of 1964 was taking effect. Among its other provisions the act forbade discrimination in all places of public accommodation, in job hiring, and in voting. The act also gave the federal government the authority to withhold funds from school districts that remained uncooperative.

Congress of Racial Equality (CORE) members immediately tested the Civil Rights Act by motorcading into "Little

Dixie" to towns like Hugo, Idabel, and Durant, where they integrated restaurants, motels, and hotels. Although some whites made threats, no violence occurred. Meanwhile, black Oklahomans began testing their new political rights. In November 1964, four African Americans were sworn in as legislators in Oklahoma, thereby marking a first in the modern South (*Black Dispatch* 1964). Those black legislators helped get a state public accommodations act through the legislature in 1965. On the national level, under President Lyndon Johnson's dynamic leadership, a voter registration act was passed in 1965 and an open housing ordinance in 1968. Moreover, Johnson's Great Society program targeted the poor nationwide, and many black Oklahomans living below the poverty line received aid (Tolson 1972, 197–99; Teall 1971, 257).

As the decade of the 1970s dawned, black Oklahomans could point to many accomplishments. Yet in what could have been a time of celebration, another issue arose which divided the races: busing. Throughout urban America (and Oklahoma was no exception) resegregation of housing had occurred in the 1960s as great numbers of whites moved from the cities to the suburbs. That resegregation of housing meant new segregation of schools. In addition, as whites fled the cities, they took the financial tax base with them. Blacks thus "inherited" school districts with little or no money and with reduced public services. As the answer to the resegregation of schools, activists pushed the busing of children to schools outside their neighborhoods. White Oklahoma resisted that measure. In early 1970 the legislature passed an antibusing bill, which blacks strongly protested but which Governor Dewey Bartlett signed on April 15, 1970 (see *Daily Oklahoman* 1961*b*; *Black Dispatch* 1970*a*).

Meanwhile, racial discrimination in the state apparently increased, judging from news headlines. For example, African American staffers at radio station KBYE walked off their jobs, charging discrimination in hiring and promotion practices and complaining that the station completely ignored the black community's needs (*Black Dispatch* 1970*b*).

Additionally, more ominous events occurred as the Ku Klux Klan experienced a revival in the state. In August 1971 Klan activities centered around McAlester; there, the organization planned a giant rally near the Anderson community (on private property). Biracial opposition committed to racial conciliation, however, became so intense that Judge Robert Bell delivered a restraining order blocking the racist rally. That caused Klan reaction; Robert M. Shelton, head of a national Klan group, and Lloyd French, of the United States Klans of America, an organizer in Oklahoma, vowed to continue their efforts in the state.

Indicating a renewal of Klan strength, organizer French met with the Tulsa City Commission in early January of 1971 and expressed his intent to hold a Klan rally within the Tulsa city limits. The rally would include, he said, instruction about communism in America and would close its ceremonies with the burning of a forty-foot-tall cross. By taking no action whatsoever, the commission gave French tacit permission for his rally, which fortunately produced no violence (*Black Dispatch* 1970*b*).

Meanwhile, both the national and the state focus had shifted back to busing. The heart of the opposition to busing appeared to be racist. Bishop Stephen Spottswood of the NAACP maintained that in almost all Southern school districts there was less busing than there had been under segregation. Hence, he said, "there is no other way to interpret opposition to busing for integration than as opposition to integration or inexcusable ignorance" (Quint, Cantor, and Albertson 1972, 418). In Oklahoma, F. D. Moon, a black educator in Oklahoma City, simply said that he really could not get worked up about busing because for years black children in and around Oklahoma City had been bused up to seventy miles a day round trip—past white schools—to enforce segregation. Most whites, however, continued to oppose busing (*Oklahoma City Times* 1971).

Despite opposition, Judge Luther Bohanon ordered a busing proposal, known as the Finger Plan, to be implemented in Oklahoma City. Drawn up by a Rhode Island educator, the plan called for new attendance zones for senior and junior high schools and a new network of fifth-grade centers for primary schools. The plan was made effective February 2,

1972. It was unpopular but was enforced (*Oklahoma City Times* 1972; Boulton 1980).

Black Oklahomans in the Recent Era

From the 1970s to the 1990s many critical issues continued to confront black Oklahomans. Education remained a crucial issue, with white "flight" to the suburbs continuing the trend toward resegregation. By the 1990s more than 60 percent of African American students still attended predominantly minority schools. Furthermore, Oklahoma's public school dropout rate remained greater among blacks than among whites, and among adults twenty-five years old or older, only slightly more than 60 percent of the African Americans had four years of high school or more compared to 80 percent of the whites.

In the 1990s demographic trends among black Oklahomans show a continuing migration into the larger towns and cities, particularly the four Standard Metropolitan Statistical Areas (SMSAs): Oklahoma City, Tulsa, Fort Smith, and Lawton. The census of 1990 divulged that of the 233,801 blacks in Oklahoma (9 percent of the total population), more than 70 percent live in the SMSAs. Although many among the growing black middle class settled into suburbia, more African Americans joined the impoverished of the central cities. Approximately 30 percent of the urban-dwelling Oklahoma blacks fell below the poverty line.

As was also true nationally, social problems plagued Oklahoma's black family structure in the 1990s. More than 50 percent of black children were born illegitimate and lived in female-headed one-parent households, many of which were dependent on welfare programs. Unemployment remained chronic among young blacks who quit high school, drugs were ubiquitous in the core cities, and blacks constituted at least 40 percent of Oklahoma's prison inmate population. All these statistics suggested community disintegration.

In some areas, however, progress was obvious. In public accommodations blacks finally gained equal access. If white Oklahoma's approval came haltingly, at least the law was obeyed. Moreover, even with periodic economic recessions the economic position of the black middle class seemed to be improving, especially in view of equal opportunity regulations.

However, even as Oklahoma seemed to solve some of its old racial problems, new ones emerged. Occasionally, as in 1980 in Idabel, racism again raised its ugly head, and racial clashes intensified as the Klan continued its presence. At Oklahoma State University in the late 1980s several members of an all-white fraternity painted their faces black, grabbed banjos, mimicked what they thought might be the behavior of slaves, and became minstrels, all for the attention of some sorority sisters. When several of the leaders among campus blacks protested, out came the rebel flags, some of which still fly. The white message was thus sent to African Americans.

Some blacks appear to be fighting back at the system but tragically do so illegally and create a far worse "system" that must be suppressed; urban warfare defined by violent ethnic gangs in Los Angeles made its appearance in Oklahoma in the late 1980s and grew rapidly, as did the illegal drug trade that served as the gangs' financial underpinning. Additionally, at an opposite extreme, the number of homeless people grew in Oklahoma, and blacks comprised a significant minority of that dispossessed group (O'Hare et al. 1991; *U.S. News & World Report* 1991, 18–28).

Despite some of the alarming facts and figures given above, the long historical overview gives historians some grounds for optimism. Blacks in Oklahoma, like their counterparts throughout the nation, have come far since the slave days as the gains of the civil rights movement attest. This is particularly important because in Oklahoma there was more of a racial triad—white, black, and red—than existed in some other parts of the country. Middle-aged blacks and whites all remember the old days of segregation and of blatant discrimination and can agree that a virtual revolution was wrought in the 1950s and 1960s. A strong people, black Oklahomans will continue the struggle to succeed.

CHAPTER 4

Ethnic Adaptations to Oklahoma: The Germans, Mexicans, and Vietnamese

DONALD NELSON BROWN

Adaptation, whether to the natural or social environment, is a universal and ever-changing process. In this chapter Donald N. Brown considers Oklahoma as a social environment to which the adaptation of three ethnic-national groups takes place: Germans, Vietnamese, and Mexicans. He explores the question of the fit between the host environment and the cultural emphases brought by the immigrant groups—even as the host culture of Oklahomaness constantly undergoes change. He simultaneously paints a portrait of the rich cultural diversity within Oklahoma and of the interactive process between these diverse cultural groups that in fact create, renew, and redefine Oklahomaness. Although Brown does not focus on Native Americans, blacks, and many other groups whose experience could have been cited, his comparative study of adaptation helps to establish a base line analogous to Gary Thompson's chapter on cultural geography.

The relatively brief history of non–Native American settlement in Oklahoma allows the researcher an opportunity to examine the motivations and aspirations of the new settlers who were attracted to the territory. Questions that in other studies are often indirectly answered in letters and documents can be answered directly through interviews with individuals who participated in the early settlement. These very personal accounts also provide insights into the problems faced and the solutions achieved by these new settlers as they adapted to their new environment. "Adapted" in this case means the way one's group or social characteristics fit into the needs and norms of the new or host system. For groups which were culturally different from the majority, this process of adaptation frequently resulted in the formation of unique communities with focused economic activities. Even in urban areas of Oklahoma, occupational specialization and residence in identifiable neighborhoods became characteristic of these culturally different groups.

Many of the new settlers on Oklahoma lands in 1889 were born in Europe and had come to the United States seeking better economic opportunities. They brought with them their languages, religions, and other customs. The variety of European cultural backgrounds is not surprising when it is considered that the development of Oklahoma corresponded with the period of the greatest flow of immigrants into the United States. In the 1880s over 5.2 million immigrants entered the United States. In the next decade the total of immigrants dropped to 3.7 million, but the first decade of the twentieth century saw the highest flow of immigrants into the United States in the history of the nation: over 8.8 million new arrivals.

In this chapter, relying primarily on oral interviews conducted in 1980 and 1981, I shall briefly examine the adaptations of three ethnic groups to Oklahoma. The Germans formed the largest population of the early European settlers. They sought landownership and business opportunities in order to build a new permanent home. They found an area with few of European descent and little economic development by European standards. Two decades later, Mexicans became a significant population in Oklahoma. Rather than landownership, they sought employment opportunities in an area with an established farming economy and an emerging industrial economy. Except during the Depression years of the 1930s, their labor was welcomed, and many remained to make Oklahoma their home. The Vietnamese came to Oklahoma in the mid-1970s as political refugees. They brought with them economic skills which could be translated into employment and business opportunities. Although many Vietnamese initially expected to return to Southeast Asia after a brief residence in Oklahoma, they have remained and found security in their new homeland.

The German Adaptation

By far the largest number of identifiable European settlers were of German descent. The 1910 census listed over 27,500 residents of Oklahoma as either born in Germany or of German parents (Table 4.1). They were concentrated in the north central counties (Hale 1975). Most were farmers, but a number were successful businessmen. A study by Rohrs indicates that the Germans settling in three central Oklahoma counties had spent an average of sixteen years in the United States before arriving in Oklahoma. Most had migrated across the northern states, while a few entered the United States from either Galveston or New Orleans (Rohrs 1981, 6). Once concentrations of German populations were established in Oklahoma, other settlers migrated directly from Germany.

For many German settlers the primary reason for coming to Oklahoma was the opportunity for landownership, as indicated in the following account of participation in the 1889 land run.

Mama's folks lived in Kansas and they all came down on the run. Papa, he had a covered wagon and put grandma in it and they had a cook stove in it, and a bed. My sister was about six months old. So grandma came with them and they made the run. Dad was trying to get us close to Oklahoma City. He wanted to get to Oklahoma City, but then they had to bring enough along that they would have something to eat and drink. They brought a few chickens in a coop; they would have eggs to eat. They brought the cow along so they'd have milk to drink. And they had a stove in the covered wagon. All four of them stayed in the covered wagon and they had the cow tied on the wagon in the back.

When they crossed at Cottonwood Creek one of the wheels fell

Table 4.1. The Ethnic Population of Oklahoma

Ethnic/Racial Groups	1910*	1970*	1980 Foreign-Born	1980 Ancestry
Black	137,612	171,892	204,658	
American Indian	74,825	98,468	169,292	
Chinese	139	999	2,461	
Japanese	48	1,408	1,975	
German	27,599	21,475	6,768	178,615
Russian	13,160	5,463	613	1,942
Austrian	7,684	1,893	271	N/A
Irish	6,309	2,386	285	158,897
English	5,794	7,307	2,690	400,283
Canadian	4,123	7,811	2,729	N/A
Italian	3,867	3,531	625	11,469
Mexican	2,645	6,071	5,531	N/A
Scottish	2,335	1,718	386	10,825
Other Foreign-Born				
Czechoslovakian			374	
French			762	24,136
Greek			425	1,892
Dutch			370	20,927
Spanish			305	
Asian Indian			1,514	
Iranian			3,193	
Korean			2,256	
Lebanese			656	
Philippine			1,221	
Thai			646	
Vietnamese			3,769	
Cuban			446	
Colombian			393	
Other Ancestry Groups				
Hungarian				1,552
Norwegian				4,413
Polish				7,665
Portuguese				785
Swedish				6,928
Ukrainian				587

*1910 and 1970 figures are for "Foreign Born" and "Native of Foreign or Mixed Parentage" categories.

off of the wagon and he couldn't get no further. There was a house not far from there and he went to that house and they helped him. The guy gave him a wheel and he finished making the run.

He was on his way to Oklahoma City and he thought he was pretty close to Oklahoma City. Mama's folks, grandpa got tired. He was going to stop and he said, "I want to get where there's lots of brush and water." He stopped on the creek, that was mama's folks, and he did have brush and water. That's about all he had. And then, dad stopped right on the next quarter west of him. Then my dad built a dugout in the back of the creek there. That's where they lived, four of them and I had two sisters born over there in the dugout.

Even those who had been unsuccessful in the land run were able to purchase land.

My family came from Alsace-Lorraine. . . . First they landed in Pennsylvania and they just kept on migrating west till they landed in Kansas. And then when this Cheyenne-Arapaho country opened, course everybody was after free land then, my grandfather made the run, but he failed to get a claim. So then he came back, just how soon after the run I couldn't tell you. But he came back and bought this old homestead. Give $400 for it. Then he went back to Kansas to get the family. While he was there he contracted typhoid fever and passed on. He already had this farm down here, and so my grandmother and these seven kids came. She raised those kids there by herself. How she did it I don't know, but in the run her dad got a claim and he was down here and I think he helped her quite a bit.

Another motivation for coming to Oklahoma was for the dry climate and its influence on health.

My mother had asthma and the doctor advised her to go to a drier climate. In 1903 my father came to Oklahoma. He had a friend, Mr. B. B. Post, that was living at Kingfisher. So he came to Kingfisher, and he and Mr. Richard Pappe took him out to look at some farms. He selected a farm out east, northeast of Kingfisher. He bought a half section, and it was quite a deal to buy that much land. He paid $13,000 for the half section. Then he went back to Illinois and made preparations to sell his farm in Illinois and as soon as my mother would be able to move why we were coming to Kingfisher. We moved here in February 1904. The house on the land that my father bought was just a little old shack, so he rented a house on the quarter just east of our place. There was a pretty good house on that place. We lived there until my father built a two story house, and when that was finished we moved into the new house.

In addition to farming, other Germans became successful businessmen, as demonstrated by the following account from an individual who lived in Kingfisher:

My grandfather was a baker by trade. He was also what you would call a whiskey merchant and he was a real estate man. By that I mean he bought and sold property and then built rental houses and things like that. He was responsible for bringing quite a few German immigrants to this country by finding farms for them. And then they came over here and settled on the farm. Those that came from Germany to settle these farms couldn't speak any English, quite difficult for them in those days. Also, there's a few families he brought down here out of Illinois that he found farms for. Basically he was real estate and after he got into real estate business why I don't think he operated the bakery anymore. And certainly when statehood came, he didn't operate the saloon anymore.

After the initial settlement of Germans in Oklahoma, they established a number of institutions to support their communities. German-language newspapers, churches, schools, and social clubs were begun in the 1890s. At least sixteen German-language newspapers were published in Oklahoma (Rohrs 1980, 24).

While the economic life of the Germans was essentially the same as that of other settlers in western Oklahoma, the use of the German language formed the primary boundary marker for the German ethnic group. With the entry of the United States into World War I, many non-Germans in Oklahoma challenged this boundary marker, as shown by the following account of attacks on Germans at that time:

They done everything to you, a German. Let's see. You had to buy bonds or something. If Germans wouldn't buy any, oh my, they'd take after him. The Germans bought so much more than the English people. At that time there were so many Germans in the grocery stores and even in the dry goods stores. There was some Jews there in the dry goods store at Kingfisher. You could go in there and they would understand the German women, what they wanted. They had German clerks. You couldn't talk German in the street. Some of them Englishmen heard you, they could go and whip the thunder out of you. That was alright, cause you was a German. That was a hard time for the Germans, because that's when they were so against the Germans. The German boys had to go to the army, but still they persecuted the family. I didn't think it was right. They had a hard time. That's why they changed Kiel to Loyal, cause Kiel sounded like a German name.

The response to these attacks was to cease speaking German, Anglicize names, abolish the German language schools and newspapers, and Anglicize the church services.

From what I gathered from my folks there was quite a bit of prejudice against people that spoke German and of German heritage. My mother, she could write and speak German, and dad, he could understand it and talk it some. This prejudice that was building up so I can remember yet dad said, "Well, if that's the way it's going to be, then we just won't have anymore of that." So that was the end of the German speaking at our house. See, we never learned anymore after that, and I wish today that I knew some of it, but I don't.

By the 1930s the boundary between the German ethnic group and the other residents of Oklahoma had largely vanished, and only memories remained of the once influential German institutions. In the 1980 census more than 178,600 residents of Oklahoma listed their ancestry as German. Today, the Germans are no longer an identifiable ethnic group in Oklahoma. Yet several Oklahoma communities celebrate Octoberfest in recognition of German influence and historical heritage.

The Mexican Adaptation

The earliest Europeans to visit Oklahoma were sixteenth-century Spanish explorers from Mexico, and in the nineteenth century a number of Mexican cowboys worked on ranches in Texas and Oklahoma, but it was not until after 1900 that large numbers of Mexicans came to Oklahoma. In 1900 only 134 Mexicans were listed as living in Oklahoma. By

1910 the number had grown to over 2,600. By 1920 the population had again doubled to almost 6,700 (Smith 1981, 10–11).

This increase reflects two social processes. First, the social and economic problems which developed in Mexico in the late nineteenth and early twentieth centuries made life difficult for many rural residents of Mexico. Second, the close proximity of the United States and the need for workers there attracted many Mexicans. The Mexican influx came when there was a growing demand for labor in the West and Southwest. The federal immigration laws had excluded the immigration of Chinese and Japanese workers, but the railroads, mines, and agricultural developments needed workers, and Mexican workers became available to meet those demands.

Many of the Mexicans who came to Oklahoma came from the states of Jalisco, Guanajuato, Michoacán, and San Luis Potosí in central Mexico. The Mexicans from the northern states of Mexico had taken available jobs near the border, so those from central Mexico moved further inland to the plains area of the United States, including Oklahoma. Most of those Mexicans initially came as single workmen, leaving their families behind. They intended to work only a few months and then return to their homes and families with their accumulated earnings. It was not until the second decade of the twentieth century that other family members began to accompany the workmen to Oklahoma. The following account tells of the early economic experiences of one Mexican in Oklahoma:

When I came in here from Mexico I was twenty-one, which was in 1927. I cross the border in El Paso on the 10th day of April 1927. In those days there were officers there, used to send you, direct you, to work on the railroads. So they took us out from there. Came into work on the Santa Fe. They sent us over here to Mulhall, Oklahoma. That's where I live, right there on the Santa Fe railroad. From there I work until 1929 which was during when Hoover was coming in, and then the depression starts. Then they turn us loose. They say they were going to send us back to Mexico, or we can go somewhere else if we would like. Well, I decide I better stay here because I didn't want to go back to Mexico.

So I took the freight trains from here to there and everywhere looking for work. There was no work from '29 until I came back over here in 1930. I never did pick cotton, and I went to pick cotton over here by Shawnee, Oklahoma, place where they call Meeker— kind of small village. We pick cotton there about three or four months, and then from there I came back to Oklahoma City. I really did like Oklahoma City, but I found me a job on the Rock Island railroad. Went to work from here to Hartshorne, Oklahoma, until we run out of work, too.

As this statement shows, economic specialization was characteristic of the Mexicans. They found work on the railroads and in the fields throughout Oklahoma, in the mines of the southeast, and in the packing houses of Oklahoma City.

The Depression years severely affected the Mexicans in Oklahoma. Jobs became scarce, and the few jobs available were frequently reserved for U. S. citizens. By 1940 the population of Mexicans in Oklahoma had dropped to 1,425 (Smith 1981, 11).

Because most Mexicans coming to Oklahoma were attracted by the available wage work, they rarely became landowners. Also, the rural nature of this population and its mobility precluded the establishment of many of the institutions which might have provided social support for the group. Because most of the workmen were illiterate, Spanish-language newspapers were not published. It was not until 1915 that a Catholic Carmelite mission was established to serve the Mexicans in southeastern Oklahoma, and six years later a mission was founded in Oklahoma City (Smith 1980, 57–58).

In addition to the Catholic church, several mutual aid societies developed in Oklahoma as Mexican families began to settle in Oklahoma in the 1920s and 1930s: *La Comisión Honorífica* (the Honorary Commission), *La Cruz Azul* (the Blue Cross), and *La Sociedad Benéfica Nacional* (National Benefit Society) (Smith 1980, 55). More recently several additional organizations have been formed, including Catholic Action, Los Amigos Lions Club, and the American GI Forum. These organizations have sponsored a number of activities within the Mexican community, such as fiestas celebrating Mexican Independence Day and the Day of the Virgin of Guadalupe.

Except for restaurants, the early Mexican residents developed few business establishments. One couple described the development of their restaurant in Oklahoma City as follows:

Then we fixed a café, a take out. Later on when we got more customers, why we let them come there and eat. We served Mexican dishes—*albondigas*, mole, and *sopa*, and tacos, enchiladas, mostly beans. I never cooked so many beans! Well, I didn't cook the beans, my husband did. I played a part in making the mole and flour tortillas. During those nine years we rolled out a hundred pounds of flour from Yukon Mill. I'd go there and get a hundred pounds a month. That's what it took for our customers. Then I had about five regular customers that would take from ten to fifteen dozen every two weeks or three weeks. We had a lovely life, you know. We didn't have much.

Social activities for many Mexicans centered around the activities of the Church, the fiestas sponsored by the Mexican organizations, or the "home dances":

We used to have the dances, you know, home dances. Never go to public dances, never did. They were beautiful. Just real good. See, you don't have to dance too close cause they're pushing you around; they're dancing in a room so many of them. It was fun. . . . Then they had a waltz, called them ladies' waltz. Then the girls come and pick you up to dance. We have a kind of orchestra, but not what you call that many. There was about three, fiddle, guitar, sometimes two fiddlers, and they play real nice, real nice music, Mexican music. . . . We used to be together. We'd go to a dance, then this fella would invite us to their home and to a dance the next week. We get together again, nearly most of the time, the same old crowd.

These home dances apparently ended in the mid-1940s.

The Mexicans in Oklahoma experienced some forms of discrimination, as reported by a woman who came to Oklahoma City in 1918:

We came from San Francisco del Rincón, State of Guanajuato. I had two brothers that were already here and my dad, but then he went after us. He brought my youngest brother, my oldest sister and myself, and my mother. We all came.

They put us in school. My sister was real tall, and she quit school because they were always making fun of her. They put us in the first grade. That was out because she had already been in the fourth grade in Mexico, and they put her in the first grade. I stayed in school, but they sent a note, pinned a note to my dress and said I had to learn some English before I could come back to school. They wouldn't let me go to school. So I learned a little bit of English here and there with the children around the neighborhood. Then I went back to school.

When I was in elementary school, it was really hard for me because there was a lot of prejudice, really, the school where I was; it was Garfield School on south Robinson. When we'd get out of school the children would push me off the sidewalk and make me walk out into the middle of the street. Good thing there wasn't hardly any traffic. And my brother would take me to school and talk to the teacher, and the teacher said anything that happens on the school ground we can supervise it; but anything after school, we cannot do anything about it. So, my sister would always go after me to school and take me back home because that was the only way I could stay on the sidewalk. Otherwise they would push me off the sidewalk, make me walk out in the middle of the street.

For the Mexican ethnic group in Oklahoma, religious affiliation and language provided the primary boundary markers between themselves and other social groups. Within the Mexican community, social events, such as the fiestas and home dances, reinforced the sense of group solidarity. The nearness of Mexico to Oklahoma allowed visits back to their homeland, which helped the Mexican residents of Oklahoma maintain family ties and a sense of cultural continuity. Today the Mexican communities in Oklahoma, primarily in the major urban areas of Oklahoma City and Tulsa, maintain a strong sense of Mexican identity and continue to use their language as the primary boundary.

The Vietnamese Adaptation

Until the mid-1970s there were few Asians living in Oklahoma. In 1910 there were only 139 Chinese listed in Oklahoma, of which 101 were in Oklahoma County, and forty-eight Japanese, half of whom were in Logan County. The restrictionist laws which limited Asian immigration to the United States after 1882 may account for this low Asian population in

Table 4.2. 1990 Ethnic/Racial Population of Oklahoma

Group	Population	% of Total Population
American Indian, Eskimo, or Aleut	252,420	8.02
Black	233,801	7.43
Hispanic	86,160	2.74
Mexican	63,226	2.01
Puerto Rican	4,693	0.15
Cuban	1,043	0.03
Other Hispanic	17,198	0.55
Asian	32,002	1.02
Vietnamese	7,320	0.23
Chinese	5,193	0.17
Korean	4,717	0.15
Asian Indian	4,546	0.14
Philippine	3,024	0.10
Japanese	2,385	0.08
Thai	942	0.03
Laotian	902	0.03
Cambodian	307	0.01
Hmong	207	0.01
Other Asian	2,459	0.08
Pacific Islander	1,561	0.05

SOURCE: Oklahoma Data Center, Oklahoma Department of Commerce.

Oklahoma. In 1990 the Japanese population had grown to 2,385 and the Chinese population to 5,193 (see Table 4.2).

In 1975, with the fall of South Vietnam, Oklahoma became the home for a number of Indochinese refugees, mostly Vietnamese. By 1980 the number of Indochinese refugees living in Oklahoma was estimated to be about ten thousand. Most of this group are located in the Oklahoma City area, with a smaller number in Tulsa. These Vietnamese refugees have made a remarkable adjustment to their new homeland.

The route to Oklahoma was for most Indochinese refugees a long and dangerous journey. Most Vietnamese did not plan to come to the United States when they fled South Vietnam. They were simply trying to escape the battle zone and expected to return home after the battles had ended, as shown by the following account:

In 1975 I was really not thinking of leaving Vietnam. I married in 1973 and in 1975 I was really pregnant. My husband was a Captain in the Navy. He said that he would have to leave because if the Communists came in they would kill him because he was in the Navy. I said that I would have to visit my parents before I left. So my husband said, "Okay. I'll take you over there and visit, and then we go."

The way to my parents' home was terrible—people dying and dead bodies around the streets, and children running around—really just like a "Death City"—and I was afraid. My husband borrowed a jeep from his headquarters and we went on to my parents. I told them of our plan to leave Vietnam. We didn't think that we would go to America. We thought that we would go to some island and stay there a few months until everything was settled, and then go back to Saigon. My father gave me my two brothers and a sister to take with us.

We went back to headquarters, and the last ship was broken. My husband said to get on it, and maybe he and the Captain together could fix the boat. And then we went out. We didn't know where to go. We had been out one day, one night, and a big Navy ship came by, and we got on it. They took us to Subic Bay in the Philippines. We stayed there three or four days. Then an airplane took us to Wake Island, a very small island out in the ocean, and we lived there for three months. Then we arrived at Fort Chaffee and stayed there for one month. We got to Oklahoma City after that. The Oklahoma Carmelite Sisters sponsored us. They helped us in everything. They are Catholic, and since we were Catholic the relations were real good. They talked with us. They were excellent.

The Vietnamese refugees did not represent a cross-section of Vietnamese society. The refugees generally were those who feared the Communist takeover. Many were former residents of North Vietnam who had fled south following the division of Vietnam in 1954. Others were Catholics who feared Communist persecution. Still others were military and police personnel and former employees of the U.S. government in Vietnam. Many professional people also fled, including about 25 percent of all physicians in South Vietnam (Brown 1981, 14).

The Vietnamese faced many hurdles in adjusting to the United States. They had to learn a new language, adjust to new foods, find employment, and learn a new culture. Increasing the difficulty of initial adjustment was the sponsorship program of the U.S. government, which resulted in spreading the refugees across the United States and did not initially stimulate the growth of Vietnamese communities. In the last decade many of the Vietnamese have moved from their initial resettlement locations to areas with greater concentrations of Vietnamese population. Oklahoma City has become one of these growing areas.

As refugees the Vietnamese had little time to plan their exodus from the homeland. Unlike other immigrant populations such as the Germans, who came to Oklahoma seeking land and business opportunities, the primary motivation of the Indochinese refugees for coming to the United States and ultimately to Oklahoma was survival. They were forced to leave behind family members and ancestral homes which had been the core of life for the Vietnamese. Initially, many Vietnamese did not expect to stay in the United States for a lengthy period. They hoped to be able to return to their families and their former lives. After more than a decade in the United States, though, most now recognize that their stay here will last an indefinite time.

Today many Vietnamese own and operate businesses, including restaurants, real estate firms, insurance offices, tailor shops, and grocery stores. Federal and state offices employ others. Still others, especially physicians, have been able to practice their professions in their new homeland. Many now own their own homes and other property. Overall, the Vietnamese have made a remarkable adjustment to life in the United States. The Vietnamese American Association, a mutual assistance association, has sponsored a number of programs for language training, employment training, and orientation to American life. A Vietnamese-language newspaper has been published in Oklahoma City, and a weekly radio program is broadcast in Vietnamese. Perhaps the institutions which have been most influential in assisting the adjustment of the refugees to their new life have been the church and the pagoda. Catholic services are held weekly in Vietnamese with a Vietnamese priest, and a pagoda has been established for Buddhist activities. These institutions have provided some continuity with their homeland for the refugees.

We have identified language as the primary boundary marker of the German ethnic group and the Mexican ethnic group. Language plays a similar role in the life of the Vietnamese community. On the other hand, the annual celebration of Tet, the Vietnamese new year, has also become a significant event in the life of the Vietnamese in Oklahoma. In Vietnam, Tet is a family celebration, an opportunity for individuals to return to their ancestral home and honor their parents and ancestors, teachers, and neighbors. Tet in Oklahoma City has become a community celebration for all Vietnamese in the region. It reinforces traditional orientations and values and provides an opportunity for traditional forms of entertainment. Participation in the celebration of Tet is another boundary marker between the Vietnamese and other social groups.

Overall, Vietnamese residents view Oklahoma in a very positive manner, as seen by the following two statements.

I think Oklahoma City is a "Boom City." In the future I think Oklahoma City will be a big city because of the many companies that have opened here. Industries are growing here. People feel that they can get a job easier here than in another state. Also, in Oklahoma they have a quiet setting; not quite so busy and noisy like California.

I think Oklahoma is a good place for us. The people that live in Oklahoma City, they are very nice. None of them have too much trouble in Oklahoma City. We have a Vietnamese American Association, you know. That's why we have lots of people. They like to stay here because if they need help, they can ask for it from the Vietnamese American Association.

Conclusions

In this chapter we have examined the adaptive responses of three ethnic groups in Oklahoma: the Germans, the Mexicans, and the Vietnamese. Each group viewed Oklahoma from a different perspective. For the Germans, Oklahoma offered the opportunity for landownership and the development of business. For the Mexicans, Oklahoma offered opportunities for wage employment. For the Vietnamese, Oklahoma offered a safe haven and an opportunity to begin a new life in a new land.

These differing perspectives resulted in different patterns of adaptation and strategies for maintaining boundaries between the ethnic groups and other social groups. For the Germans such institutions as churches, schools, newspapers, and social clubs were established. Language provided the primary boundary marker between the Germans and other groups. With the outbreak of World War I and the oppression many Germans felt, the language, and with the language the other institutions which supported the German ethnic group, largely disappeared.

For the Mexicans few supportive institutions were initially established. They maintained contact with relatives in Mexico and expected to return to their homeland after accumulating some funds. Only after other family members began to accompany the Mexican workers did supportive institutions develop in Oklahoma: the Catholic missions and churches, the mutual aid societies, and the social clubs. Today, language and affiliation with the Catholic church remain the primary boundary markers for the Mexican community.

The sudden unplanned departure of the Vietnamese from their homeland and their unexpected arrival in the United States has influenced the adaptation of this group. They brought with them many skills and experiences which could be transferred successfully to their new context. They also brought their language and religions. Today the Vietnamese language, religious affiliation with the Buddhist pagodas or the Catholic church, and the celebration of Tet remain as the primary boundaries markers for the Vietnamese.

Three ethnic groups, three perspectives, three patterns of adaptation—yet today all are woven into the fabric of life which makes Oklahoma distinctive.

CHAPTER 5

Complexities of Ethnicity among Oklahoma Native Americans: Health Behaviors of Rural Adolescents

ROBERT F. HILL, GLENN W. SOLOMON,
JANE K. TIGER, AND J. DENNIS FORTENBERRY

The empirical discovery of great variation in cultural identity in rural southeastern Oklahoma, by Hill and colleagues, is important not only for social science and the humanities but also for Oklahomans' and non-Oklahomans' sense of what and who Oklahomans and "Indians" are. Stereotypes abound, not just of Native Americans, but also of rural, small-town folk, religious fundamentalists, adolescents, and many other groups in Oklahoma and elsewhere. This chapter challenges the overly simple, sometimes romantic, sometimes racist, often politically or ideologically motivated cultural stereotypes of Native American youth. Although the focus of this chapter is on health-related behaviors, or what some might call preventive medicine, the cultural issues discussed are no different from those for any public problem: What is a person? How do a person's varied social relationships and identifications affect his or her behavior in a highly differentiated society?

The language of this chapter, more so than any other in this volume, is the language of science. Thus, the story it tells is a story of numbers, of statistics, of study variables and their associations. The cultural identifications behind the numbers are no less real or important for the general reader. The authors' main purpose is to test empirically the value and utility of the concept of cultural identity systems in relation to health issues.

The authors also wish to demonstrate that culture can be measured—that numbers complement personal life experiences, stories, or literary texts, and vice versa.

Most studies of Native American ethnicity and of Native Americans in Oklahoma focus on a particular tribal affiliation or background and assume a substantial degree of "Indianness" or identification with a particular set of traditional values, beliefs, and behaviors. The empirical data presented in this chapter suggest otherwise: "Indianness," at least among rural, southeastern Oklahoma adolescents, is much more inclusive and complex, embracing Americanness, Christian religion, and Oklahomaness.

In this chapter we explore the relationship between cultural identity systems and selected health behaviors (Hill, Fortenberry, and Stein 1990) among a large sample (N=620) of rural Oklahoma adolescents. We focus specifically on the approximately 16 percent of our sample who identify themselves as Native Americans—predominantly of the Seminole and Creek tribes.[1] We show that presumed ethnic identity as Native American is of only limited value in explaining whether or not one is overweight, or uses automobile seat belts, tobacco, marijuana, or alcohol; that one's "pure" or "mixed" tribal background means little with regard to these behaviors; and that involvements in other cultural identity systems such as religion, family, and school, are of much greater significance in our comprehending the lives of rural Oklahoma adolescents, whether they are of Native American or any other ethnic background. Thus we demonstrate not only the complexity of Native American cultural identities but also how Oklahomaness and Americanness symbolize much of their identities.

Background

All the adolescent subjects in our study sample attend public school in three small rural communities of the southeast central region of Oklahoma. Because of the sensitivity of some of the health behaviors studied, both the towns and the schools will remain unnamed. The health-related behaviors are self-reported seat belt use, tobacco, marijuana and alcohol use; eating problems as reflected by body weight; and music preference. Each behavior has been identified as a risk factor in the growing literature on adolescent medicine (see Friedman, Johnson, and Brett 1990; King 1988; Winfree and Griffiths 1983; Maron et al. 1986; Moore 1990; Earls et al. 1989).[2]

The information presented here is the first part of a larger, on-going quantitative study of cultural identity systems and health behaviors among Oklahoma youth in the four quadrants of the state. Additional study sites will be chosen based on the predominant Native American tribal group in each of the remaining quadrants and, as with the present study, will include subjects from other ethnic backgrounds as comparison groups.[3] Besides providing a quantitative test of the theoretical model described more fully in the first chapter of this book (and in Hill, Fortenberry, and Stein 1990), such an investigation will provide a more comprehensive view of the complex relationship between culture and health in Oklahoma.

Previous studies in Oklahoma and other locales have tended to reduce explanations of this complex relationship to one or two primary factors (Scott 1974; Jones-Saumty et al. 1983; Snow 1974; Horwitz and White 1987; Ramsey, Abell, and Baker 1986; Fletcher 1988; Aro and Hasan 1987; Jarvis and Northcott 1987; Lenkoff et al. 1988). Clarissa Scott (1974) and Loudell Snow (1974), for example, focus on ethnicity as the primary determinant in the complex decision process behind the seeking of medical care. Deborah Jones-Saumty and her colleagues (1983) focus on psychological functioning and family background as determinants of alcoholic disability. A. V. Horwitz and H. R. White (1987) believe gender role orientations govern the choice of and degree of involvement with health-harming behaviors in adolescence. In this study we will be able to compare the relative statistical associations of many of these cultural identity factors to commonly studied health-harming or -protective behaviors, with special emphasis on Native American adolescents. We will also be able to compare the relative degree of ethnic or tribal identifications with wider, societal (American and Oklahoman) identifications such as music preference, gender, Christian religion, and the primary institution for vocational choice and achievement in this society, school.

Methods

Data for the statistical analysis presented in this chapter come from survey questionnaires completed by 620 students from three schools in grades 8–12. Each of the five grades was almost equally represented (range 13–25 percent of the total), a slightly greater proportion being in the higher grades. As noted above, about 16 percent of the study sample identified themselves as Native American, 12 percent as African American, 4 percent as Asian American, 3 percent as Hispanic American, and the rest as the residual "white" (or, as some "nonethnic" respondents playfully wrote on their survey forms: "honky," "white-boy," "white-girl," "caucasian," "American," or "100% pure white"). The proportion of nonwhite or minority students in our study sample is about double their representation in the state at large. Indeed, in one of the schools minority students make up almost half the student body.

Almost three-fourths (74 percent) of the total study sample identified themselves as members of a church, with Baptist, Methodist, and other common Oklahoma Protestant denominations overwhelmingly favored. This was also true for our Native American subsample, although several specific church listings contained a Native American qualifier such as Indian Nations Baptist Church or First Indian Presbyterian. Only one Native American respondent made reference to affiliation in the Native American Church, thought to be important in this region of the state (Wiedman 1990). The total study sample was almost evenly split into male (52 percent) and female (48 percent). Almost two-thirds (64 percent) were from two-parent families; 17 percent were from single-parent (usually mother-headed) families. Other family configurations comprised 19 percent. African American students were significantly more likely to be from single-parent families. Native American family configurations did not differ significantly from those of whites.

In order to quantify involvement in cultural identity systems, each cultural identity system (ethnicity, religion, family, and school) was represented by four questionnaire items assessing degree and quality of participation or both, leadership role at group meetings, and a summary rating. Response to each item was limited to three choices—low, medium, or high—so that each dimension of each cultural system could be quantified and scored, with one point for low involvement, two points for medium, and three points for high, making each cultural system total between four and twelve points. Health behaviors were handled similarly but were limited to one questionnaire item per behavior. This made it possible to consider health behaviors in two ways: (1) as a series of health-harming behaviors for cross-tabulation with the above identity system involvements, and (2) as an additional health identity system domain with four items (seat belts, tobacco, marijuana and alcohol), with score ranging from four to twelve. (See Table 5.1 for a listing of abbreviated sample questions from the survey form.)

In addition to the above variables of cultural identity system, sex (gender) identification was included as a categorical either-or marker of gender culture to be more fully assessed in future studies (Hill, Fortenberry, and Stein 1990). Likewise, music preference is treated here as a health-harming variable for one part of our analysis (see King 1988). Virtually all of our study sample (97 percent) reported listening to music "often" or "frequently (sometimes daily)." The kind of music they listened to varies greatly, however. An open-ended question on music preference produced the following frequency percentages: (1) country-western, 11 percent; (2) rock and roll, including "soft rock," 35 percent; (3) heavy metal, 15 percent; (4) rap (favored by most African American students) 8 percent; and (5) other (including classical, folk, Christian, and popular, or a mixture of categories), 31 percent.

In the presentation of findings which follows, we show

Table 5.1. Cultural Identity System and Health Behaviors: Sample Questions

ID Domains (Abbrev.)	Health Domains (Abbrev.)
1. Strength of identification	1. Buckle seat belts
a) stronger than theirs	a) usually
b) about average	b) often
c) not as strong	c) seldom or never
2. Attendance at group meetings	2. Use tobacco
a) often	a) never
b) once in a while	b) often
c) seldom or never	c) daily
3. Leadership role at meetings	3. Use marijuana
a) often	a) never
b) occasionally	b) often
c) never	c) daily

how categorical or typological variables for Native American tribal background (comparing Seminoles and Creeks with other tribal permutations), ethnicity (comparing Native Americans, African Americans, and others), sex (comparing males and females), and music preference (for heavy metal or rap) can be statistically cross-tabulated with continuous or numerically scaled variables for cultural identity systems of ethnicity, religion, family, school, and health (range four to twelve each). The last system—health—was constructed specifically for this chapter, combining an average score for degree of health preventive or protective behaviors: use of seat belts, and refraining from use of tobacco, marijuana, and alcohol.

Findings

In Fig. 5.1 we present scores for average group cultural identity system, on a scale of four to twelve, cross-referenced against homogeneity of tribal background. Four distinctive background groups were constructed. Group 1 includes all those students who identified their tribal background as homogeneously Seminole, Creek, or Seminole-Creek. This group comprises forty-four of our ninety-nine Native American respondents. Group 2 (sixteen of ninety-nine) includes those

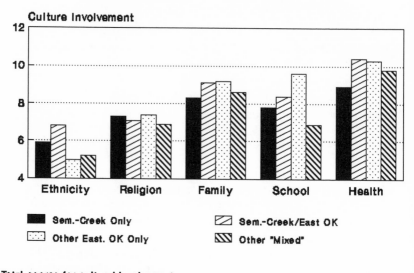

CULTURE INVOLVEMENT BY TRIBAL GROUPING AND IDENTITY SYSTEM (n-99)

* Total scores for cultural involvement
(range 4-12) derived from sum of 4
items for each system.

Fig. 5.1. Cultural involvement by tribal grouping and identity system (N = 99). Total scores for cultural involvement (range 4–12) are derived from the sum of four items for each system.

who indicated a primary tribal identification with Seminole-Creek but one also mixed with other eastern Oklahoma tribal groups, mostly Cherokee or Choctaw. Group 3 includes those who indicated a single or homogeneous tribal identification that was mostly of the eastern Oklahoma tribes but not Seminole-Creek; it comprises twenty-two of ninety-nine respondents. Group 4 (seventeen of ninety-nine) includes mostly eastern regional groups (none Seminole-Creek) mixed with other ethnic permutations such as black, Hispanic, Navaho, several western Oklahoma plains groups, and, most commonly, white.

Fig. 5.1 clearly shows that Native American respondents as

a group report a higher degree of cultural involvement with religion, family, school, and health identity systems than they do with ethnicity. In fact, only eight of ninety-nine Native American respondents reported a "high" involvement with their tribal or ethnic backgrounds. This was significantly less than the involvement of African American respondents (chi sq = 10.9, p < .027). Despite one's tribal or ethnic label, one may well be more culturally Oklahoman or American than exclusively Indian. Moreover, according to these statistics, categorical differences in tribal homogeneity appear unrelated to the degree and kind of other cultural identity systems with which these students report involvement. We assume that a self-reported high identification with a school that is not symbolically "Indian," a main-line Protestant church that is not symbolically "Indian," and/or a family configuration that includes predominantly mother, father, and dependent children (the American ideal) suggests cultural identifications and social structures that are not predominantly "Indian."

In Fig. 5.2, variables of cultural identity systems are cross-tabulated with variables of health-harming behavior for the larger sample of 620 students. Health variables are shown in combined negative form for seat belt and substance use and categorically for overweight and heavy metal–rap music preference. Likewise, ethnicity and gender are used here in categorical form. With the larger, total sample, it becomes possible to show results of statistical significance tests for those cultural identity systems which differentiate among health-harming variables.

As shown in Fig. 5.2, religion, family, school, and gender account for more differences in health behavior than does ethnicity. Moreover, cultural involvement with school has a stronger statistical association with health-harming behaviors than do any of the other cultural systems. In other words, the more positively involved one is with school, the less involved one is with tobacco, marijuana, or alcohol (see Dreyfoos 1990).

In Fig. 5.3 we present correlation coefficients (degrees of association) for selected health behaviors associated with

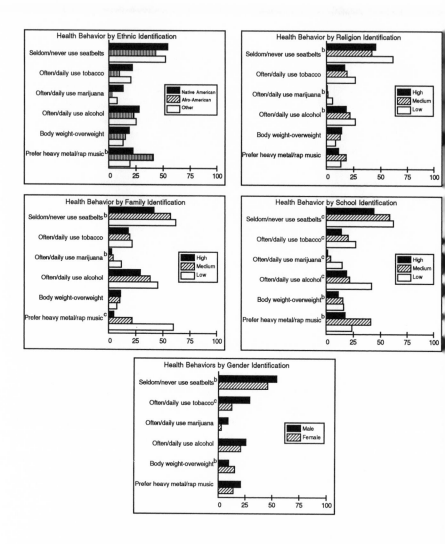

a = Statistical analyses based on 3-way continuum for each variable except music, ethnicity and gender.
b = significant at < .05 level, chi square test.
c = significant at < .001 level, chi square test.

Fig. 5.2. Health behaviors by cultural identification systems in percentages (N = 620).ᵃ

other study variables. As presented, each correlation, or *r* value, has a probability value of chance association at less than .0001. This figure shows the close interassociation between most of the health-harming and -protective behaviors—seat belt, tobacco, marijuana, and alcohol use—and substantiates the connections between health and school, religion and music preference highlighted in the previous figures. In order to streamline this figure, frequency of use for health variables as well as direction of association between variables (positive or negative) are shown together and covered under the general rule "all correlations in the expected direction." Thus it can be seen at the top of the figure that buckling one's seat belt is positively associated with membership in a church and negatively associated with using tobacco.

The multiple correlation coefficients shown in Fig. 5.3 demonstrate the close interrelationships of study variables and provide additional confirmation of cultural influence in health-related behaviors. It can be shown, for example, that gender and alcohol use are highly associated with tobacco use, that heavy-metal music preference and alcohol use are highly associated with marijuana use, and that tobacco and marijuana are highly associated with alcohol use. It seems that health-harming behaviors go together.[4]

Discussion

In this chapter we have presented empirical data and analyses which contrast sharply with the common stereotype of Native Americans in Oklahoma. We have shown that "Indianness" among a sample of rural Oklahoma Native American adolescents does not include a high degree of involvement with self-reported conscious tribal or pan-Indian affiliation. Moreover, contrary to the stereotype, Native American background appears relatively unrelated to the health-harming behaviors that might be precursors of serious substance abuse in adulthood (May 1982; Earls et al. 1989; Mills, Dunham, and Alpert 1988; Baumrind 1987). Indeed, according to our study criteria, Native American students are strongly identi-

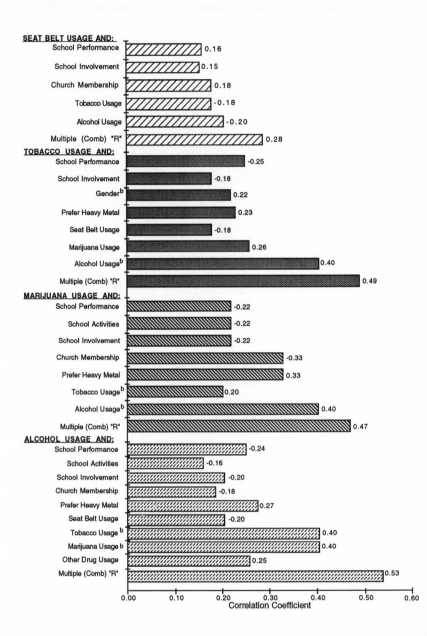

a = p<0.0001 for all correlation coefficients. All correlations in the expected direction. Multiple "R" based on SAS multiple regression procedure.
b = Variables contributing the most to overall associations with each specific health behavior, based on multiple regression analysis, τ test, p

Fig. 5.3. Correlations of specific health variables and cultural system variables.[a]

fied with health protection. As we noted earlier, only a hand-ful of Native American subjects rated their involvement with their tribal or ethnic American background as "high." This was significantly less than the responses of African American students. But in neither case did they match the reported involvements with Christian religion, school, and family.

It is possible, of course, that Native American students' re-sponses to the questionnaire items did not truly reflect their personal involvements with the cultural identity systems and health behaviors under study. We think that is unlikely for several reasons. First, as shown in Fig. 5.1, the frequency distributions for cultural involvements did not differ signifi-cantly across tribal groupings, suggesting very little differ-ence in individual responses. Second, the frequency distribu-tion for health behaviors was reasonably close to those reported in other studies (Maron et al. 1986; Geer and Resnick 1988) and within several percentage points for seat belt, tobacco, and alcohol use. Third, self-reported substance use has been found to be reliable and valid in a rigorous methodology study when compared to data obtained by personal inter-view in the home (Needle et al. 1983). Finally, our finding of a strong statistical association among family, school, religion, and several health-related variables was even more convinc-ingly shown in previous quantitative studies by Richard Jessor and his colleagues at the Institute of Behavioral Science of the University of Colorado in Boulder (see, for example, Jessor and Jessor 1977). We should also note that student sub-jects in our study seemed remarkably compliant with the tasks of questionnaire completion. Only three survey forms of more than six hundred had to be discarded because of missing data. Only one form contained unsolicited negative remarks. We conclude that there was a high level of acceptance of study procedures and content of questions.

We do not believe, however, that low self-reported involve-ments with tribal or ethnic cultural systems in this study mean that study subjects may not manifest traditional, and cultural patterns of thinking, feeling, and acting in their daily lives. Such questions go beyond the limited aims of this study. Howard Stein and Robert Hill refer to this as the distinction between "ideological" or self-conscious ethnicity and "behavioral" or unself-conscious, often "hidden" ethnicity (1977a, 14). George Devereux has made a similar distinction between ideological "ethnic identity" and behavioral "ethnic personality" (1975). What Stein and Hill wrote in 1977 seems equally applicable today:

Ethnicity is assimilated into the syncretic, fluid nature of American culture in general. . . . Much of what can be called "hidden ethnicity," for instance, food preferences or attitudes toward health and illness based on values and ethnic personality structure, is highly valent in private and public social life. . . . "Hidden" refers to the fact that the common American culture may not be aware of them, or even that the ethnics themselves, engage in activities that are in accordance with specific values, without knowing why. (1977a, 22–23)

Determination of the presence of traditional culture in family life, peer associations, and the social meaning of various health-related behaviors among Native American adolescents must await intensive, qualitatively oriented ethnographic studies such as that of David Moore (1990), who studied the social meaning of drinking among ethnic skinheads in Australia. Moore showed that alcohol use among Australian skinheads is a highly ritualized, symbolically laden behavior: "While drinking features in most skinhead group activity, it assumes different forms which are defined by the situation at hand. Therefore . . . we may say that an agent is constrained to drink heavily in a scene which requires high levels of consumption. The combination of skinhead (the agent), drinking (the act) and a night 'in town' (the scene) produces a *known* style of action" (Moore 1990, 1268; Moore's emphasis). Interestingly, Moore describes skinhead ethnicity as an "invisible ethnicity" which seldom makes its way into public consciousness.

Numerous studies over the past decade have focused on substance use among Native American youth (Holmgren, Fitzgerald, and Carman 1983; Barnes and Welte 1986; Welte and Barnes 1987; Winfree and Griffiths 1983; Murray et al. 1987; Hall and Dexter 1988; Oetting, Beauvais, and Edwards 1988). While rates of use vary greatly (tending to be much higher in reservation areas of the southwestern United States and differing little from those of whites in nonreservation schools in such regions as New York State), all of these studies suffer from the same problems: they do not measure the degree or quality of involvement with ethnic or tribal culture; they do not take into account presumably wide variation in tribe, region, and local social or cultural context; and they do not elucidate the social meanings of the various health-harming behaviors under study and their relation to youth or adolescent cultures (Moore 1990; Hill and Fortenberry 1990).

By contrast, Philip May (1982) has proposed a conceptual model which does take into account regional-tribal variation and wider social context. May sees susceptibility to greater substance use to be a function of two factors: degree of traditional Native American cultural integration and degree of acculturation stress. The higher the integration and the less the acculturation stress, the lower the susceptibility. As May describes it:

Tribes which have low traditional social integration and are undergoing acculturation stress will produce people who abuse drugs and abuse them for longer periods of time. Those tribes which are highly integrated and are isolated from rapid change and modernization will have lower levels of abuse. Individuals who are well integrated in modern and traditional Indian ways, and identify with both are the least susceptible to drug abuse. Those who are not well established in a socially integrated role of either white or Indian society are the most likely to abuse drugs (May 1982, 1205).

The predominant tribal backgrounds of our study sample for this chapter (Eastern Oklahoma Seminole, Creek, Cherokee, and Choctaw) appear to fit into the paradigm proposed by May for "high traditional integration," "high acculturation stress," and "high social integration in white society." The relative frequencies of substance use found in the present study seem to fit reasonably well with May's hypothesis as well. May's model does not, however, explain why the cultural identity system and health behavior profiles of the Native American adolescents in our study do not differ substantially from those of our non–Native American comparison group. Nor does his model explain the close similarities we observed across and within tribal groupings. Further discussion must await additional studies.

What is a Native American? What is a Baptist? What is a Native American of Seminole-Creek tribal background? What is a Seminole-Creek, Native American, adolescent male of rural, small-town southeastern Oklahoma who plays tackle on the school football team, sings in the choir at the First Baptist Church, occasionally attends a local Indian pow-wow with his favorite uncle, and does not prefer country and western music? These are only a few of the possibilities. Human beings are not one-dimensional in their cultural identities and should be seen, not in broad stereotypes, but, as the poet William Blake put it, in their "minutely organized particulars" (Blake 1979). According to a popular Oklahoman cultural stereotype, one shared nationally if not worldwide, Native Americans or Indians are not only a distinctive, defining cultural category of Oklahomaness but also a category that culturally contrasts with "cowboys" or "whites." This chapter has shown, if only in a preliminary fashion, how complex "Indian" culture in Oklahoma is, and how much it departs from popular simplifications inherent in Oklahomaness.

In the final chapter of this book Howard Stein and Robert Hill review the various ways in which Blake's "minute particulars" are organized into a sense of Oklahomaness. For Native American Oklahomans (or Oklahoman Native Americans) the intrapsychic and social realities are no less complex. According to anthropologist Eugene Roosens, who studies Native Americans in Canada: "Each individual always belongs to several social units: a nation, a profession, a family, a political party, an ethnic group, a religious organization and so on, and *belongs to all of them at the same time*" (1989, 16, our emphasis). It is the circumstance which dictates how or even whether any of these identities will be emphasized. In some circumstances, for example, "Indianness" may be of great significance; in other circumstances it may mean little or nothing. Roosens writes further: "Given our current knowledge, nobody could maintain that ethnic identity is a 'feeling' that is determined by genes or by 'the blood' and that one carries it with oneself in all circumstances of life" (1989, 16;

see also Weissman 1990). One could, of course, say the same thing about each of the other identity systems to which one belongs, including Oklahoma. For Native Americans, as for whites, neither is Indianness nor Oklahomaness the only circumstance influencing identity choices in their lives.

Notes

1. According to Swanton (1979, 181) the name *Seminole* is a relatively modern tribal designation dating from the early 1800s. It is a Creek (Muskogean) word for "runaway" or "refugee," referring to Creeks who took refuge with Oconee speakers, becoming assimilated with them during the military and political turmoil of that early period in Florida before their forced emigration to Oklahoma. Very few if any persons continue to speak these original languages, although the specific genealogical linkages with Creek, Seminole, or Oconee still exist for some persons. Before the early 1800s, in Florida, Oconee Indians consisted of the Hitchiti, Chiaha, Mikasuki, Apalachicola, Sawakli, and Tamathli bands (according to Swanton), although these distinctions seem relevant only to historians and genealogists today.

We have chosen to use the common term Native American in this chapter to refer to decendants of the culturally diverse groups of people who occupied the lower half of the North American continent before European immigration and colonization. The preference of this term over *American Indian* is congruent with the current trend to recognize all North American ethnic minorities in the same way (African Americans being the latest group to choose this format) and to bring everyone except nonhyphenated "whites" into a system of special entitlements based on (sometimes) tiny fractions of "blood" or "ethnicity" in their ancestry (Roosens 1989, 13). The choice of Native American over Indian American also appears to serve the need to distinguish the former from those who may have come to America from the country of India on the South Asian subcontinent, although we doubt that common usage will easily follow this logic. We also wonder about possible hidden agendas in the common preference for Native American over other possibilities. Could this designation imply that others who have been born in America might have a lesser claim on this land? And might not the same logic also apply to that space called Oklahoma?

2. Besides the work of Paul King (1988) at the University of Tennessee College of Medicine in Memphis, numerous national and local parent groups are today concerned about popular music which contains explicit lyrics about sex and drugs, believing that such music contributes to sexual promiscuity, teen pregnancy, sexually transmitted diseases, suicide, violence, and drug abuse. Tipper Gore, the wife of U.S. Senator Albert Gore

(also from Tennessee, and a recent presidential candidate) has gotten considerable national publicity for this "health problem" through a national group called the Parents Music Resource Center. In November 1988 the American Academy of Pediatrics issued a position statement warning parents about the "new rock" music, not to be confused with the "old rock" music of the 1950's and 60's, which also created a large public outcry (American Academy of Pediatrics 1988).

3. The tribal headquarters of the Seminole Nation of Oklahoma is located in Wewoka, Oklahoma, and is responsible for serving the needs of the Indian people of Seminole County, the majority of whom are members of either the Seminole or Creek tribe. In an effort to acquaint the tribe with the proposed study, we met with the governing officials of the tribe to discuss the purpose of the study and to assure that the results obtained from the survey would be made available to the tribe to use as they deemed appropriate. Lucy Harjo, manager of the Johnson O'Malley Education Program, Seminole Nation, was our primary contact and assisted us in our efforts to gain the consent and cooperation of tribal officials. The Johnson O'Malley Act, from which the program originates, was first introduced in the U.S. Senate as S.B. 2571 by Senator Hiram W. Johnson of California on February 2, 1934. A similar bill, H.R. 257, under consideration by the House of Representatives, was written by Thomas P. O'Malley; it requested consent for the Senate to provide federal assistance to supplement local school funds for educating American Indian children in public schools. Today J.O'M. program funds are allocated through contract with tribes, incorporated Indian education committees, public school districts, or a state department of education to provide supplementary program activities to meet the unique educational needs of eligible Indian students attending public schools. Tribal contractors, such as the Seminole Nation of Oklahoma, provide teacher aides, tutorial services, Indian cultural activities, incentive programs, parental cost, student assistance, and coordination with Title V-C Indian education activities.

Lucy Harjo's role in the study team's efforts to reach a viable agreement with the tribe was invaluable, for she represented the interests of the parents of the Indian children enrolled in the county's rural schools. The meeting with the tribe's governing officials was deemed successful, and they expressed a deep appreciation of our efforts to involve them in the decision-making process. School principals and staff from study sites were also very cooperative and helpful.

4. Additional multiple regression analyses, not in the table, showed that church membership contributed the most to variation in seat belt use ($r^2 = .08, p < .003$); gender to tobacco use ($r^2 = .24, p < .0001$); preference for heavy-metal music to marijuana use ($r^2 = .22, p < .0001$); and tobacco use to alcohol use ($r^2 = .28, p < .0001$). Multiple regression is a technique which allows investigators to hold some study variables constant while they assess the relative associational strength of other variables.

CHAPTER 6

The Cultural History of an Oklahoma Identity

CHARLES W. NUCKOLLS

If every culture—ranging from tribal to ethnic to corporate— has an origin myth (or multiple origin myths) that accounts for how the group started, every culture also has foundation or explanatory myths that imbue the group with core meanings and values. In this chapter, Charles W. Nuckolls imaginatively and persuasively argues that much of Oklahoma culture and its history can be understood as a living out of the legend of King Arthur and the Knights of the Round Table. It is a mythic system that is rarely explicit in Oklahoma culture, yet Nuckolls shows how it can be seen as an underlying cultural glue that unifies elements of "capitalistic adventurism" and "romantic sociability" within Oklahoma. He traces the more than century-old cultural history of the Oklahoma identity system through this organizing myth and those who personify and embody it. To illustrate his explanatory approach, he not only gives accounts of life histories of two prominent Oklahomans, David Payne and E. W. Marland, but he also artfully draws upon his own life and family in the oil exploration business. He literally brings home, as native and observer, the profound influence of Oklahoma culture in the lives of its citizens.

Western concepts of civilization typically fall into two groups. In the first, civilization is equivalent to personal potential and realizes itself through utilitarian calculations of means versus ends. It consists of techniques and institutions (means) which produce happiness for the greatest number of people (ends). It is the perspective of eagerness and anticipation: the emancipated initiative of free individuals will create a future utopia. We will call this the egocentric view. It can be interpreted to mean that hard work pays off. Adam Smith, Jeremy Bentham, and John Mill were among its exponents.

In the second view, civilization is equivalent to social solidarity and the network of structures which creates and sustains it. The value of the group and its unity is paramount. It is the perspective of tragedy and nostalgia: the past and the primitive (the past's representative) offer a benign world of shared dependency that is now or will soon be lost. We will call this the sociocentric view. The early Karl Marx, Auguste Comte, Emile Durkheim, and Max Weber were among this view's founding exponents.

With these distinctive viewpoints in mind, it is interesting to compare Max Weber's turn of the century impressions of two important American places within the civilized world. Of Chicago, Weber wrote:

It is an endless human desert. . . . When the hot, dry wind from the deserts from the southwest blows through the streets, and especially when the dark yellow sun sets, the city looks fantastic. In broad daylight one can see only three blocks ahead—everything is haze and smoke, the whole lake is covered by a huge pall of smoke. . . . With the exception of the better residential districts, the whole tremendous city is like a man whose skin has been peeled off and whose intestines are seen at work. (Weber 1988, 286)

His impression of Oklahoma was much different:

Nowhere else does old Indian romanticism blend with the most modern capitalistic culture as it does here. The newly built railroad from Tulsa to McAlester first runs along the Canadian River through veritable virgin forest for an hour. . . . The larger streams, like the Canadian River, have the most Leatherstocking romanticism. . . . There is a fabulous bustle here, and I cannot help but find tremendous fascination in it, despite the stench of petroleum and the fumes, the spitting "Yankees" and the racket of the numerous trains. Nor can I deny that in general I find the people pleasant. . . . I believe I have not been so merry since my first semesters at the university as I have been here with these people who are as naïve as children and yet handle any situation. . . . This is a more "civilized" place than Chicago. (Weber 1988, p. 293)

What is interesting is not only that Weber visited Oklahoma shortly before statehood, but also that he liked it for what many (especially Oklahomans) consider its most distinctive feature: the social cohesion, friendliness, and independent initiative of its people. He saw in Oklahomans what he wanted to see in other places—social solidarity—but also something more. In his description of Oklahoma, Weber suggests that civilization should consist of productive industry whose human face preserves the countenance of a buoyant and slightly naïve child. This chapter follows Weber's insight in arguing that a synthesis of values—capitalistic adventurism and romantic sociability—constitutes the conceptual background for an important identity: the Oklahoma adventurer.

King Arthur and Camelot in Oklahoman and American Identity

American identity, too, includes elements which contradict each other and which only occasionally find resolution in the formation of a "compromise" identity. Americans are drawn to the self-effacement and competitiveness of the corporate world. One public figure who best embodies these qualities is the football player. "Like the corporate executive," as L. Drummond remarks, "the football player is virtually faceless; his individuality has been consumed by the voracious demands of his function" (1986, 83). At the same time, Americans also are drawn to the self-expression of independence. One public figure who embodies these qualities is the rock star, who, "glorying in the wildest flights of egotism, screams for the death of the corporate state" (ibid., 84). Both football player and rock star invoke highly valued but highly contradictory American cultural ideals (see also Bellah et al. 1985).

"Compromise identities" synthesize and represent contradictory ideals in a such a way that they no longer appear contradictory. One of these is the enduring cinema favorite,

James Bond, who reconciles autonomy and dependency by putting his flamboyant individualism at the service of the state. To make the synthesis work, however, the character of Bond must give up something: his conscience. After all, he is a man of action, not a man of reflection. If Bond possessed a conscience, he might have to decide between the contradictory ideals (individuality and obedience) which constitute his dual nature.

On the other hand, consider the culture hero King Arthur, as he is known to American audiences through the ever-popular musical *Camelot*. Individualistic young Arthur sets out to fulfill his personal destiny and does so, creating the community of Camelot. Problems emerge when members of his community (for example, Lancelot and Guinevere) also act individualistically, putting themselves ahead of their group loyalty. Arthur must decide between vengeance and reconciliation, between individualism and community. Such a hero can internalize the paradox and make his own psyche a battleground for the conflict between opposing ideals. The result is a paralyzing ambivalence. Or he can do the reverse: externalize the conflict and project its competing obligations onto the outside world. The world can represent *either* the demands of dependency and obedience *or* the demands of individualism and personal fulfillment.

When the hero sees the world as full of overwhelming forces which threaten him with absorption or annihilation, he responds with rebellious self-assertion to protect his own autonomy. When he sees the world as too chaotic, and thus in need of protection and direction, the hero responds as a benevolent autocrat and paternal overlord. It all depends on which role he is playing; when he is one, the world becomes the other.

The cultural model of King Arthur and the Knights of the Round Table comes close to the one I describe for Oklahoma, itself a distillation of the broader American identity. Consider the model's basic constituents (Cavendish 1978). His noble destiny implicit but unknown, the Arthurian "type" rises from humble beginnings and discovers a tool which gives him special power. With it, and sometimes with the special knowledge acquired from a sage or teacher, he creates a loyal fraternity. Together they pursue a fabulous goal. Peace and happiness reign throughout the land. A Camelot exists. But a flaw inherent in the system, in the king or in the kingdom he creates, eventually causes the goal to be lost and the fraternal group to disintegrate.

The identity I discuss is by no means the only (or, arguably, even the most important) Oklahoma identity (see also Stein 1984, 1987c; Hill and Stein 1988). It is simply the one most familiar to me as a native Oklahoman. It consists of two closely linked but ultimately conflicting elements generated in the symbolic construction of Oklahoma as a border zone and configured by the discovery of petroleum and development of the petroleum industry in Oklahoma. The two elements are (1) pursuit of a social cause, and (2) formation of a social group.

Several important qualifications follow. First, central to the cause is a compulsion to risk everything, even the prospect of its ultimate achievement, in the cause's lifelong pursuit. Second, the formation of a group follows from a sense of mission and the charismatic quality needed to convey it, which attracts a loyal following in pursuit of the cause. Third, the identity is prototypically male. This does not mean that only men express it, but that as conventional attributes its constituent elements attach more readily to expected male rather than female roles—the case of Belle Starr notwithstanding. It follows that the group that constitutes itself around the charismatic identity is a fraternity composed mostly of young men who devote themselves loyally to the leader and his cause.

The model of the Arthurian type is useful because of its heuristic value. Nowhere in the Oklahoma source material I discuss is King Arthur mentioned. Yet the Oklahoma identity I discuss reveals the history of a noble but self-defeating Arthurian type. Of course, it constitutes the formative background against which many types of epic tales and stories of heroic adventure take shape in western society since the twelfth century (Cavendish 1978). The frequent likening of President

Kennedy's administration to Camelot is a case in point. Here, I use "the Arthurian type" only as a heuristic device. Its usefulness will be measured by the extent to which it helps illuminate Oklahoma identity.

Oklahoma is by no means unique as a ground against which the figure of the Arthurian type distinguishes itself. By tracing its origin to Oklahoma's pre-1889 status as an "unassigned land," part of my analysis considers why the Oklahoma version of the Arthurian identity is special. The symbolic creation of the state as a border zone, followed a generation later by the discovery of oil and the formation of an oil-based economy, makes the Oklahoma identity special, if not altogether unique.

The method I use to identify personalities that seem Arthurian draws on the concept of the social "cynosure" introduced by Weston La Barre (1980). A cynosure represents in extreme form values and attitudes strongly "selected for" in a culture. Serving as a benchmark against which people judge their conformity to accepted ideals, it stands out and attracts attention. Public figures as well as literary characters and media personalities known for their charismatic appeal are obvious candidates (for example, President John F. Kennedy and Martin Luther King); so are those who seriously offend publicly accepted standards of social behavior (for example, Adolf Hitler and Charles Manson). Analysis of such individuals as case studies reveals the values that are most salient to the formation of cultural identity.

My analysis begins in reverse chronological order with the study of the cultural world I know best, my family. The two case studies that follow are from a public world. The first is E. W. Marland, founder of the Marland (later Conoco) Oil Company and governor of the state in the 1930s. The second is David L. Payne, leader of the Boomer movement in the 1880s and "father" of Oklahoma.

Are these men social cynosures? They certainly meet the primary criterion of cynosureship; Payne and Marland attracted great public attention, inspiring thousands of people with visions of Oklahoma as a social utopia—a promised land which Payne wanted to seize from the federal government and which Marland, a generation later, believed would constitute the foundation for a new order that would rival the East's power and prestige.

But there is another reason to examine Payne and Marland as social cynosures. Payne participated directly in the creation of Oklahoma in its most important cultural form, *as a symbol*, well before the land it occupies was opened to white settlement. He led the Boomer movement, embodying and publicly representing its values. Three decades later, Marland shaped these symbolic features into their currently most recognizable form by linking them to the oil business and the oil business to state politics.

Popular biographies are my main source of information (Rister 1942; Mathews 1951). The biographies of Payne and Marland are especially useful for two reasons. First, they are written narratively, with little attention to detail and a strong emphasis on telling a good story. Since they are popular, not scholarly, works, we can assume that their narrative structure—the structure of heroic narrative—was chosen to appeal to a broad readership within the state of Oklahoma. The choice of the heroic narrative as a model, whether deliberate or accidental, is telling. It asks us to reflect on the salience of that model as a framework for understanding an Oklahoma identity. This narrative structure, as a cultural construct that took on a distinctly Oklahoma form, is the subject of this analysis.

The second advantage these books possess is that they are overly sympathetic as biographies go. Both authors (Oklahomans) make no effort to conceal their uncritical adoration of their subjects. Far from attempting to distance themselves, in fact, the authors try to get as close as possible, even to the point of calling their subjects by their first names ("Dave" for David Payne and "E. W." for Ernest Whitworth Marland). Sources are generally unattributed; important contextual material appears without reference. Uncritical praise is valuable, however, because it reveals what must have been important in the publicly inspiring public images of these two men.

In the next section I begin in the present, with reflections on my own family, my mother and my father. It is in my father's legacy to me that I first noticed the existence of the Oklahoma identity that is my subject.

Personal Symbols

My father was a drilling contractor (later an appraiser and consultant) and my mother was a schoolteacher (later a tax commission clerk). I was raised in Oklahoma City. The stories I tell below are from memory. They stand out for me in the same way signatures do, as immediately recognizable tokens of personal identity. To recall them I simply asked myself, "What stories best represent the members of my family?"

A Story about My Father

What follows is a story my father has told for almost as long as I can remember. It is the story of "the water can," presented below as my father narrates it:

> One night I was home in bed and the telephone rings.
> "Hello?" I said.
> "Hello, Bill, this is Curt."
> Curt is my tool-pusher.
> "Curt, what the hell are you doin' callin' me at 3:00 in the morning?" I asked.
> "We need a new water can," he said. (Now, that's a five gallon Gott water can and costs about five bucks.)
> "Curt," I said, "what the hell are you doing callin' me about a goddamned five dollar water can. You can go to the supply store and pick one up in the morning!"
> And then Curt says:
> "The derrick fell on it."

It was 1963. A tornado passed through the Hennessey area and struck my father's rig, toppling the derrick and destroying everything. We surveyed the wreckage the next day. The huge steel derrick lay flat, pushed up here and there by the objects it had crushed on its way down: the tool box, the dog house, the trailer, and, of course, the water can. It was a total loss. The rig was carried away, bit by bit, and sold for scrap. The well was plugged and abandoned. My father never fully recovered from his loss. He hung on for a few more years until he liquidated the business. That was just before the Arab oil embargo, when the price of oil shot up and the domestic oil business began to boom.

The story celebrates risk as well as admits powerlessness before mighty outside forces. It invites the listener to admire the splendor of an operating rig but also calls upon one to contemplate the magnificence of great machinery once it has been reduced to wreckage. For me, thinking about the rig is like contemplating the ruins of an ancient civilization. Both represent the spectacle of magnificence destroyed by forces beyond anyone's ability to control.

A Story about My Mother

"Be careful." If there is one phrase I associate with my mother more than any other, it is that. When we took leave of each other, either in person or over the phone, this was what we said. Later I wondered, What was I supposed to be careful of? The stories my mother told were short and didactic, punctuated by cautionary remarks. One is from her college days in the mid-1930s: "In college I took a course in government. The professor had us read the *New York Times* every day. I didn't do well, and went to see the professor, who told me to drop the course. I refused; I believe in sticking with something, in playing by the rules, no matter what. So I did, and got a D." Another illustrative account is so often repeated that it represents a central moral catechism of my childhood: "My father carefully managed his investments. His motto was, 'Invest your money, let it work for you, and never spend your capital.' That's what supported my mother after he died, and that's what supports us now. Your father has never believed in saving and investing. Whatever else you do, you should get an M.B.A. . . . so that you know how to carefully manage money."

The point of these stories is cautionary. They warn against making decisions precipitously, based solely on the probability of success or failure or on one's likes or dislikes. Instead, they advocate a determination to obey the rules and to persist no matter what the outcome. Lose gracefully, the first story says, and look for ways to do better the next time around. The second account stresses thoughtfulness and planning—in deliberate opposition to the theme of my father's story.

A Story about Myself

An account from my own life illustrates how themes in the preceding stories interact. It is the story of "the petition."

When I was in the fifth grade, I began a petition against the school lunch service for serving food nobody could eat. My mother then started making me a lunch to get me to stop. But I persisted because of the principle of the thing. It took me a year—until I was halfway through the sixth grade—to collect a hundred signatures from other students.

Parents of some of the children refused to let their children sign; others called my parents and told them to stop me. The principal of the school called my mother and told her that something had to be done. My mother told me to stop. She said to me that I was making waves, rocking the boat, offending people, and not trying to get along. The principal, meanwhile, took me to another school to show me that our school's food was better than its. I agreed with her, as a matter of fact, but I didn't see what difference it made.

Finally, after collecting the signatures, I planned to submit the petition in person to the director of food services at the Oklahoma City Board of Education. But somebody had to drive me. My mother refused. But my father agreed. He said then what he often said: "Sometimes you just gotta rare up." He took me there, parked, and waited outside as I went in and deposited the petition on the director's desk.

My mother cautioned against individualistic display whenever it risked offending or alienating people, especially people in authority. She stressed adherence to the rules, hard work, and honesty. My father never stressed hard work or adherence to the rules, but opportunity and adventure. He looked down on employment by others as a waste of one's natural talents and energy. The idea of working in an office, behind a desk, and for a certain number of hours each day was abhorrent to him.

The story of my petition drive encapsulates a confrontation of values. Risk-taking as a value comes to me through my father. The story of the rig has helped me at various times to overcome fear, to temporarily ignore danger, and to respond to disaster with the same feelings I felt when I first saw the wreck of my father's rig—feelings closely akin to remorse, nostalgia, and awe. Caution as a value comes to me through my mother. The stories about herself and her father have helped me to see the value of working within the system and planning for the future. The narratives themselves conflict, of course, as much because their authors want them to as because they represent different orientations to personal experience. The values they convey are not the same, yet each paradoxically needs the other.

Oklahoma Adventurism: The Cultural History of a Regional Type

My interest in mythic Oklahoma heroes is part of the legacy I attribute to my father—a legacy of what I will call "Oklahoma adventurism." It is not the same as adventurism we associate with such other western stereotypes as the cowboy or the gunslinger. Typical cowboy adventurism always culminates in itself, not in the creation of large organizations, such as oil companies, and not in the attempt to realize a vision of the ideal society. King Arthur more nearly represents this Oklahoma image than does Clint Eastwood.

Now, my father has never referred to himself as King Arthur or to his enterprise as Camelot. What links the two is the element of contradiction. The Arthurian type with his fraternal cohort struggles against external constraint to build a new world. The contradiction is that once the desired world exists, it constitutes the external constraint against which the hero naturally struggles, resulting in destruction or abandonment of the created world and the transformation or demise of its heroic creator.

My father's career is a good illustration. A business was interesting to him as long as it provided opportunities for adventure, which depended on keeping the distinction between (individualistic) self and (autocratic) world intact. In a business's early stages, when opposition to its growth is greatest, maintaining this crucial distinction is not difficult. But later, once the business becomes better established, the distinction likely becomes blurred. Then adventurism gives way to routine, and the creator, seeing his independence compromised, may turn on his creation, either to reinvigorate it by adding new surprises or to destroy it by neglecting its operation.

My father built and abandoned many businesses over the years. As I was growing up, I wondered why our family always seemed to approach but never quite grasp the success which my father's business ventures held out for us. I see now that there is something more frightening to the Oklahoma oil field adventurer than failure, especially when success threatens loss of autonomy, independence, and initiative. To avoid such losses the adventurer must abandon or radically transform his world once it takes on the characteristics of a constraining external force. My father never directly destroyed any of the things he created, but his benign neglect, following almost immediately the creation of anything new, eventually assured the collapse of his endeavors.

As we look back on my father's story of the rig destroyed by a tornado, its special power to represent him should now be clear. The story condenses all the major symbols of heroic legend: fraternity (between my father and his employees), fearlessness (in the face of disaster), and final destruction. What made the wreck magnificent was the suddenness and finality of its destruction, the perfect end to a heroic creation. That is why the wreckage seemed so wonderful to us. It was possible to contemplate it, like the ruins of Pompeii, as a remnant of a heroic age. My father's other business disasters did not lend themselves so well to this kind of thinking. They took place too slowly and resulted too obviously from indifference to a business-centered way of life once it had become routine.

The oscillation between authority and autonomy apparent in my family history constitutes the defining feature of the Oklahoma oil field adventurer. This identity represents a cultural ideal. Is it any wonder, then, that individuals like my father might seek to realize it in their own lives? The question I want to consider now is, How did this identity develop and where did it come from?

Ernest Whitworth Marland

E. W. Marland was born in 1874 in Pittsburgh. His father, Alfred, had immigrated from England at the time of the Civil War to help the South in protecting its culture "from the hordes of Northern tradesmen bent like the Huns on destruction" (Mathews 1951, 6). His grandfather had been a famous mathematician and headmaster of the Whitworth School for Boys, near Manchester. "But mathematicians," as Mathews notes, "no matter how famous, were restricted by the rule of the patricians in England and did not have the means or the freedom possessed by the landed gentry" (ibid., 5).

This is a theme common to the biographies of famous Oklahomans: the notion that the best of European aristocratic values could be preserved in the New World (see Harlow 1928). Alfred Marland thought that America could nurture a classless society that still held on to the best of English aristocratic tradition. So he sent his son, E. W., to attend the Arnold School, a Tennessee institution created by Thomas Hughes, British author of *Tom Brown's School Days* (1857).

The Arnold School and the surrounding colony, "Rugby," did not survive for long. Marland completed his education in Pittsburgh. Nevertheless, his father tried to instill aristocratic values in his son and to persuade him that duty and dignity were foremost as virtues. Yet the lure of wealth and power were stronger. Marland fused the roles of prince and businessman and thus became a blend of English aristocrat, with his noblesse oblige, and American tycoon, with his profit motive.

Marland's quest began when he abandoned the search for coal in Pennsylvania and, without a penny to his name, journeyed to Oklahoma to look for oil. Oklahoma and its unexploited mineral wealth provided the perfect nurturing environment. The state was open and free, and its boundaries and constituents were newly created. Its mineral wealth could be used to create the new society. Oklahoma also represented the place in the New World where all that was best in the Old World could take root. Oil exploration possessed everything a heroic quest requires, including the sudden discovery of unseen wealth (oil) in a new land (Oklahoma) and battle with a terrible giant (Standard Oil Company).

Mysterious encounters often presage heroic achievements. Prospecting for drill sites, Marland noticed an unusual land formation in an area owned by Ponca Indians. It turned out to be the place where the tribe disposed of its dead by placing their wrapped bodies on braided mats and exposing them to the elements. "The reality of the hill excited him, and he decided to drill for oil just down from the crest toward Bodark Creek—down from the crest of the hill to escape defiling the Poncan dead" (ibid., 81). Thus located on a site whose cosmological significance could only be hinted at, Marland began his search for the bounty of oil. Visions of success and possible failure pursued him as the well got deeper and deeper:

Most times when the pumps disturbed his sleep with their hateful "dollar, dollar" talk, he would walk out into the darkness and abandon himself to his fear of losing his independence. He saw himself with a dinner pail working for someone else. He felt that he had staked his future on a hole in the ground, for which he would not be able to pay if oil didn't ooze up and flow to make it an oil well. Even on cool nights he sweated at the thought of being a nobody. Might as well be lying on a wicker platform, as he called the funeral scaffolds, as be unknown among the millions of unknowns. (*Ibid.*, 83)

The appeal of the unknown was balanced by Marland's fear that he might turn out to be an unknown himself. Worse still, he might become the anonymous employee of somebody else.

We are told that Marland's wooden derrick stood alone, the highest point within miles, and challenged the lightning and the sky. (Half a century later, a cover photograph from *Oklahoma Today* magazine appeared to re-create almost perfectly this fabled scene; see Fig. 6.1.) Then they struck oil, and Marland, as transformed by this event as Arthur was by pull-

Fig. 6.1. Oil rig and lightning, summer 1978. (Reprinted with permission of *Oklahoma Today* magazine.)

ing the sword from the stone, said, "I am sorry for the man who has missed the big thrill that comes to the wildcatter when his well, on which he has worked night after night and day after day, comes in a gusher" (ibid., 85).

The building of the new world began in a typically Arthurian fashion with the arrival of a Merlinesque seer (Professor Irving Perrine) from a temple of learning (the University of Oklahoma). Using the knowledge Perrine gave him, Marland expanded his operations, buying leases and drilling wells throughout the Cherokee Strip. The Arthurian adventurer needs a quest and the knowledge to pursue it. Marland now had both. His status as an independent oil field adventurer was nearly complete.

What Marland lacked was a band of loyal followers. He began by hiring a young man, John S. Alcorn ("a handsome opportunist") to be his right-hand man. Alcorn was quick and aggressive and became the conquering hero's charioteer: "He drove the Cadillac to carry E. W. and Dr. Perrine across the wind-singing prairie of the western Osage" (ibid., 92). Then Marland brought in loyal comrades from Pennsylvania and, nearer to home, whole classes of undergraduate geologists from the University of Oklahoma. In the period just after World War I, he vigorously recruited, from among the ranks of demobilized soldiers, ready-made knights of the Round Table "who would follow his fantastic activity without question" (ibid., 109). Collectively he referred to them as his "lieutenants." The Arthurian Marland then created his Camelot, Ponca City.

Ponca City took shape in the early years after Marland's first successes. He bought land and dedicated it to the homes of his employees. He started a bank, to help ordinary people, and built parks, gardens, golf courses, swimming pools, and polo fields all for the free use of the citizens, saying, "We are going to pay dividends in happiness to the community" (ibid., 102). Marland then went among his people to know their needs, recalling the ancient motif of the king who disguises himself as a peasant and goes among his subjects.

Great heroes need great enemies. Marland's enemies were monopoly businessmen and bankers, whom he called "the big boys" and "the still-faced boys." A writer for the *Wichita Beacon* remarked as early as 1921: "Periodically the great majority of oilmen have hoped that a great, new independent concern will arrive and do battle with the Standard" (in Mathews 1951, 144). Marland saw this as his mission. Money was not the object: "Long before that I had all the money I wanted and had ceased trying to make money for myself." The goal was victory over a giant: "I was ambitious to build a completely integrated oil company that would take its place in the petroleum industry and compete for markets with the Standard Oil Companies" (ibid.).

As the 1920s advanced, Marland spent less and less time building and improving his kingdom. Instead, he lavished money on himself and others, purposefully disregarding how much he spent or where the money came from. The decline of King Arthur's Camelot begins in the descent into passion, as Arthur's affection for Lancelot and Lancelot's love for Guinevere undo the bonds that unite the Round Table. For Marland's world as well, passion and possessiveness were its undoing. Marland's biographer refers to the 1920s as "a partial reversion to barbarism" (ibid., 148), his people turned into slaves of their own material success, and Marland himself, threatened by a loss of autonomy to the very empire he had created, began to act with a recklessness surprising even to his closest friends: "He was with his staff like a spoiled, irresponsible woman who makes no attempt to keep check stubs on her allowance, and whose husband must sweat to keep her account straight" (ibid., 150).

The feminization of Marland, even in metaphor, is revealing, since it represents a departure from the adult masculine ideal he previously embodied. The same deterioration besets Arthur, who cannot even lift a finger when an evil knight abducts his queen and demands ransom. What was strong, chaste, and responsible is now weak, greedy, and profligate. Soon it became impossible for Marland's loyal lieutenants to "refill the sack into which he had plunged his hand" (ibid., 150). At such times Marland grew annoyed, and when discussion turned to his financial improprieties, he either left the room or lay down on the office couch and pretended that he had gone to sleep.

The most extravagant of Marland's acts was the construction of a hunting camp, on the Arkansas River southeast of Ponca City, complete with electricity, a sewage disposal system, and running hot and cold water. The guests could hunt quail with bird dogs, shoot ducks along the river, hunt raccoons at night, or run coyotes across the prairie. There was also fox hunting on imported horses, with imported hounds, on the scent of imported foxes. Most of the foxes were eaten by coyotes before they could be caught.

An episode from his later years captures key aspects of Marland's persona. One night in the mid-1920s Marland sat drinking in a friend's kitchen when someone asked him, "E. W., why don't you have Jo make a statue to the vanishing American, a Ponca, Otoe, or an Osage—a monument of great size?"

Women were sitting about in short skirts, putting their knees awkwardly together as they backed up a chair to sit down, continually tugging at their inadequate skirts to cover an exposure of pale thigh. They shook their bobbed hair back like emergent swimmers, and lit cigarettes as if they expected them to explode. They saw the obscenity and missed the point in jokes, which, incidentally, were few and pale when E. W. was present.

E. W., in a pontifical manner which often offended those who didn't know him well, said, "The Indian is not the vanishing American—it's the pioneer woman."

Quite possibly he had not thought about this before that moment as he sat with his Scotch and soda in his hand. He assumed the attitude of "I tell you what I'm gonna do," and the idea of the statue of the pioneer woman was born. (Mathews 1951, 180)

Apparently, if the story is true, one of the premier Oklahoma icons owes its origin to E. W. Marland's sudden antipathy to chain-smoking flappers in short skirts. But the episode is revealing in other ways. On the one hand, "E. W." enjoyed drinking and gambling and wild behavior. This was the Marland who fought on the side of the independent oil producers against the eastern monopolies, "the big boys." On the other hand, he liked to create large autocratic structures himself— the oil company, his own great mansion, the statue itself— and to preside over them with unchallenged pontifical authority. This was the Marland who deliberately failed to invite

Will Rogers to the unveiling of the *Pioneer Woman* statue because he thought Rogers's "common touch" might demean the ceremony and the Marland who ridiculed "Alfalfa Bill" Murray, his immediate predecessor as governor, for growing onions in the capitol garden and for wearing sagging socks.

By the early 1920s Marland was devoting more of his time to the consolidation of old acquisitions and less to the discovery of new ones. It probably bored him. His business no longer provided a creative outlet for his adventurism, and so he turned to personal pleasure as the only domain in which his pursuit of individual achievement could be realized. That this also interfered with, and possibly even impaired, the workings of his company might actually have been functional for Marland. It vented his frustration at the business which had been a source of stimulation but now constituted a source of creative restraint. His behavior also served to inject a degree of unpredictability and adventure and thus to keep the business alive as a locus of creative involvement.

Nevertheless, Marland still maintained good Arthurian intentions. "He thought that the gift of freedom implied happiness." But he found that the utopia he had tried to create only encouraged greed and licentiousness among its intended recipients:

He didn't realize that the high salaries which he paid his executives and the heads of departments freed men who didn't know how to use freedom. His company officials, having no economic fears, expressed their natural urges rather freely. But they soon satiated their appetites, and there was nothing else. Even the Mecca of all inlanders, New York City, became dull to them. The women of New York suffered a fading of their glory with familiarity, and so did whisky and champagne.

There was excitement and maneuvering, and the chance to make money; there was polo, and poker, and visits to New York. And there were women everywhere, with short dresses and shingled hair, who, barbarically binding their breasts, attempted to look like shapeless boys. (*Ibid.*, 158)

In an Arthurian world, success always spoils the heroic vision of the adventurer. In Marland's world, materialism became the means and measure of happiness. Masculine camaraderie, so essential to the Arthurian myth, became debased as relationships to women and their powers of distraction grew. There is no individual woman—no Guinevere—to represent the symbolic power of women to corrupt. Marland's empire itself became feminized as men gave themselves up to pleasures that were seen as essentially female.

Thus weakened by concupiscence, but wanting more regardless of the price, Marland finally sought financial help from his ancient enemy, the bankers. He obtained it, but only by relinquishing ultimate control of the business. This led almost immediately to his demotion to a figure-head position, to the dismissal or resignation of most of his loyal lieutenants, and finally to the end of the empire itself. Not long after assuming control, the bankers even changed the name of the company from Marland Oil to Conoco, the name by which it is known today.

The end of one Camelot only served to begin the search for another, as Marland gave up the oil business for politics. In 1932 he was elected to the House of Representatives; he served one term and then in 1934 ran for governor of Oklahoma. He served one term as governor and then lost his bid for reelection in 1938. He ran for office on an avowedly pro-Roosevelt platform. He supported the extension of state control and the creation of new authorities. As one of his friends pointed out, such actions seemed to violate his principles. Marland's answer is revealing: "I'm governor of the state—I'm not an oilman any more."

Marland sought success in two forms. He wanted to be an individual who set and met independent objectives despite conventional wisdom and the nay-saying of established authorities. Marland thus embodies the familiar American stereotype of the rugged individual—a stereotype consonant, in political terms, with traditional Republican values. He also wanted to use material achievement to create a fraternity of like-minded men and to extend the benefits of their association to the whole community, starting with Ponca City and extending ultimately to the state and the nation. It is the vision of oil-based utopia—a Camelot with derricks. In this form, upholding the values of community solidarity and group responsibility for happiness, Marland much more closely represented a Rooseveltian Democrat. The two images contributed to Marland's strength but also created, at least in the eyes of his closest friends, a noticeable contradiction.

It could also be argued that the contradiction was very real, since Marland's vision depended on defining himself as the heroic individualist who realizes a dream against the opposition of large autocratic structures. But when the new world seemed imminent or close at hand, as it did in Ponca City at one time, Marland found himself in the position of autocrat and his creation no different from the great structures, such as Standard Oil and the Mellon Bank, he had fought against. Competition with the established authorities (the "big boys") threatened Marland's independence where it mattered the most—in his definition of himself as a swashbuckling oil field adventurer. The more he competed with them the more he became like them and the more his adventurism made him resist transformation. This culminated in the highly contradictory image Marland presented to his associates: the powerful and autocratic chief executive who went to sleep when talk turned to matters of his own financial responsibility. He died in 1941.

Marland's public persona had two sides, one independent and adventuristic, the other domineering and autocratic. Yet Marland, like my father, never manifested both aspects at the same time. When he was one, the world became the other, in a continuous oscillation that occupied many years. What makes Marland's career unique is the vast arena within which this oscillation played itself out. First, its scale was huge, extending throughout the state. Second, its realization was diverse, all the way from presidency of an oil company to governorship of the state. And third, it attracted great public attention.

Neither Marland nor his heritage was unique. Many famous Oklahoma businessmen and politicians were (or were said to be) descendents of minor European nobility. The biographies of E. K. Gaylord, Frank Buttram, and Charles Colcord, to name just a few, all make references to their subjects' European aristocratic heritage in order to explain the character and extent of their public largesse as well as the magnificence of their business creations (Harlow 1928).

In Marland's career we see a cultural response to the opening of a new frontier and the building of a new society, a response in which the publicly proclaimed values of freedom and democracy went hand in hand with the slightly more muted but no less salient values of aristocratic privilege and noblesse oblige. Syntheses were often attempted; indeed, the cultural histories of people like the Rockefellers and of places such as Newport reveal a few of the different permutations. But these histories failed, for the most part, to become the gathering points for larger social movements because the models of aristocracy they drew on were forms only and lacked compelling social substance.

Now consider Marland. His background, as it was popularly understood, made his attempted synthesis of European and American values seem all the more likely in retrospect. But the model that underwrote Marland's synthesis was the model of heroic adventure, of putting a leader's creative individualism at the service of a united group in common pursuit of cause. The cause had less to do with making money than with creating a happy world. That is what made the assimilation of European aristocratic values possible for Marland and is what made Marland himself so charismatic in the eyes of so many Oklahomans.

David L. Payne

"Oklahoma" originally refers to the Unassigned Lands, the area central to what later became the state which the federal government took away from the Indian tribes after the Civil War and opened to white settlement more than twenty years later in the famous Run of 1889. That the same name eventually stood for a much larger area is important, because the larger area that became the state derived its cultural identity from the original Oklahoma of the Unassigned Lands. We must look to that core area, and to what happened there, to understand the symbolic formation of the state and the reason why some personalities, like Marland's, eventually became representative of it.

Until almost the end of the nineteenth century, the original Oklahoma remained largely untouched and untraveled by the westwardly expanding white population. All that changed after the end of the Civil War, but not because of increased travel or because the discovery of natural resources made the land suddenly more desirable. The transformation had more to do with developments outside the area than within it: "For three centuries the white man, in the name of God, in the name of Civilization, in pursuit of liberty, fought his way through the wilderness of America. In blood and sweat the frontiers fell before him until only one remained. Chance and circumstance and governmental policy had left one great area, bounded by Kansas, Arkansas, and Texas, comparatively untouched" (Glasscock 1937, 11). Oklahoma's value grew in direct proportion to its status as the largest remaining area where settlement by whites was prohibited.

David Payne did not create the myth of Oklahoma; he popularized it. By the end of the 1880s, largely through Payne's efforts, the Unassigned Lands had taken on the status of an American Eden. Payne's technique was simple. He would lead a small band of settlers into the forbidden zone, set up camp, and wait for the military to arrive and eject him. Returning to his staging ground on the Kansas border, he would describe his visit to the promised land and tell tales of its magnificence and grandeur. He repeated the process several times in the early and middle 1880s, with the result that Oklahoma became, in the view of many, "a virgin land, inexhaustible in its wide variety of resources; with mines, forests, and prairies; with mountains, cataracts, and canyons; and with valleys and streams. Here were the brightest skies, the grandest sunsets, the softest twilights; and the most brilliant moon and glittering stars, smiling their welcome to visitors. . . . God had reserved it as man's paradise on earth" (Rister 1942, 76).

Payne, meanwhile, was busy selling settlement shares to the men and women whose appetites for land he had whetted. He made a fortune, and later lost it, without ever delivering anything. Payne died of a heart attack in 1884 at the age of forty-eight. He is described in his biography as "an Oklahoma hero and border adventurer of much the same mold as Buffalo Bill Cody, Kit Carson, Ewing Young, and Sam Houston" (ibid., vii).

Oklahoma adventurism, as I have discussed it, leads paradoxically to the fight against authority and to its creation, usually in the form of an organization or system of centralized control that eventually overwhelms and rejects the creator-adventurer. During the period when "Oklahoma" existed only as an idea, the basic constituents of this identity appeared in David Payne. They emerged in the circumstances which defined his public persona.

David Payne's history, as it is known to most Oklahomans, follows his development as a border fighter and rebel from his youth in Indiana, where he was born. At the age of twenty-one he went to Kansas, attracted by the adventure of a military campaign against the Mormons and then by homesteading. He tried farming, rail splitting, and hunting but soon gave them up because "regions farther west wooed him" (ibid., 10). He was a scout for a while and then enlisted in the Kansas Volunteers at the outbreak of the Civil War. He left the army in 1864 to run for the Kansas House of Representatives. He won and served out his term, then reenlisted in the army. He was present at Appomattox when Lee surrendered to Grant. Payne then served as sergeant-at-arms of the Kansas Senate during the sessions of 1866 and 1867 and afterward became postmaster at Leavenworth.

Payne's biographer, drawing on well-known and popular legends, constructs Payne as the kind of man who had taken on the characteristics that later made him famous as leader of the Boomers even before he had heard of Oklahoma:

Dave had emerged from his border and Civil War experiences with traits which were to characterize him in later years. Stirring days had left him restless and intolerant of humdrum life, not content to settle down to the quiet ways of peace. For many years he had been associated with rough, untamed characters who were accustomed to pillage, bloodshed, and war, and he had gradually taken up their habits of drinking, cursing, and gambling. He had also evinced an amazing disregard for money. He was careless not only with his own money but also with that of his friends. One who knew him said: "If there was a man among his contemporaries from whom he did not borrow, or to whom he did not lend, it would be interesting to know what character of man he was. He did not borrow because he loved money. On the contrary, he hated it." (Ibid., 15)

Such characteristics also make Payne comparable in temperament and taste to Marland and my father. This is especially true with respect to their indifference to money and their quest for adventure. Money was valuable only to the extent that it could be used to support heroic adventure; otherwise, in the absence of heroic possibilities, money was simply a means of entertainment as one escaped from external constraint and waited for the next adventuristic opportunity to appear.

Not surprisingly, Payne gave up his positions in Kansas to respond to "the ringing call for border service against hostile Indians on the frontier" (ibid., 15). Shortly after Custer massacred Black Kettle's camp of Cheyennes on the Washita, Payne accompanied General Sheridan to the site and helped bury the dead. This was Payne's first visit to the land that would become Oklahoma. He continued in the frontier service until 1869, when the campaign against the Indians ended. But the border zone still attracted him.

For a while Payne tried homesteading and farming and even went back to the Kansas Legislature. But he found such jobs too boring. Payne left Kansas in 1876 for Washington, D.C., and got a job as assistant doorkeeper in the House of Representatives, but when he lost the job he returned to Kansas. If nothing else had happened, Payne might have continued this oscillation, seeking and losing jobs, trying to create and trying to avoid stability, and always hearkening back to the frontier. But just about that time, the *Chicago Times* published a lengthy article on the unoccupied lands in Indian Territory known as Oklahoma. This was to be the turning point for Payne.

Newspapers republished the story throughout the country, resulting in a settler stampede toward the border towns near the territory. Thousands of emigrants moved toward the Indian Territory, "and their trains of white-topped wagons in the broken lines along the roadways appeared in the distance like patches of snow" (ibid., 44). But lacking an effective leader or any form of organization, the would-be settlers were driven back by the military as soon as they tried to colonize the territory. Payne possessed the leadership qualities they needed; people said later they could see it in his eyes. As soon as he arrived from Washington in Wichita, he created the "Oklahoma Colony" to plan the invasion of the territory and the creation of a settlement in its center, to be called "Oklahoma City."

Payne's sudden transformation from assistant doorkeeper to planner of invasions might be difficult to interpret if his history up to this point were unavailable. The unknown and the inaccessible, however, clearly exerted an influence on him. Just as clear, of course, is his deep antipathy to settling down, to financial responsibility, and to detail, which made it impossible for him to succeed in a homestead once the struggle for its acquisition had ended. The irony is palpable—that a man who could not stand settling down defined himself as leader of people who wanted only that. But in this Payne is hardly unique. Marland and my father, as we have seen, evinced the same qualities in pursuit of similar ends.

In 1880, Payne led the first invasion and established a settlement of twenty-one men near present day Oklahoma City. A cavalry squad from Fort Reno arrived and escorted them back to the border. When Payne returned to Wichita, he advertised the land he had just seen and had been forced to leave. Eager homeseekers bought membership certificates in Payne's Oklahoma Colony and awaited the results of his next attempt. That came just two months later, in July 1880, and ended as before, with one difference: Payne was arrested and bound over for trial in Fort Smith. That was his objective. A public trial would force the issue of Oklahoma settlement through the courts and result in tremendous free advertising for the settler movement.

Galvanized by Payne's "sacrifice," the Boomer movement reached the height of its popularity. Over four thousand names were enrolled on the colony roster in Kansas alone, and mass meetings and subsidiary colonies were created in other border states. Entrepreneurs throughout the Midwest, in Chicago and in Saint Louis, lent their support—not because they wanted to settle in Oklahoma, but because they knew that those who did would need the goods and services they would supply. Members of the clergy, too, responded enthusiastically to the Boomer movement as if to a holy cause. At one of Payne's settler camps, for example, a chaplain preached from a passage in Exodus, speaking of President Hays as Pharaoh, Oklahoma as Canaan, and the colonists as the Lord's people (ibid., 83). Settlement became a spiritual quest.

The classic confrontation between the independent Oklahoman and the authoritarian outside world occurred in Payne's trial before Isaac Parker, the famous Kansas City judge, in 1881. Payne argued that the Unassigned Lands were open to settlement because they constituted "reacquired" public domain and as such were subject to homestead entry under the Homestead Law. The government argued that the lands were still part of Indian Territory and therefore closed to white settlement. Parker, in deciding for the government, concluded that the disputed area was intended for the benefit of Indian resettlement when it was "reacquired" by the government from the Creek and Seminole nations after the Civil War.

Payne's legal plight did not impede the Boomer movement, for the Oklahoma adventurer always has a way to circumvent authority. Within a year, advertisements appeared in all the regional papers offering more shares in the Oklahoma Colony. Payne sold thousands (including five thousand to the *Chicago Tribune*). Few could resist his charismatic appeal, despite repeated references to him as "a professional dead beat" and "a worthless drunken loafer" (*ibid.*, 122). Payne, meanwhile, grew more hyperbolic in his commitment to settlement, declaring that "I would rather have my arms cut off, my throat cut and the streams run red with blood than to be arrested and prevented from settling in Oklahoma" (ibid., 126). Under his command, the unsuccessful invasions continued into Oklahoma for the next two years.

In 1884, Payne suddenly died. "What Daniel Boone is to Kentucky," his eulogy read, "David Payne will be to Oklahoma" (ibid., 187). Still, his movement survived and grew and finally forced the government in Washington to act. In 1889, the Unassigned Lands were opened. Yet very few of Payne's closest associates profited by it. Payne's common-law wife lost her claim to land when a high court ruled that settlers who started from railroad camps within Oklahoma, instead of from sites along the Oklahoma border, did not possess valid claims. She moved to Oregon and died in poverty. Payne's other close confidant and successor as leader of the Boomers, W. L. Couch, made the run and went on to become Oklahoma City's first mayor, but he died in a gunfight in 1890, less than a year later.

Payne and his closest associates flourished when Oklahoma still existed as a concept, not a reality. What we know of Payne suggests that he was drawn to borders; if the borders surrounded a land that was inaccessible or remote, so much the better. Payne did not want to become a settled citizen in a land that had been tamed. His dream centered on the quest itself—to lead an army of like-minded men into a promised land—and on his own extraordinary ability to gather and lead a band of loyal followers. The dream was self-defeating, or probably would have been if Payne had survived, because it was limited by an *attainable* goal. Such a goal, once achieved, would have resulted in the destruction of the loyal band through its dispersal as individual interests prevailed over group ones, as they did for other Arthurian types, such as Marland and my father, in the next century.

The legend of Payne is important for bringing together elements that soon became central in the cultural construction of the Oklahoma adventurer. These elements included charisma and a quest; flamboyant optimism in the face of terrible odds; carelessness; and tragic destruction. Political careers, like Payne's, lent themselves well to the process of identity construction in the early days as Oklahoma was being created. But soon the scene shifted, and oil, not land, became the new frontier as new personalities, such as Marland's, evolved to represent it. It may be only speculation, but if the model of

Oklahoma identity I have described really exists, then it is very likely to survive the eclipse of the oil business. Just what new form it may take is hard to say, as I explain below, but certain candidates have already begun to appear on the scene.

Conclusion

What I earlier described as the "egocentric" definition of civilization asserts that private interest is the foremost goal of human action; it alone creates the ordered world of free individuals in mutually advantageous association with each other. The "sociocentric" definition of civilization, by contrast, asserts that the bonds which unite people are intrinsically nonutilitarian, that among these bonds the highest and best are unity in a noble quest. The definition emergent in the cultural construction of Oklahoma combines these two into one: civilization becomes synonymous with an entrepreneurial enterprise made up of men who are loyally devoted to each other and to their charismatic leader. This is what Max Weber seems to have noticed on his trip through Oklahoma in 1904. The problem is that these elements are hard to sustain in balanced combination. It is too easy for independent entrepreneurialism to turn into authoritarian big business and for loyal men to turn into profit-seeking loners. It is the possibility for a synthesis, as well as the inevitability of demise once the synthesis is achieved, that defines the Arthurian type.

If an Arthurian ethos permeates Oklahoma identity, then what sustains it generation after generation? Perhaps it is the symbolic existence of Oklahoma as a perpetually renewable frontier. Oklahoma remains this because of its oil and natural gas, both real and wished for. Its fantastic wealth-generating potential is always immanent. The search goes on, not only for oil but also for the world we believe our wealth might create, thus sustaining not only the cycle of boom and bust but also the cultural system which applauds individuals who embody its chief characteristics: individual initiative, group fellowship, and the search for something always just out of reach.

Are there contemporary counterparts to Payne and to Marland? Oil field adventurers still abound, but none (so far) has the prominence or public appeal that it takes to make a cynosure. For the charismatic embodiment of entrepreneurial adventurism there is only one obvious modern candidate: the "televangelist" Oral Roberts.

For adventure, Roberts offers a war between God and the Devil; for fellowship, the community of the born-again; and for rewards, the promise of spiritual salvation and the risk of eternal damnation. The frontier is the human soul—potentially as renewable as that other unseen frontier, oil, and like it, holding out the promise of rediscovery. The problems endemic to this quest remain, too. Success engenders loss of vision, dissolution of fellowship, and decline into greediness and passion. Oral Roberts's Camelot—the City of Faith—may or may not survive, but the cultural order that created it will no doubt endure, even though we cannot now foresee its forms.

CHAPTER 7

Spa in the Dust Bowl:
Oklahoma's Hidden Paradise

J. NEIL HENDERSON

The distinction between wetness and dryness is central to the feeling and image of Oklahomaness, both to Oklahomans and to outsiders. In this chapter J. Neil Henderson examines this profound cultural polarity through the local history of Sulphur, Oklahoma, the site of a mineral-water spa. What Henderson demonstrates for Sulphur applies not only to the symbolism of that spa town, but also to the entire state: that water is far more than a necessity of life. It is a symbol of life itself, of renewal. Its absence reawakens the specter of death. Much of Oklahomaness can be understood not only in terms of the dread of literal dryness (aridity), such as that associated with the Dust Bowl, but also in the sense of all that dryness means and feels, whether the absence is of water or of oil. Through and in water one can be religiously born again. Henderson's chapter shows how the symbolism of water in Sulphur and throughout Oklahoma has a sacred, even revitalizing, as well as secular, practical connotation. It shows how spa symbolism offers a rich counterpoint to the theme of dryness in general and the Dust Bowl in particular.

Even the oceans do not hold enough water to fill the nation's image of Oklahoma's dry Dust Bowl days. As Robert F. Hill and Howard F. Stein (1988) report, four other neighboring states were severely affected by the multiyear drought, but only Oklahoma acquired its barren image. This stark image was impressed upon the public by John Steinbeck's powerful Pulitzer Prize–winning book, *The Grapes of Wrath* (1939), and visually fixed by the 1940 Academy Award–winning film starring Henry Fonda. More than fourteen million copies of *The Grapes of Wrath* have been sold, and it has been translated into most western and eastern languages. University of Oklahoma historian William Savage paradoxically notes that the altruistic and noble aspects of the Joads have been lost to readers and replaced with the pejorative "Okie" appellation (a California term for a poverty-stricken Oklahoma refugee from the ravages of the Dust Bowl) (DeFrange 1989).

Also lost in Oklahoma's dry Dust Bowl image was the active spa resort town of Sulphur, which featured cold mineral water, mineral-water baths, and mud baths as the perfect therapy for a multitude of ills. Paradoxically, the peak year of activity for Sulphur's mineral-water resort industry was 1937, the height of the Dust Bowl. As a state, Oklahoma countered the Dust Bowl experience by developing numerous water projects. Very large lakes were constructed from small streams dammed to back up water. Today, marketing brochures portray Oklahoma as an aquatic vacationland, with a preponderance of pictures showing lakes, skiers, and sailboats. This type of adaptation to unpredictable, noxious change is a way to revitalize a community's "life blood"—in a sense, to be "born again."

The Spa: Sulphur, Oklahoma

The purpose of this chapter is to show the ways in which the Dust Bowl image of Oklahoma exists in spite of large water resources even during the Dust Bowl. The town of Sulphur, Oklahoma, is a microcosm of the wet reality that contrasted with the dry Dust Bowl image. Also, Sulphur reflects other important Oklahoma themes such as boom-and-bust cycles, allegiance to the work ethic glorified in Oklahoma's motto "Labor Conquers All Things," and a "born-again" revitalization scheme to keep the community economically vital. The last two are part of the fundamentalism of Oklahoma Protestants, who far outnumber Catholics, Jews, and other non-Protestants. Protestant fundamentalism in Sulphur is linked with another healing tradition now headquartered in Tulsa, Oklahoma. Oral Roberts's faith healing and laying-on-of-hands brought him to Sulphur, where he met his wife and from where he continued to minister to adoring audiences.

The spa town of Sulphur in south central Oklahoma is in the part of the state recently designated "Lake Country" by marketing promoters. It is in an area of forested rolling hills with a geologic uplift that produces a ridge known as the Arbuckle Mountains. In correct geologic terms, the Arbuckles fall short of being mountains by several thousand feet. Still, they rise distinctly above the surrounding terrain.

The Arbuckles were geologically uplifted in a region in which former seas laid down horizontal sediments which became hard strata. The uplifting inclined the horizontal strata to a near vertical tilt, which is apparent at the present ground surface. Because of erosion, the surface sometimes shows parallel rows of flat rock that appear to have been set upright in the ground like tombstones.

Sulphur's mineral springs, seven miles away, are related to this hilly topography and "tombstoning." Rainfall seeps between the vertical strata, gathering minerals from the rock, and then emerges at the base of the uplift as mineral springs. Sulphur itself is in a relative valley alongside the uplift ridge. One feature of the ridge at Sulphur is Bromide Mountain, the north face of which has a prominent rock outcrop visible for miles. From it people have viewed the wooded valley below for millennia. Directly under the rock outcrop, and at the bottom of Bromide Mountain, was one of the biggest mineral wells in the area; it yielded water of the type for which Sulphur's "mountain" is named.

Sulphur has weathered severe dry heat waves in the mid-1930s, early 1950s, and early 1980s. It first experienced rapid growth as its mineral-water fame spread in the early 1900s, but that growth was followed by drastic cycles of change in weather and the popularity of mineral water. By the mid-

1950s community leaders developed a vision of a future in which a water supply would be under complete human control from a lake to be constructed nearby. Oklahoma communities statewide benefited from man-made lakes such as Lake Texoma near Durant and Lake Murray near Ardmore (both about forty to fifty miles from Sulphur). Sulphur's vision was realized when the Lake of the Arbuckles was constructed in the late 1960s. The lake has become the main attraction for Sulphur's tourist traffic, taking precedence over the nearly forgotten mineral springs.

Why have the springs and other aquatic features in the area been forgotten? Murray County, of which Sulphur is the seat, boasts a seventy-seven-foot waterfall and numerous coldwater mineral springs. In fact, well before the Dust Bowl, Sulphur developed as a spa resort town in Indian Territory, later to become Oklahoma. The waterfall, Turner's Falls, seven miles from Sulphur, has also become a tourist attraction. How could such a bustling, water-driven community as Sulphur have vanished from Oklahoma's national image?

Oklahoma Culture under Construction

In the late 1930s a remarkable twist of fate led to the collision of two developing images of Oklahoma. One image centered around Oklahoma's spa resort at Sulphur, and the other image developed from the powerful photographic display of the worst of the Dust Bowl in western Oklahoma. That the Dust Bowl image emerged as the long-range winner is testimony to the power of visual examples, or icons. Still photographs and the film *The Grapes of Wrath* are black-and-white, chemically produced icons of Oklahoma which the nation readily accepted as representative of all the state's ecological regions and history. As symbols, icons represent that which believers want them to represent.

Yet earlier in the century, Sulphur had enjoyed a meteoric rise in fame as a place of healing waters and miracle cures. Are journalistic photos and Hollywood movies alone powerful enough to have derailed that wet image of Oklahoma?

Actually, the power of the press and other media is enormous, but the Dust Bowl press unknowingly had an ally which siphoned away any chance for Sulphur's wet spas to become the predominant Oklahoma image.

In order to understand Oklahoma culture as expressed in Sulphur during this century, some historical developments of the spas need to be specified. Then the Oklahoma cultural themes of the "Dust Bowl," "boom-and-bust cycles," "work conquers all," and "born-again" can be seen in action.

Sulphur's Healing Waters

It was during the hydrotherapy health craze that Sulphur, Indian Territory, developed as a frontier spa resort featuring healing mineral waters for drinking and bathing and for mud baths. The historical development of Sulphur is well delineated in *Oklahoma Oasis*, by Palmer H. Boeger (1987). Boeger shows that by the 1890s the mineral-water springs were beginning to attract Anglo settlers. A neighboring town's newspaper referred to Sulphur Springs as a "great health mecca and summer resort" (Boeger 1987, 42). By 1905, commercial hotels and bathhouses were established around the mineral spring sites. In 1906, Congress designated the immediate area surrounding the springs Platt National Park.

Soon the town of Davis, seven miles west of Sulphur, had replaced stagecoach service to Sulphur with a twice-daily "Health Special" train on the Sante Fe Railroad. In 1908 the fame of the mineral water in Sulphur was sufficient to spark discussion of developing the spring sites as a sanitarium which would serve as a magnet to health specialists from throughout the world. For the first time, however, interest in conservation began to be expressed by the national park authority. One of the park management's regulations placed a one-gallon limit on bromide water taken away from the springs. At the same time, many mineral-water wells had been drilled on private property outside the National Park Service jurisdiction, and those wells provided the necessary mineral water to sustain the private-enterprise spa industry.

The new State of Oklahoma began to issue proclamations from Oklahoma City, the capitol, touting Sulphur's mineral water as a tourist attraction. The Oklahoma governor in 1921 stated in a promotional letter that the springs' mineral waters "have cured thousands of sufferers and in the millions of gallons that daily continue to bubble from Artesian wells and springs there is renewed vitality and zest for living for the visitor. . . . As the Executive of the Commonwealth I extend to you a hearty invitation to enjoy at an early date the benefits of these health giving waters." In addition, Oklahoma's state health commissioner and the Murray County Medical Association endorsed health claims about the mineral waters.

As cars became more numerous and roads improved, visitors began to come to the springs in greater numbers. Most came from near and far throughout Oklahoma, and a significant minority came from Texas and Arkansas. Of the 50,000 visitors who camped in 1927 (there were also 250,000 non-camping visitors) Boeger states:

Half the campers admitted to coming for their health. Every morning during the visitor season, people spilled out of the city hotels or boarding houses in town and strolled into the Park. Often the trails to the springs were as full of people as a city street. Everyone carried a small folding tin cup. Gentlemen put their cups into their pockets, while ladies carried theirs in their purses. Ladies outnumbered men in these health excursions. Nobody hurried. Some rode to the springs in their automobiles. All were visibly lighthearted, happy, their spirits buoyant. Parties chattered merrily on these jaunts to the fabled waters. (1987, 117)

Use of the park continued to increase, so by 1928 Platt National Park and its mineral waters had the second highest use of all the national parks although the park was the smallest in size.

Visitors used the mineral springs at Sulphur three ways: they drank it as a health tonic, bathed in it at bathhouses, and bathed in its mud, usually by standing ankle-deep in mineral-water ponds formed by runoff and applying the thick black mud to the body as a poultice. All three therapies were widely used. Hotels and bathhouses sprang up as support industries in service to the pilgrims to Sulphur.

Anecdotal testimonials have long been used by spa resorts to prove the medicinal efficacy of their mineral waters. Detailed accounts of testimonials by mineral-water users who came from throughout Oklahoma and neighboring states to Sulphur have been recorded by Palmer Boeger (1987), Opal Hartsell-Brown (1977) and Opal Hartsell-Brown and R. Garrity (1981). For example, one user reported: "Have been at Sulphur eight days, drinking Bromide water for kidney trouble and nervousness. Gaining in weight and can sleep ten hours at a stretch. Have received more benefit by drinking Bromide water eight days than by five weeks of treatment at Hot Springs. G. R. Langtree (Sulphur, Oklahoma 1913)." In a few decades, however, Sulphur's waters would stop healing.

A radical shift in health beliefs began to occur in the scientific community during the late 1800s and early 1900s with research by Edward Jenner, Joseph Lister, Louis Pasteur, Alexander Fleming, and Howard Florey, to name a few. The grand scheme of naturopathic health, and the broad values of cleanliness and order of the Sanitarian Revolution, were gradually supplanted by the understanding that specific microorganisms cause specific diseases. The Doctrine of Specific Etiology was the new banner for health belief and health care.

The Doctrine of Specific Etiology had crossed the Atlantic just as its sanitarian predecessor had done. Palmer Boeger's detailed recording of the history of Sulphur and its mineral waters reflects the effects of this change in health belief. Boeger (1987, 155) notes that in 1937 the amount of mineral water taken from the park reached its peak, but by 1941 very few gallon jugs of water were being sold in the city. Boeger (1987, 157) also reports that by 1942 there had been a shift in the origin of users of mineral water for health purposes. The primary users by then were "old folks [who] lived in the vicinity," not health pilgrims (1987, 157). During the war years, soldiers from a nearby air base visited the park on leave but had no interest in the mineral waters. World War II seemed to be the watershed for belief in the mineral waters at Sulphur. The Doctrine of Specific Etiology had finally taken its toll. As Boeger writes: "The resort hotels and bath houses in town never again attracted the vacationing crowds as before, and some of them closed. Visitors did not flock to the mineral springs as they once had. The heyday of mineral baths and spas—the Age of the Springs and their healing tradition—was drawing to a close although the old-timers would not yet admit it" (1987, 161).

The decline in use of the mineral waters occurred just as the development and widespread use of antibiotics such as penicillin skyrocketed. The shift in belief about public health was complete; Sulphur's waters stopped healing.

Oklahoma Themes

Dust Bowl Theme

I have examined the paradox of the spa during the Dust Bowl by analyzing the coincidence of the drought in western Oklahoma at the same time that belief in mineral water as a health tonic died. Had it not been for the drought, and its powerful dramatization in Steinbeck's (1939) novel, the wet reality of Oklahoma could just as easily have been one of the main image makers of Oklahoma. Of course all of Oklahoma is not Lake Country now, nor was it in the past. Yet, this fraction of Oklahoma reality might also have stood a chance to become *the* stereotypic feature of all Oklahoma realities, just as readily as others have, under different conditions of promotion. (For other examples in this volume, see chapters by Lamar regarding free land, Nuckolls regarding oil field adventure, or Tramel regarding big-time football.)

The current post–Dust Bowl cultural themes of Oklahoma derive from some deep-seated western culture and Protestant religious ethics. They are not necessarily a direct product of the Dust Bowl. Nevertheless, these themes were played out in the context of the Dust Bowl of Oklahoma and have therefore become interwoven with Oklahomans' life experiences, which prominently include Dust Bowl days themselves and the national perception of Oklahoma as the place of the Dust Bowl.

Boom-and-Bust Theme

The pioneer frontier experience was an array of feast or famine: too much rain, too little rain; too much regulation, too little law and order; pockets of eastern urban "civilization" in the middle of an overnight, muddy boom town. The newness of Oklahoma as a state had preserved a bit of the Old West into the 1900s, delaying the comparatively steady conditions of commodities, law enforcement, public utilities, and public health enjoyed by older states. This delay left Oklahomans more subject to the unsteadiness of boom-and-bust cycles.

Weather, oil, and cattle are features of Oklahoma's natural environment only partially subject to human control. Now it is clear that mineral water is not a stable commodity either. Sulphur experienced a boom-and-bust cycle, not because of oil gushers and dry holes, but as a result of a change in the belief about mineral water as a health tonic. The thriving resort spa was a boom town based on a "wet" commodity initially more important than oil. But then came the bust for Sulphur when the spa in the Dust Bowl became just running water.

Born-Again Theme

Communities adapt to the ever-changing experiences of life in a patterned way (Linton 1943; Wallace 1956; La Barre 1972). When people experience a change that undermines former belief systems, established patterns of behavior, or workable economics, the community adapts toward a way of life that brings a new sense of order and renews the community's sense of cohesion, success, and economy (Wallace 1956). It is as if the community was re-created and born again, only better. Such processes are called revitalization movements. One type of revitalization movement—the "cargo cult"—typifies the Sulphur experience (Worsley 1959).

Cargo cults were first described among nonwestern societies whose life-ways had been severely disturbed by European invasion or contact. To the natives, it appeared that the Europeans intercepted commodities really meant for them and that the alien invaders must know some special ritual formula to bring such vast amounts of technology and goods from the cargo holds of ships and airplanes. The natives then changed certain parts of their former life patterns in an effort to acquire the desirable cargo and reestablish the former sense of balance in life.

Cargo cults as seen in American society are not actual cults but are an organized response to increase community viability (cf. Burns 1978). Part of Oklahoma's post–Dust Bowl days involved a statewide interest in developing lakes by damming small rivers. Although a constructed lake with a one-thousand-mile shoreline is within forty-five miles, the town of Sulphur decided to apply this proven strategy in their own backyard. The development of such a freshwater resource in the Sulphur area was calculated to recapture interest and money (that is, "cargo") that the mineral waters had formerly brought to Sulphur. According to Boeger, the idea of a lake near the mineral-water springs was "originated by a group of citizens who first met informally, [and then] the lake became a Chamber of Commerce project. Its promoters anticipated tourists, jobs, and new area growth. Businessmen believed that the lake would give a much-needed boost to the lagging community. . . . These discussions about a lake revived dreams of a greater Park" (1987, 180).

By 1970, Sulphur had a new nearby lake, and the national park property boundaries were extended to incorporate not only the mineral-water springs but also the Lake of the Arbuckles. The name of the entire service area of the park was changed to Chickasaw National Recreation Area. Today a campground surrounds the mineral-water springs. Those springs, which in the past drew so much attention as a health resort, have been preserved and are well used by campers, though not as a health tonic but for their natural beauty. The mineral-water springs sometimes go dry, but the lake, which is a few miles long and a mile wide, should always have water. As Boeger relates, "If Platt's Springs quit—a distinct possibility—the public still has the lake" (1987, 192).

The lake has attracted around this farming community a series of water-related industries. For example, there are now dealers which sell only boats and boat motors and marinas that sell all manner of equipment for water recreation. There are permanent boat docking facilities and fishing tackle shops. All these are products, or cargo, of this newly developed commodity, the lake. The quest by Sulphur for a revitalized economy has met with at least some success. With its own new water, Sulphur has been "born again."

Work-Conquers-All Theme

Most of Sulphur's mineral-water springs have stopped flowing, but not so the spirit of its townspeople. A new drive toward recognition recalls the old days of the mineral-water spa in the logo, "Sulphur—City of Springs," emblazoned on city stationery, caps, visors, flying discs, and a canvas bag which (tongue-in-cheek) lists notable world-class sites: "London-Paris-Rome-Sulphur." But modern reality is reflected on a large multicolored billboard on the interstate highway ten miles west of Sulphur. It features a water skier with water spraying from under the skis. Five specific attractions are mentioned on the sign. Mineral water is dead last.

Another marketing effort refers to Sulphur's county with the alluring slogan, "Murray County—Southern Oklahoma's Hidden Paradise," revealing the self-awareness of the lost image of Oklahoma's water resources in the bright glare of the Dust Bowl image: it was unknown, lost, but now is an attainable Eden, paradise. In purposeful allusion to a favorite Oklahoma church-goer's hymn, Sulphur's waters were "lost but now are found."

Sulphur marketing brochures from 1913 to the present show a change in self-perception related to the changing tides of Sulphur's waters. In 1913 the brochure emphasizes the healing waters of Sulphur, with pictures of the springs, and resort hotels, ordering information for gallons of mineral water, and dozens of testimonials to the sure cure by Sulphur's waters of seemingly all diseases imaginable. In the early 1950s a picture-packed brochure designed for mailing mirrored the post–Dust Bowl era and contemporary enthusiasm for antibiotic cures. Sulphur is redefined as the "Home of Platt National Park *and* Capital of Hereford Heaven." Out of ten pictures of the park's mineral springs (one is in a bath house), two mention the water as being healthful. The others are recreational scenes. Of the twenty-seven pictures in the brochure, eight relate to the park's waters in recreational terms, and only two mention mineral water for health.

In the 1990s brochure the front surface is a full-color picture of a water skier with immense water plumes spraying into the sky. The top reads, "Discover Southern Oklahoma's Hidden Paradise," and below, in big print, is "Murray County." There is no mention at all of healing mineral waters. The attraction to Sulphur is still to water, but to the Lake of the Arbuckles.

The Oklahomans of Sulphur have worked hard to revitalize their community from a spa ghost town to a paradise of water recreation. Water is still the main attraction in Sulphur, but now it should stay outside the body. Moreover, Sulphur's promoters, in concert with promotional efforts by Oklahoma state officials, admonish non-Oklahomans to "discover" Oklahoma in general, as the state boundary marker signs read, and specifically the hidden paradise of Murray County. As Oklahomans work at their state image, so must the visitor do some work at discovering. Remember, *Labor Omnia Vincit*, labor conquers all things.

Acknowledgments

The author wishes to thank the following for their very useful information and insight. Of course, any inaccuracies are the author's responsibility. Many thanks to 'berta S. Stumpff, Jo Alice Lochmiller, Patricia S. Henderson, Jamie Petitte, Ruby Townsley, Opal Hartsell-Brown, Carl Reubin, Inez Greene, Buster T. Robb, Jean Phillips, Evelyn McGeehee, Juanita Peveto, Frank Townsley, Lori Williams, Ike and Opal Henderson, Mr. Ballard, and Mr. McDonald. I also wish to express my appreciation to Deborah McPherson for processing the draft.

CHAPTER 8

The Significance of Sports in Oklahoma

BERRY WAYNE TRAMEL

If every society has some distinction between what constitutes "work" and "leisure," in this chapter Berry Wayne Tramel dispels the notion that sports are necessarily mere play. Through historical research, documentary analysis, interviews, and his years as a sportswriter, Tramel shows sports in Oklahoma— especially football and baseball—to be a feature of the core identity of Oklahomaness. He describes the pervasive presence of sports in family, school, community, and state life. He shows how inextricably tied the emotional significance of sports is to the legacy of the Great Depression and the Dust Bowl, with sports as the culturally most important element relied upon to reverse the status and come out a winner. Tramel thus shows how sports is about far more than the game itself. Many Oklahomans incorporate and manage their very self-image through the medium of sports.

While no single symbol can tell us everything about a culture, in every society there are key symbols that condense much that is important. In that sense, to understand sports is to understand Oklahoma. When the University of Oklahoma (OU) board of regents met in December 1945, the discussion turned to state morale. The Great Depression, coming on the heels of an agricultural recession in the 1920s, had given Oklahoma a generation of hard times. And the clincher came in

1939, with the publication of John Steinbeck's novel, *The Grapes of Wrath*. The novel brought a cry of rage from virtually every segment of Oklahoma society, which (mistakenly) thought it libelous in its depiction of Oklahoma sharecroppers forced to flee for California.

"It's unbelievable how Oklahomans thought in the thirties and early forties," remembered George Lynn Cross, OU's president from 1943 to 1968 and a member of its faculty since 1934, during a July 1989 interview. "They seemed almost apologetic for being here. Morale was very low. The regents . . . wondered what the university might do to instill a sense of pride." It so happened that OU was also without a football coach, Snorter Luster having just resigned "because of ill health," Cross said. "The ill health being he couldn't beat Texas or [Oklahoma] A&M" (Cross 1989).

Lloyd Noble, an oil driller from Ardmore and one of the most influential regents in university history, "was sitting back and said, 'The war's coming to an end; we're going to have a four-year crop of high-school athletes. If we could find them and get some of them.' . . . He didn't use the term instant great football, but that's what he meant" (Cross 1989).

In January 1946, OU hired Jim Tatum, who had coached at the University of North Carolina in 1942 before directing a navy team during World War II, to replace Luster and brought with him a thirty-year-old assistant coach named Bud Wilkinson. It was Wilkinson who would succeed Tatum the following year and take the program through the most successful stretch of seasons college football has yet seen.

In Tatum's season, OU defeated Oklahoma A&M (now Oklahoma State) 72–12, reversing a 42–0 setback from the previous year, and played Army, the college football power of the day, to a virtual standstill before losing in the final minutes, 21–7. This success, and Wilkinson's which followed, gave Oklahoma football, fifty years old at the time, a new commission. Football was overtly converted from one of many campus activities—which drew marginal interest outside the area—to *the* state institution. "It was very effective," said Cross. "Wilkinson did more for Oklahoma by way of favorable publicity than any individual other than Will Rogers"

(Cross 1989). Before the hiring of Tatum, "I don't think football was thought of as anything but just recreation for the
university. We didn't think of using it in the sense the regents
later did. I was instructed by the regents to do it, and we did
it. We may have overdone it, but we did it" (Cross 1989).

Perhaps Cross had just such an expansive notion in mind
when, in February 1951, he appeared before the joint House-
Senate Appropriations Committee of the state legislature to
appeal for $3.6 million more than Governor Johnston Murray
had recommended. After a thirty-minute presentation, during which Cross explained in detail the financial need,

a sleepy-looking senator, just to my right on the front row, raised his
hand and said: "I'd like to ask the good doctor why he thinks he
needs so much money to run the University of Oklahoma." For a
moment I was completely nonplused. Then came the depressing
realization that I had failed to get my message across. After groping
for an answer, I concluded that nothing by way of logic would
impress my questioner, and so I replied that I would like to build a
university of which the football team could be proud. My remark
brought a laugh and scattered applause but when Governor Murray's budget was finally approved, I didn't get the funds I had requested. (Cross 1977, 145)

That has long been the paradox in Oklahoma. The university—and all education, for that matter—has long been near
the bottom in appropriations nationally, yet the university
football team has long been among the nation's best supported and is the primary supplier to an athletic department
that receives no state funds but has an eleven-million-dollar
surplus.

While Will Rogers and the Rodgers and Hammerstein musical *Oklahoma!* are football's only rivals as the chief source
of state pride, the sport has not always brought such favorable publicity to Oklahomans. OU football in the 1970s and
'80s has been involved in numerous scandals, culminating in
a six-week period beginning in December 1988 that included
National Collegiate Athletic Association (NCAA) probation
and five felony arrests in three separate incidents. Oklahoma,
although the majority of its residents did not seem to com-
prehend it, became the epitome of the tail wagging the dog: a

college football program out of control: "Think about what the pursuit of football victories has done for the University of Oklahoma. On a national level, it has made the school a laughingstock, a caricature of a greedy, low-minded, hick institution that can find satisfaction only in beating somebody at a violent game, sort of like a hillbilly who just loves wrasslin' fellers till they cry, 'Uncle!'" (Telander 1989, 132–33).

What is this phenomenon that can transform the psyche of a state, that can boost its morale seemingly overnight, that can make it lose its moral consciousness? How can it have such a grip on Oklahoma culture? Chuck Edgely, an Oklahoma State University (OSU) professor of sociology, says: "The drive to win doesn't come from OU or OSU. It comes from the population of the state. It's fan-driven, it's ethnocentrism driven. This state is not well known for much of anything except football. And the one thing we've done historically and traditionally well, they want to be the best at it of anybody" (Edgely 1990).

That is how the University of Oklahoma found itself in such a reputational quandary with its football team. That is how OSU President John Campbell found himself the subject of a state government probe in January 1990 after he asked for the reinstatement of several athletes after they failed to meet university requirements. That is how Oklahomans can define themselves by what is done on a rectangular field with an oblong ball.

Oklahoma is not unique in its obsession with football. Most of the southern United States, from Florida to Texas, use the game, on both high school and college levels, as a chief source of identity. But Oklahoma's propensity for athletics goes even deeper. Dr. John F. Rooney, an OSU professor of geography, has conducted research in the field of the geography of athletics and has defined regions of the nation by their attitudes toward athletics. He has tagged the Deep South's attitude the "Pigskin Cult." He writes that "Oklahoma is part of that Pigskin Cult region, but Oklahoma is unlike most of the Deep South. Football is still king, we put a lot more of our emotion into it, yet somehow baseball has always thrived here. Some individual sports, like wrestling, have always thrived here.

Women's sports have always thrived here. Oklahoma and Texas are slightly different. They've provided greater opportunity for participation" (Rooney 1990). Rooney is unsure why Oklahoma, despite being involved in the Pigskin Cult, avoided many of its snares. "Maybe it goes back to the newness of Oklahoma," he says. "It's really a complex problem that I don't think anybody has the full answer for" (Rooney 1990).

It appears, though, that Oklahoma Sooner football is not the cause of this mentality but is merely its most overwhelming effect. Certainly sports were a major part of Oklahoma culture before Jim Tatum and Bud Wilkinson. The "ill health" of Snorter Luster, Tatum's predecessor, in 1945 can attest to that. Harold Keith was sports information director at OU from 1930 to 1969 and said of Sooner football before World War II: "Everybody in our state was crazy about it. There's always been a big public interest" (Keith 1989). Responding to a 1929 Carnegie report, which characterized collegiate athletics as commercialism, subsidization, exploitation, bribery, gambling, and proselytism, OU's administration reminded the public "that our educational institutions are committed to the maintenance of sound educational standards . . . [and] intercollegiate athletics is incidental to the major purpose of imparting knowledge to students" (McBride 1965, 6). Yet one of the symptoms of the excesses mentioned by the Carnegie report was the large number of huge football stadiums erected between 1900 and 1928—and OU changed its system of athletic control for the very purpose of raising its own. The Athletic Council, formed as part of the athletic association in 1907, became a separate entity in 1924, independent of the university. In 1928 it incorporated, primarily so it could borrow money and finance the construction of Memorial Stadium. Such an undertaking fits in with Chuck Edgely's theory that "These kinds of patterns exist in an area where they've been essentially deprived. If you laid out a map, those places that are successful in major-college sports would be on the bottom in terms of everything else. Football gives us an identity. Sports give us national recognition. How much national recognition do you think we'd get if we relied on the high-technology industry, or the price of wheat, or the fate of red meat?" (Edgely 1990).

OU football's transformation in the psyche of the people can be divided into three groups: the early years, when it was little more than a recreation for students; the middle years, from the 1920s through World War II, when it became successful on a regional basis under head coach Bennie Owen and began drawing enough attention that Memorial Stadium was needed by the end of the 1920s; and the post–World War II years, when Bud Wilkinson and his legacy took the institution of football to unparalleled heights. Thus Edgely's belief that "deprived" areas can be tied to the embracement of sport connects with Oklahoma history. The first thirty years of its existence, from the opening of the Unassigned Lands in 1889, were marked by unbridled optimism, during which there is little evidence that athletics played an overbearing role in the state culture. But the agricultural depression of the 1920s quickly ended such a spirit among Oklahomans. By the end of the decade, football was a major force. After the Great Depression of the 1930s, unbridled pessimism would more accurately describe the state, and the chain of events that led to today's fascination with football in particular and sports in general began.

The football mentality is impressed upon Oklahomans at an early age. Little league sports, complete with scoreboards and referees, are organized for children as young as five years old. As children reach adolescence, school teams usually replace little leagues. They serve as the hub of communities. High school athletes become the most prominent citizens of a town under such circumstances, but such status has its price: championships are the desired goal, and a lack of success often spoils the union of athlete and community. For example, Lance Rentzel was a star athlete at Casady High School in Oklahoma City before playing football for OU and three National Football League teams. In 1970, while a member of the Dallas Cowboys, he was arrested and charged with indecent exposure, his second such offense. Rentzel was subsequently traded to the Los Angeles Rams, who as a condition of employment required him to attend therapy. Dr. Louis

West, chairman of the University of California, Los Angeles, psychiatry department and formerly of the University of Oklahoma, treated Rentzel and wrote the following appraisal of him:

It is only because of a minor quirk in Lance Rentzel's sexual maturation that the exaggerated importance he places on winning has come to his attention. Exhibitionism is a relatively mild sexual symptom, almost a trivial one compared with other more frequent manifestations of sexual maldevelopment that rarely come to light . . . [but] the role of defeat or loss is often found to play a major part in the appearance of self-exposure as a symptom. It is as though the patient suddenly needs to be certain that his manhood is intact, and is impelled to demonstrate that fact to a female. . . . On the rare occasions when Lance Rentzel experienced the impulse to exhibit himself he was feeling like a loser. And while other elements compounded the problem, his preoccupation with being a winner as a football player was always involved. (Rentzel 1972, 271–72)

The win-win-win mentality did not arrive with Jim Tatum and the success of Bud Wilkinson. It has a long history in this young state. In 1911, four years after statehood, the Oklahoma State High School Athletic Association was formed to enforce eligibility rules, yet abuses remained widespread. "One documented case involved a coach who persuaded a mother to move a few belongings into an empty house in another school district, satisfying the bona fide resident rule, though both mother and son return home for the weekend" (Diffendaffer 1929, 14). A 1929 survey asked school superintendents the most frequent reasons for coaches changing jobs. "Failure to win games" was surpassed only by the opportunity for a better job (Diffendaffer 1929, 18).

The Oklahoma Secondary Schools Activities Association (OSSAA), the successor to the state athletic association, added music and speech contests in 1963 and cheerleading and academic contests in 1989. But make no mistake, the OSSAA is first and foremost an athletic association. Of the OSSAA's five full-time administrators, four are involved in athletics and the other in music and speech. A part-time administrator conducts the academic competition. Eighty percent of the association's operating revenue comes from its expansive basketball playoffs, and quite revealingly, neither H. J. Green, the executive director of the OSSAA, nor Junior Simmons, its administrator for music and speech, can say exactly how many of its schools compete in music and speech (H. J. Green 1989). Yet Green can immediately relate how many field football teams (250 out of 486) and basketball teams (every member except Oklahoma School for the Blind) compete.

Another interesting element of the OSSAA's activities is its music contests, which have as long a history in Oklahoma as does athletics. According to on-going research by George McDowell, the first state music contests in the United States took place in Emporia, Kansas, in 1912; Oklahoma's first state-wide contest was held in 1913, three years after its first district contest. In all the music competitions held—vocal choir, solo, and ensemble and all the various band and orchestra categories—only one, the state stage band contest, produces a "winner." All the others are based on the festival concept, in which contestants are given ratings, from excellent to poor, and there is no limit to how many excellents are awarded. In other words, the thirst for victory that is rampant on Oklahoma's athletic fields and courts does not bleed over to its artistic stages. Oklahoma, as Edgely (1990) pointed out, sees itself as doing one thing well, and that one thing is athletics.

Little league sports thrive in Oklahoma, even to the point of employing scoreboards, cheerleaders, and state tournaments. Like their collegiate and high school counterparts, they show widespread abuse of regulations. The Moore Junior Sports Association, which provides tackle football competition for boys ages five through twelve, included 850 youngsters in 1987, but that figure dipped to 650 in 1988 and "would have been 400" in 1989 (Patton 1989). The trouble, the association learned, was that a rival organization in Oklahoma City had no boundary rules and allowed teams to form with players who lived anywhere. Since Moore had school boundary regulations, coaches could recruit the best players from Moore and enter the Oklahoma City league with virtual all-star teams. What did the Moore association do? It dropped its boundary rules and allowed coaches to recruit players from any school, thus forming powerhouse teams that were far superior in strength and talent to the neighborhood teams that had formed the core of the association. Thus the Little League teams, which seek to duplicate the success of the state football team that dominates Oklahomans' loyalties, have also duplicated some of its excess. "As a Little League program, we need to keep this in perspective," said association president Hal Patton. "This isn't the major leagues, this is Little League ball" (Patton 1989). It may be Little League ball, but in Oklahoma, that does not make it a playful children's game; it is deadly serious.

Still, Oklahoma's penchant for sport has had positive effects. The state, despite a poor record in its treatment of minorities, was nevertheless ahead of other Southern state universities in athletic integration. OU's first black football player was Prentice Gautt in 1957. By contrast, the ten-member Southeastern Conference did not have a black player until 1968, and the universities of Arkansas and Texas, perhaps the most similar institution to OU in terms of athletic mentality, did not have a black player until 1970.

Gautt, now associate commissioner of the Big Eight Conference, tends to attribute his breakthrough to two factors. One—a group of black professionals in Oklahoma City had provided him with an academic scholarship—has nothing to do with the Pigskin Culture, and one, namely that Wilkinson made the decision to allow him to play at OU, does: "I think Bud was a little different. Bud was his own person. I think he was a little ahead of his time. Regardless of the pressures he was experiencing, there was a very positive reaction I got from Bud. I would imagine without the support of the head coach, I couldn't have made it" (Gautt 1989).

Cross, who was president through all of the school's integration turmoil, has no answer for why OU football did not turn to blacks even sooner, but he does credit its renaissance in the 1970s to OU's ability to attract black athletes. While Southwest Conference schools were just becoming integrated, by 1970 OU began routinely recruiting the best black players from Texas, a pivotal factor in the return to the glory days of the 1950s.

When Gautt was playing, Wilkinson pushed the integration issue, but only to a point. The Sooners used to spend

Friday nights before home games at the Skirvin Hotel in Oklahoma City, but "the Skirvin wouldn't take Prentice. They took him once, then said Bud couldn't take him anymore" (Cross 1989). So Wilkinson moved his entire team to the Biltmore. On the other hand, when Gautt's eligibility expired, OU returned to the Skirvin. And when OU played Texas in the annual State Fair game at Dallas, Texas' Jim Crow laws forced Gautt to stay in a separate hotel.

Cross remembers an example of the uneasy acceptance of black players. The morning after Gautt starred in OU's 21–6 victory over Syracuse in the 1959 Orange Bowl, he and a teammate were walking through the hotel lobby when they were stopped by an intoxicated man who said, "You black son-of-a-bitch." Cross was afraid "Prentice would hit him and kill him. While I was holding my breath, he put his arm around Prentice and said, 'You're the best God-damn football player I've seen on a football field. I just wanted to congratulate you'" (Cross 1989).

Even more pronounced than its acquiescence to black athletes is Oklahoma's role in women's sports, primarily on the high school level. Oklahoma, which is hardly a feminist state, has nevertheless always had a history of high school girls' sports, even dating back before statehood. Title IX, the 1973 congressional legislation mandating equal opportunity in state or public education, brought an avalanche of female sports across the nation, including Oklahoma, but high school girls' basketball has been part of the state association since 1924 and surpasses the boys' teams as the prime form of entertainment in many small Oklahoma towns.

Girls' athletic competition on a statewide basis dates back to at least 1910, when girls' basketball was added to OU's interscholastic meets, which had begun with boys' track and tennis in 1905 and baseball in 1907. Girls' tennis was added in 1915. The first recognized state championship in any sport was boys' basketball in 1918, and although the state association did not sanction a girls' championship until 1924, Central Normal in Edmond hosted an unofficial girls' state tournament in 1919, and OU and Oklahoma A&M alternated it in the following years.

Yet it is high school football that dominates many an Oklahoma town.

Texas and Oklahoma towns are the epitome of the high school football culture. . . . In many towns, the game is life's biggest diversion, and in the autumn the game schedule controls the tempo of activity from Friday evening to Sunday afternoon. High school sports programs are a mirror of community attitudes and values. Some are designed to breed major-college and pro athletes who will bring prestige to the homeland and win at all costs. Others promote mass participation and encourage a lifetime of physical activity. (Rooney 1974, 137)

Although Rooney places Oklahoma in the Pigskin Culture, he acknowledges that its status there is precarious, since other sports have thrived as well, a factor foreign to most of the Deep South: "How an area becomes infatuated with football, or any other sport, cannot be easily explained. Something intangible accounts for the great interest and prolific output of talent from certain areas. Such factors as economic and occupational structure, ethnic and racial composition, and climate surely play a role. But perhaps most important is the degree to which a community provides social and financial support for its schoolboy warriors" (Rooney 1986, 42).

Rooney theorizes that the football cultures of Oklahoma, Texas, and Louisiana developed in the first half of this century "when the southwestern oil boom pulled workers from northeastern football hearths like Ohio and Pennsylvania . . . into those southern states" (Rooney 1986, 38). He suggests that the following hypotheses (from Rooney 1974, 137–38) be tested concerning the football cultures of Oklahoma and Texas:

1. "There is an above-average emphasis on rugged individualism or 'ruggedness' which finds expression on the gridiron, either through direct participation or an intense identification with the participants."

2. "There is an above-average emphasis on militarism which is reflected in an attraction for games which demand considerable self-discipline, i.e., football."

3. Obsession with state and local identification "which seems to reach a zenith in Texas and Oklahoma, finds a micro-

expression at the local level, so that community prestige is more vital than in other sections of the country. The football team is a tangible instrument by which prestige is judged. This state-oriented nationalism is reflected in the great reverence for such songs as 'The Eyes of Texas,' 'Deep in the Heart of Texas,' and 'Oklahoma.'"

4. "The fine autumn weather provides ample time for a long season including 'playoffs.'"

5. "There is an absence of intervening opportunity so that greater emphasis is placed on football—in other words, there is little else to do."

6. "There are numerous local opportunities to play major-college football."

Some of these hypotheses are documented by the voting behavior of Texas and Oklahoma congressmen and a casual observation of editorial comments in the region's newspapers. This is part of the nation where the individual believes himself to be more self-reliant than many of his fellow Americans. It is an area where provincialism supersedes nationalism on many fronts, where support for the war effort in Vietnam was strong, where the fraternity-sorority system still thrives, where D.A.R. membership is high, and where urban problems are less acute, or occupy a very low position on the priority list. The great involvement with football is a clue to the character of Texas and Oklahoma and other places which have so completely embraced the game. Hypothesis three can be reduced to cover the community as well as the state scale. At the local level, football may be the only outward manner by which a town can demonstrate its superiority over another town and show its character. (Rooney 1974, 138)

The preoccupation with athletics in Oklahoma has formed an uneasy alliance with education, particularly on the university level. Since that December day in 1945, university administrators have dealt with athletics disproportionately. For example, consider John Campbell's involvement in the scandal at OSU—a university president asking for the reinstatement of students who quite obviously had not met the requirements to remain in school and bypassing the college deans to do so, solely for athletics. Campbell said he intervened because "what was at issue was academic progress, getting these students back on track academically so that they might have some reasonable likelihood of graduating from OSU. . . . Athletic eligibility . . . was not an issue or a consideration" (*Daily Oklahoman* 1990, 1). Yet Campbell asked for the reinstatements only after meeting with athletic officials, and he admitted never intervening for a nonathlete.

John Thornton, chairman of the OSU Faculty Council, was angered by Campbell's intervention: "OSU faculty are angry, upset and disgusted" (*Daily Oklahoman* 1990, 1). He compared it to the Dexter Manley incident. Manley, who went on to a standout career in the National Football League, played at OSU in the early 1980s and later acknowledged that he could barely read or write while he was at the university. OSU admitted him after he scored a six on the American College Test. Of the seven players reinstated at Campbell's request, five were eventually suspended again; the other two remain at OSU.

Although the faculty was outraged at Campbell, a significant faction of the general public was outraged at the rough treatment of Campbell: "I've seen the letters that have come in since the scandal. 'You're going to ruin our football team. You're going to hurt our ability to recruit.' Never mind that there's some fundamental issues here. Don't get me wrong, I like sport. In and of itself, it is very good. But you couple it with a state that doesn't really know what education is but does know what football's about, does know about Cowboys and about Sooners" (Edgely 1990). Campbell's action brought to mind the stated goals of OU President Dr. William Banowsky in 1985 concerning the athletic department: "1. To preserve the tradition of excellence that the University of Oklahoma has enjoyed; 2. To have a program which is truly student-oriented as opposed to one becoming more highly professionalized while being as excellent as we can; 3. To avoid abuses which have scarred too many of today's university athletic programs" (Bibb 1985, 7).

Winning—the preservation of excellence—is the first priority, ahead of student interest and integrity. People think of state universities in athletic terms even in academic endeavors. In 1989, OU, OSU, and the other six members of the Big

Eight Conference, an athletic league, formed the Association of Big Eight Universities as "a vehicle for cooperative programs that can create significant benefits for member institutions, their students and faculties," according to an OU news release. The new association replaced the Mid-America State Universities Association, which had been active since 1960 coordinating a limited number of joint activities. The result may very well be positive, but the message nevertheless remains that these schools are defining themselves in athletic terms. Another example of such definition is the annual salary comparisons among faculty at Big Eight schools.

The irony of the situation was illustrated on January 15, 1990, when classes began for OU's spring semester and the university's Faculty Senate met and discussed school holidays, including the traditional "Texas Monday," the Monday following the OU–Texas game when classes are suspended. "It seems ironic," said the senate's chairman, Andy Magid, "to be talking about a holiday for football while the university is ignoring the holiday honoring Martin Luther King and the Civil Rights movement" (*Oklahoma Daily* 1990, 1). And the most obvious example of all is the repeated intervention in athletic matters by regents, especially at OU, where the presidents, for all practical purposes, have had virtually no control over athletics.

Cross, who tried to act as a buffer between the regents and the athletic department, remembers talking with his successor, Herbert J. Holloman, after his 1968 retirement:

> I kept . . . I wouldn't say tight rein, but I kept in control. I knew what was going on. When I showed [Holloman] my organizational chart, I had a dotted line from the president to the athletic director. He said, "Do you fool with athletics?" "Yes Herbert, there's no greater source of trouble for a president than athletics, especially if he has a winning team." He said, "Hell, I'll have a vice-president for non-academic affairs." I thought to myself, "You sure are opening a way for a lot of trouble." The coaches soon found out, you couldn't see the president, you go to some member of the board. The president lost all control. [The regents] have administered . . . athletics. [Holloman's successor, Dr. Paul Sharp,] wasn't given a chance. Without the president's recommendation, the regents would come up with salary increases, bonuses. (Cross 1989)

In 1978, rumors were rampant that OU Head Coach Barry Switzer was involved in a scandal with his defensive coordinator, Larry Lacewell, who had resigned early that calendar year. An oft-repeated story had Lacewell leaving OU because his wife was romantically involved with Switzer. Dr. William Banowsky became OU's president that year, and he asked Cross for advice on how to deal with the situation. Cross said, "You have a chance to pull athletics back into orbit because the coach's influence is weakened. I'd get Barry in my office and say, 'I've heard all these things. I don't know whether they're true or not'—it was true, by the way—'and I don't care. I just don't want anything like this to happen in the future'" (Cross 1989). But Banowsky apparently declined to take any action. "Banowsky was a fund-raising genius, but he didn't pay much attention to what was happening on campus" (Cross 1989).

The president's waning power in athletic matters was never more apparent than in March 1989 after the scandals struck OU's football team and it became a subject of ABC-TV's "Nightline," a late-night news discussion program. David Swank, OU's interim president, and *Sports Illustrated*'s Rick Telander were the guests. As Telander describes:

Make no mistake about it: Winning forgives all, no matter how embarrassing the situation. This point was driven home forcefully . . . [while Telander was] debating Swank about just how far a university will go before cracking down on its coach and football program. Swank had been the dean of Oklahoma's law school, and he was not, he claimed, a candidate to be the full-time president of the university. Therefore, it seemed to me, he should have felt no need to mince his words about controlling his renegade football club. . . .

Swank stated, however, that everything was pretty much under control at Bud Wilkinson Hall, that the crimes were "isolated incidents," that head coach Barry Switzer was not going to be fired, but that if there were any more transgressions by anyone on his team or staff, Switzer might get the heave-ho. One month before the crimes the Sooners were placed on three years' probation by the NCAA for "major violations," which included offering cash and cars to recruits and giving airline tickets to players. The NCAA Committee on Infractions stated that for "at least several years, the university has failed to exercise appropriate institutional control" over the football program . . . but Swank thought things were on the right track at OU.

I said that since it was clear Switzer could withstand almost any ethical turmoil on his team, the only question was, what kind of won-lost record could he survive? . . . I figured that while the commercial was running, Swank would come up with a nice, political way of saying that Switzer could lose every game from now till hell froze over as long as he maintained control of his players. . . . "Again," Swank finally said, "I don't see that an excellent athletic program is inconsistent with having a high-quality academic program. I don't know that I can give a won-lost record, but I CAN tell you that we will place emphasis first on academics at the University of Oklahoma. . . . We're not going to tolerate people, as you say, being thrown in the slammer. I can't tell you what record should exist."

[Moderator Ted] Koppel looked disgusted. "You COULD tell me that it doesn't matter to you," he shot back. "That what matters, what is important to you, is what kind of an education those youngsters get, that if [Switzer] comes in with a losing record, but creates good student-athletes, you'll be happy with him. You could say that."

Swank had a weak smile. "Well, again, I want a top-quality athletic program." . . . And then it was over. . . . I had to marvel at Swank's refusal to say he'd accept a losing record. I figured Oklahoma fans wouldn't be thrilled by a lousy record; after all, they'd almost ridden Switzer out of town when his teams went 7–4–1, 8–4, and 8–4 from 1981 to 1983. But the college president? It was plain that he was afraid that if he publicly lowered the expectations placed on Sooner football teams, the board of regents would string him up like a bad coyote. (Telander 1989, 107–109)

And so a national stage presented Oklahoma's penchant live. The "Nightline" episode is part of an ongoing drama of Oklahoma history and is not limited to President Swank. The reluctance of a university administrator to rock the athletic boat is the accepted and standard form of behavior in Oklahoma.

The athletic heritage of Oklahoma is, as John Rooney stated, a question in search of an answer. But its effects are undeniable and far-reaching, both positively and negatively. Sport, primarily but not exclusively football, has a major grip on the psyche of Oklahomans. The extreme value placed on athletic victory no matter the cost has led the state to forsake other worthwhile—maybe even essential—endeavors, such as education. But sport has also led Oklahoma to embrace progressive ideas it might otherwise have rejected, such as racial and sexual gains. The significance of sports in Oklahoma is not a random happening; it can be traced to precise developments in the state. Whatever the roots, be they historical, economic, or social, the huge significance of sports in Oklahoma is indisputable.

CHAPTER 9

Low-Style/High-Style: Oklahoma Architectural Origins and Image Distortion

ARN HENDERSON

In this chapter, Arn Henderson paints a picture of the Oklahoma cultural landscape that differs considerably from the folkloric or popular cultural view of Oklahomaness. Sod houses of Oklahoma pioneers and homesteaders and purely "functional" (no frills) architectural styles of homes and farms constitute a widespread image of what Oklahoma's built environment looks like or ought to look like. Henderson painstakingly shows, in his text and through photographs, how much of Oklahoma's architecture was influenced by national, indeed international, currents. He at once identifies those architectural ingredients of Oklahomaness and shows numerous exceptions to this popular imagination. His chapter describes not only how much visual identity is part of cultural identity (that is, how we imagine and portray ourselves is an extension of who we are), but also how that very mystique of uniqueness often neglects and contradicts the diversity of architectural style in Oklahoma.

In my work in historic preservation and my research on Oklahoma architecture and folk and vernacular buildings in the southern plains I have often been struck by the incredible visual power of historic photographic images. Photographs from institutions such as the Western History Collections

(WHC) at the University of Oklahoma and the Oklahoma Historical Society are indeed fundamentally important sources of information about our architectural heritage. These photographs tell us about our past, about the way we shaped our environment, and about the way we lived. They illuminate and edify. But they also have the capacity to distort our concept of a place, and as such, they contribute to the sustaining of myths. Among the most enduring of these myths are that in territorial days everyone lived in sod houses, everyone lived in the country, everyone was poor, and everyone had hard times.

Events associated with the Run of '89, with images of people living in tents or dugouts, contributed to the myth of our architectural heritage. Moreover, images of the Depression and dust storms by Farm Security Administration photographers Dorothea Lange, Russell Lee, and others have also distorted reality. Their depiction of lean, gaunt men and women with rough, simple clothes in the context of a run-down farm shack have, in the minds of many, become a metaphor of our culture. It is these images of "low-style" architecture, published many times, that become engraved in our consciousness and contribute to the formation of misshapen ideas of our built environment.

The popular notion of our cultural landscape is that our architectural origins are either primitive and homemade or exemplars of a gun-slinging Wild West town. The myth is that our earliest rural buildings are simply artifacts of poverty, and hence somehow uniquely Oklahoman. But our vernacular heritage, especially sod houses, are not exclusively related to just Oklahoma, but instead are representative of the entire Great Plains. In reality they represent a *regional* architectural expression, one that developed several decades earlier. Moreover, there are misconceptions about our urban architectural heritage. The buildings in the territorial capital of Guthrie are viewed by many as examples of "territorial architecture" in a frontier town and, as such, they too represent an *indigenous* Oklahoma expression. But in fact, the designs for Guthrie buildings were also based on imported concepts; architectural ideas that were popular throughout both America and Europe in the closing decade of the nineteenth century.

A Low-Style/High-Style Duality

The concept of "low-style" as distinct from "high-style" buildings has been a useful paradigm that has enhanced my understanding of our architectural heritage. High style refers to buildings that were usually designed by professional architects in one of the styles fashionable at the time. Thus, high-style architecture manifests an obvious concern for aesthetic effect. Low-style architecture is often one of expediency; the term refers to buildings that exhibit more of a concern for efficiency and economy and often reflect a particular place or local building tradition. In low-style or vernacular architecture there is less of a conscious striving for aesthetic effect. Although we may identify many vernacular buildings as having compelling visual attributes, it is not because of a stylistic affinity with architecture created by architects. Whatever visual appeal vernacular buildings have, it is often more generalized and has to do with admiration of proportions, directness of expression, and use of materials. Moreover, vernacular buildings are an important dimension of our heritage and give us a more authentic view of the relationship between humankind and the landscape of America. Since there is a direct equation between culture and the physical environment, the buildings—as material artifacts of a culture—provide opportunity for understanding this relationship. Common buildings tell us how people viewed their environment, how they lived on the land, and how they responded to the environment by design.

A useful example of the distinction between high style and low style is a comparison of the Cotton Storage House at Kinta and a commercial building in Wagoner. Both were done at approximately the same time, and both use the same materials, sheet metal. The commercial building in Wagoner is high-style architecture (Fig. 9.1). Although the design does not clearly reflect any one particular revival style popular

Fig. 9.1. Commercial Building, Wagoner, Oklahoma. Built 1895. (Photograph by Arn Henderson, 1978.)

during the nineteenth century, and is thus an eclectic design, it does exhibit a conscious striving for aesthetic effect. The facade on the upper floor is done entirely in sheet metal, a popular material for architects and building designers at the turn of the century. Moldings, finials, pinnacles, spires, and sheets of patterned metal could be selected from catalogs and ordered in a variety of sizes, shapes, and styles. These pre-fabricated parts, factory built, could then be assembled on the job into any sort of composition the architect had designed.

Fig. 9.2. Cotton gin, Kinta, Oklahoma. Built 1913. (Photograph by Arn Henderson, 1978.)

The low-style Cotton Storage House at Kinta is also a sheet-metal structure, although the skin of the building is a heavier gauge and is corrugated (Fig. 9.2). The Cotton Storage House, even though it is a rough-looking artifact, tells us much about an agricultural industry dominant in southern Oklahoma in the early decades of this century. The octagonal Cotton Storage House is the only surviving element of a cotton gin. Farmers would drive wagons loaded with cotton under the portico, and a suction fan would move the cotton through a metal tube to the top of the tower. A workman stationed in the tower then would direct the flow of the cotton into one of eight wedge-shaped bins below. The small, bottom-hinged doors in the bins allowed cotton to be moved on conveyors to the gin for seed removal and baling. The Cotton Storage House, with its form and geometry derived from its function, is listed on the National Register of Historic Places.

Low-Style Buildings

This concept of a low-style/high-style architectural duality can be amplified in the context of form-making activities associated with events of settlement. Although the name Oklahoma, derived from the Choctaw words for "Red People," was in popular use throughout the last part of the nineteenth century, the concept of Oklahoma as "free land" did not really emerge until the Land run of 1889. The date of the first Oklahoma run is of particular significance in the history of the nation. Ironically, just one year later the U.S. Bureau of the Census reported that the American frontier was officially closed. Americans could never again feel themselves dwarfed by the limitless expanses of their continent, secure in the knowledge that escape from the pressures of civilization was only as far as the next line of settlements. Though large areas of the country remained to be settled, the formal passing of the frontier had a major effect on the American consciousness. In this context, the Oklahoma run can be viewed as a symbol of the dying frontier.

Surplus Indian lands were actually opened for homesteading incrementally between 1889 and 1906 and were settled by several strategies: by lottery, auction, sealed bids, and land runs. The last—the land run—was a unique experiment in the history of American settlement and town planning. Developed by the federal government, the process was designed to provide equal opportunity for all land-seekers. The first lands made available for settlement in 1889—and settled by land run—were the so-called Unassigned Lands consisting of approximately 1,900,000 acres in the center of Indian Territory. The opening of these lands established Oklahoma Territory, even though the legal designation did not occur until passage of the Organic Act on May 2, 1890. In the following years the territory grew by successive additions of Indian lands. By the early twentieth century the formation of the twin territories was complete: Indian Territory in the eastern part of the state and Oklahoma Territory in the West.

The Unassigned Lands, which comprise six counties in present-day Oklahoma, were opened for homesteading on April 22, 1889. At noon on that day soldiers guarding the borders used pistols, cannon, and bugles to give the signal. The great land rush and race for homesteads began. Approximately fifty thousand people swarmed into the district on horseback, in wagons with whole families crowded into the back, by carriage, on trains, and even by bicycle and on foot to stake their claim for land.

In the rural areas, as settlers laid claim to 160-acre homesteads, their first concern was an immediate need for shelter. Although they might live temporarily in a tent with a wagon serving as a bedroom for some family members and as storage for possessions, they found incentive to build when sudden storms or high winds arose. Although the dugout and sod house were among the most common types of shelters initially constructed, a variety of other building materials and techniques were also used: logs; pickets; stone; and occasionally, as was commonly used in No Man's Land (the Panhandle), adobe. Often these first shelters were a hybrid of more than one technique (Fig. 9.3). In these earliest structures the dominant factor determining building form was almost exclusively the environment. In whatever part of Oklahoma Territory they lived, the early settlers invariably drew from the landscape for construction materials to build their first house.

Often this first house was a sod house—the ubiquitous low-style artifact of the Great Plains (Fig. 9.4). Sod homes were made by cutting strips of grassy topsoil into blocks and stacking them up one on top of another to form a wall. The pri-

Fig. 9.3. Dugout, Guthrie, Oklahoma, area, 1889. (Courtesy of Western History Collections, University of Oklahoma Library.)

Fig. 9.4. Sod house, Cherokee Outlet, Oklahoma, ca. 1890. (Courtesy of Western History Collections, University of Oklahoma Library. Photograph no. 68 in the A. A. Forbes Collection.)

mary tool required was a breaking plow, which consisted of a knife in the front with two parallel rods that turned the sod over in long, unbroken strips. This plow was sometimes referred to as a "grasshopper" plow because the rods resembled the wings of an insect. The sod strips were usually about four inches thick and twelve to eighteen inches wide. The strips were then cut with a spade to a length about twice their width. The sod "bricks" were laid much like regular masonry, and it was not uncommon for walls to be built of two or more widths of sod in a common bond pattern with interlocking header courses. The roof was often made by setting a forked post in the gable wall to support the ridge beam. Secondary roof members would span from ridge beam to side walls and support a sod roof.

Although sod houses were an inexpensive form of construction, they usually did not last long, because they were subject to erosion by wind and rain. Another factor that affected their durability was the time of year the sod was cut, which reflected the amount of moisture in the soil and the condition of the root system of the grass. The skill of the builder was also an important factor. Not everyone had good building skills, and some lacked the proper tools, such as specialized plows, for construction. If the sod was too wet when it was laid up, a wall might collapse. Children attending a sod school in the Cherokee Outlet referred to their building as "Old Humpback" because one end wall had begun to sag no sooner than it had been built (Cherokee Outlet Papers).

Survival on the plains of Oklahoma Territory, often in remote locations, demanded ingenuity. In constructing buildings, early settlers responded to the environment by using materials available in the landscape and by exerting control over the climate through design. Yet life could be extraordinarily harsh. The sense of isolation was pervasive, and men, as well as women, suffered from loneliness. In addition, living in primitive shelters could be difficult. Sod houses became infested with bedbugs and fleas. Centipedes, spiders, and even snakes would burrow through the sod roof and suddenly fall into the house. When it rained, the sod roof leaked. Many frontier women complained about getting mud in their cooking when they attempted to prepare a meal during a rainstorm. Just keeping a place clean was difficult. Residents in a rural area of the Cherokee Outlet known as "Gumbo Flats" were convinced that the cause of one woman's insanity was all the mud tracked into her house when it was used as a voting place on a wet day in November (WHC).

Even though sod houses were abundant, it is appropriate to view vernacular or low-style buildings, especially first-generation structures, in the context of the settlers' response to the region. Although second-generation structures sometimes reflect the cultural origins of the builder, in the initial stages of rural settlement people drew almost exclusively from the landscape for materials to shape their buildings. On the plains of Oklahoma Territory, beginning in the 1890s, settlers most often built sod houses. But this response was simply an extension of a strategy for shelter developed several decades earlier in other areas of the Great Plains— especially in Kansas, Nebraska, and the Dakotas.

The popular notion of Oklahoma in the period of initial settlement is one of a landscape of "soddies"—poor farm people who had to live in dirt houses. Similarly, photographs of the 1930s Depression depicted hard times, but in this case the sod houses were replaced by crude shacks. The inference was, and has continued to be, one of a continuity of rural poverty. But the images have distorted reality. Farmers in Oklahoma fared no better or worse than farmers in other areas of the southern plains. In the 1920s, a decade of abundant rainfall, Oklahoma farmers prospered the same as Kansas farmers did. Throughout the region farmers constructed new barns and farm houses that reflected improved economic circumstances. These new structures in Oklahoma had much in common with structures built in surrounding states. Although there are variations that reflect use of local building materials or represent folk expressions of distinct cultural groups on the plains, the vernacular architecture in the rural landscape throughout the region is more of a kind than of dissimilar types. But the images of enduring poverty, with homemade buildings, portrayed in literature, cinema, and photographs have created a mythological portrayal of rural Oklahoma architecture.

High Style: The Example of Guthrie

Settlement by land run suggests chaos, confusion, and arbitrary town development. Although the initial hours of the land run probably were frantic, considerable planning had gone into determining the location and layout of towns in the Unassigned Lands. Many of the principal towns in the area—Norman, Oklahoma City, Edmond, and Guthrie—had their beginnings as stations on the Santa Fe railroad. Surveyors for land companies laid out blocks and lots at these locations in anticipation of the land run. Unwisely, these new townsites were restricted by law to 320 acres. In Guthrie, where over ten thousand people were camped on the night of April 22, there was not room for all of them to obtain town lots on the designated 320 acres. The pragmatic and expedient solution was to develop adjacent townsites. Thus the city of Guthrie began as four separate but adjacent towns: West Guthrie, Guthrie proper, East Guthrie, and Capitol Hill.

Before the land run, it was commonly speculated that Guthrie would be designated as the territorial capital. This speculation undoubtedly contributed to the arrival of a large number of people there on April 22, 1889. It was a hectic beginning. Hamilton S. Wicks leaped from the train at Guthrie the first day of the rush and described the scene:

I joined the wild scramble for a town lot up the sloping hillside. . . . There were several thousand people converging on the same plot of ground, each eager for a town lot which was to be acquired without cost. . . .

The race was not over when you reached the particular lot you were content to select for your possession. The contest still was who should drive their stakes first, who would erect their little tents soonest, and then, who would quickest build a little wooden shanty.

The situation was so peculiar that it is difficult to convey correct impressions of the situation. It reminded me of playing blind-man's-bluff. One did not know how far to go before stopping; it was hard to tell when it was best to stop, and it was a puzzle whether to turn to the right hand or the left. Every one appeared dazed, and all for the most part acted like a flock of stray sheep. (Reps 1965)

Wicks found a corner lot to his liking, drove his stake, set up a cot with blankets thrown over it and pegged into the ground, and observed that his claim was now "unjumpable" because of the substantial improvements he had made.

The grid pattern of town blocks, usually laid out to the cardinal directions or parallel and perpendicular to the railroad track, was a simple method of preparing for the great gamble of land speculation. In the downtown areas the blocks were short with wide streets to facilitate horse-drawn traffic. By nightfall the lots in the new towns were filled with tents (Fig. 9.5). Yet this image of "instant tent towns" is deceptive in that it suggests a lack of progressive development on the Oklahoma frontier. Tents were used only a few weeks, and in many cases only overnight. Home seekers and entrepreneurs immediately began construction of wood buildings. Moreover, techniques of prefabricated construction were available and used in 1889. For example, the first store in Norman was prefabricated, brought into town, set up, and ready for business on the day of the land run. Even during the initial weeks after the opening, prefabricated squares, usually twelve-foot by twelve-foot sections, were constructed, and several of these were moved to a lot and assembled into a building in a few hours. There was no question that the townspeople in the new communities of the Unassigned Lands were prepared to meet the challenges of urban life in Oklahoma Territory.

Although the tent city image is one of the cornerstones of Oklahoma land run mythology, it is a fleeting illusion. Guthrie, as were most of the new towns in the Unassigned Lands, was an urban community from the very beginning. When Hamilton Wicks leaped from the train to search for a town lot, Guthrie had only two buildings: a new wooden Santa Fe depot and a partially finished land office. But by nightfall the ghost town of the early morning had been transformed into a bustling prairie metropolis. Over ten thousand people jammed its dusty red streets. Trains carrying lumber and building supplies followed the settlers into the territory. By late afternoon, frame buildings were already under construction, and by the time the workmen laid down their tools, the first newspaper published in the territory was available.

Fig. 9.5. Tent, Guthrie, Oklahoma, 1889. (Courtesy of Western History Collections, University of Oklahoma Library. Photograph no. 103 in the Dr. A. P. Swearingen Collection.)

The pace of development in Guthrie was staggering. Within three weeks of the opening, a Chamber of Commerce had been established. The first brick building was finished within a month after the opening. An electric street railway was franchised in June to link the central business district with the proposed Capitol Hill area. A waterworks that included hydrants at the corners of all the principal streets was operating within two months. An electric power plant capable not only of lighting the entire city but also of furnishing power to run the electric trolleys was built within four months of the opening. The hastily constructed frame buildings of the first days were soon replaced by substantial masonry structures in the central business district. Fear of fire was particularly acute in the dry Oklahoma Territory and prompted an active campaign to "fireproof" the downtown during the 1890s.

Construction fever ran high as building speculators gambled on Guthrie's future as the territorial and eventual state capital. New masonry structures were constructed using native red sandstone or brick made from red Oklahoma clay. The buildings, frequently two- and three-story structures set on long, narrow lots, had stores on the first floor and professional offices and apartments on the upper floors. Facades were often topped with a sheet metal cornice. It is likely that some of the designs for these buildings were taken from pattern books available at the turn of the century. Some of the structures are modest designs but provide good examples of vernacular commercial architecture of the times. They are important for other reasons, too. They serve as useful artifacts that tell us about everyday life in Guthrie and sometimes even the less noble impulses of our humanity. For example, the second floor of the Blue Bell Saloon was a brothel (Fig. 9.6). Located across the alley from the Elks Hotel which was frequented by early-day territorial legislators, the Blue Bell featured a connecting overhead bridge spanning the alley between the hotel and saloon. The local legend is that this iron "cat walk" was developed for the convenience and privacy of hotel patrons.

Guthrie developed an incredible array of high-style buildings. It is this ensemble of structures that gives Guthrie its remarkable visual character. In fact, the commercial district was dominated by the influence of one person: architect Joseph Foucart. Although his buildings are conspicuous, Foucart as a person is elusive as a shadow. Little is known about his background or his life in Guthrie. We do not know with certainty all of his designs. Most of the best buildings in Guthrie we believe are his, but this speculation is based largely on local oral history or stylistic inferences. There are few records that identify his buildings or give a precise account of his activities from 1889 to 1907.

Foucart was born in Belgium in 1848 and studied architecture in Ghent, where he completed the course in 1865. Early

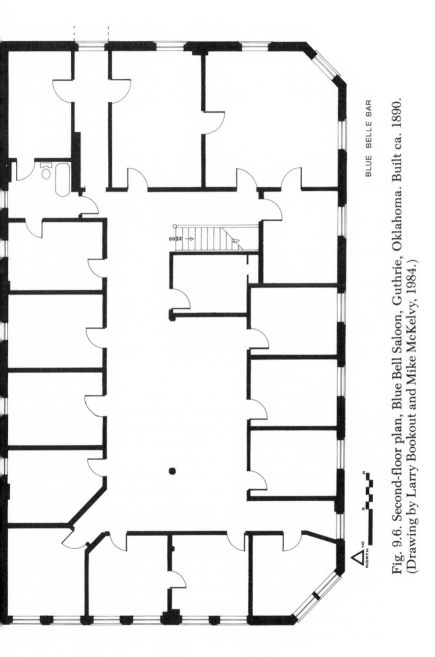

BLUE BELLE BAR

Fig. 9.6. Second-floor plan, Blue Bell Saloon, Guthrie, Oklahoma. Built ca. 1890. (Drawing by Larry Bookout and Mike McKelvy, 1984.)

in his career he worked as a mining engineer, and it was not until 1872 that he became involved in architectural projects. From then until he left Europe he worked on a number of large projects, including the new city hall in Paris. In 1888, when he was forty years old, Foucart emigrated to America. In June 1889 he appeared in Guthrie, and one month later his advertisements appeared in the newspaper: "The Parisian architects M. Villeroy and J. Foucart are very busy now getting up plans and specifications for various buildings here. They have just completed plans for the Catholic Cathedral and two brick blocks that will be completed here in the near future. These gentlemen are fine workers and should be liberally patronized. It will pay anyone to call on their office and examine their drawings" (Henderson 1980). Not long after that, their buildings began to appear. But it is difficult to sort out the influences on Foucart with so little information on his formative years. Surely the writings of the late-nineteenth-century French architectural theorist Eugene Viollet-le-Duc must have affected him. It is unlikely that most European architects working in the closing decades of the 1800s could have failed to have heard Viollet-le-Duc's gospel of an architectural trinity that embraced rational planning, structural determinism, and Gothic styling.

In Foucart's buildings we see evidence that he responded to the lessons of Viollet-le-Duc. From a planning standpoint his buildings are entirely rational and designed to efficiently serve the needs of commerce. They are most often set flush with the sidewalk to maximize lot coverage. In buildings at the corner of a block, Foucart beveled the corner and set the entry on this diagonal so that it could be seen and approached from either direction by pedestrians.

Structurally, there is little question of the buildings' integrity: they have load-bearing masonry walls, and they offer a visible argument to the spectator. There is no doubt of what is supporting what. Walls are penetrated with arched openings, the lintels of the arches are often accented with contrasting stone to signify their structural importance, pilasters and engaged piers are expressed as vertical supports, and in some cases cast iron columns are used in a completely undisguised manner.

From the standpoint of style, it is clear that Foucart's designs reveal a predilection toward the Gothic. Compositionally, they are often asymmetrical and very picturesque, which was one of the fundamental tenets of the Gothic Revival style. Yet the most telling Gothic element—the pointed arch window—is missing completely in Foucart's work. In its place we find rounded arches and arches that have a keyhole shape that evoke a Moslem feeling. There are other influences: the domes on the turrets and oriels on some of his buildings suggest a Russian influence. There is even a hint of an influence by the American Romanesque Revival architect H. H. Richardson with the rough-cut stone walls and rounded arch windows that often combine stone lintels with voussoirs of contrasting color. Thus, when we consider the question of the Foucart "style"—a style that embodies Victorian Gothic, Russian, Moslem, and Romanesque Revival elements—we conclude that Foucart's architecture is eclectic. Foucart was a product of his age, and eclecticism characterizes the entire nineteenth century in both American and European architecture. And Foucart's designs are *gloriously* eclectic and *gloriously* high style.

The early years of the decade of the 1890s were a time of rapid growth for Guthrie. They were also an extraordinarily productive period in the life of Joseph Foucart. Buildings which appear within two years of the founding of Guthrie are eloquent testimonials to the variety and range of his creative imagination. One of the most prominent early buildings was the Grey Brothers Block (Fig. 9.7). Like many Guthrie buildings located on a corner lot, the corner is chamfered, with the main entry set on the diagonal. Attention is drawn to the corner by the projecting oriel on the second floor that is capped with a Russian dome. Among the most striking yet subtle visual attributes of the building are the variations in scale. The lower portion of the facade is pierced by several large arched openings with rough-cut lintels. The rhythm of the second floor then changes to a series of closely spaced double-hung windows, each crowned with a recessed panel of patterned and corbeled brick. At the cornice is an elaborate sheet-metal band composed of a small-scale, deco-

Fig. 9.7. Grey Brothers Building, Guthrie, Oklahoma. Built 1890. (Photograph courtesy of Historic American Buildings Survey [William E. Barrett], 1977.)

rative square motif and accented by large pinnacles that extend both above and below the band and project beyond the brick surface. The effect is one of a progression of gradation of elements of different visual scales and textures ranging from large, rough elements at the bottom to small, smooth elements at the top.

Another important building completed in 1890 is the DeFord Building (Fig. 9.8). In the front facade of the DeFord Building, Foucart created an asymmetrical composition of tall, narrow arched windows and crowned it with a delicate profusion of sheet-metal ornament. The ornament, like the pattern of windows, is also asymmetrical, with a pyramidal form poised over the stair leading to the second floor as if to

Fig. 9.8. DeFord Building, Guthrie, Oklahoma. Built 1890. (Photograph by Arn Henderson, 1988.)

provide a visual landmark signifying entry. In the north elevation of the building Foucart abruptly changed the pattern, with the arched windows at the second story much wider and with several smaller keyhole windows lighting the lower floor.

Foucart's first major commission was the three-story Victor Block completed in 1893 (Fig. 9.9). The building was a speculative venture erected by one of the most successful developers of the commercial district. One of the early tenants of the building was the drugstore of F. B. Lillie, first

Fig. 9.9. Victor Building, Guthrie, Oklahoma. Built 1893. (Photograph by Arn Henderson, 1988.)

pharmacist of Oklahoma. As with other corner buildings, Foucart beveled the corner and accented it with an oriel. Although he used a great variety of window sizes and shapes, a sense of unity dominates the design by the use of common sill heights and a decorative sheet-metal cornice. The recessed brick panels in several bays at ground level are also subtle visual elements of the facade. By recessing part of the brick wall and outlining it with a strong geometric profile, Foucart maintained the continuity of rhythm established by the windows in all the other bays of the facade.

Another major commission for Foucart was the State Capital Publishing Company. It is a remarkable building, particularly for the simplicity and subtlety of the wall surfaces, fenestration, and details. The primary facades are unusually flat and restrained. Because of this facade austerity, the open, three-dimensional tower is a powerful sculptural counterpoint that draws immediate attention to the corner of the building (Fig. 9.10). The building was designed for the newspaper publisher Frank Greer in 1902 after an earlier building had burned. Greer had very definite ideas on how a building should function, and it is likely that the client exerted a restraining influence on Foucart.

Frank Greer is important in the history of Oklahoma because he played a prominent role in events which ultimately led to the removal of the capitol to Oklahoma City. Greer was one of the original Boomers who was staunchly loyal to Guthrie, and his newspaper editorials varied between glittering praise for the town he helped found and bitter attacks on those he felt might have a destructive influence. Greer's rhetoric could be absolutely scathing. In one of his editorials he described a rival thus: "Two thirds of the hell which has been raised in this town, and always in behalf of bad causes, has been raised by this mouthy egotist whose actions have always been as small as his brains. Having found a man who would loan him money enough to erect a building on lots he gained through the misfortune of a poor widow whose husband happened to be a Sooner—he has been bloviating to the disgust of all modest people on 'what I have done for this town!'" (Henderson 1980). Greer, a Republican, later became embroiled in a devastating dispute with Democratic Governor Haskell which led not only to the dissolution of state government in Guthrie but also to the demise of the State Capital Publishing Company. Nonetheless, during its lifetime of newspaper publishing it was one of the largest and best equipped operations of its kind west of Chicago. And the building, currently a publishing museum operated by the Oklahoma Historical Society, continues to dominate a corner of downtown Guthrie with a dignity and grandeur that has seldom been equaled.

During the last decade of the nineteenth century and the first decade of the twentieth, Foucart became the premier architect of Oklahoma Territory. He received two important commissions outside of Guthrie: the library for Oklahoma

Fig. 9.10. State Capital Publishing Company, Guthrie, Oklahoma. Built 1895. (Photograph by Arn Henderson, 1988.)

A&M College at Stillwater and the main building of the Northwestern State Normal School at Alva. Neither of these buildings exist today. The building at Alva burned during the 1930s, and the Stillwater building was demolished and replaced with a new structure. But Foucart did have an enormous influence on Guthrie. He left a legacy of beautiful buildings that we can use and enjoy even today.

Yet there are misconceptions about the origins of these buildings. They are frequently referred to as examples of "territorial architecture," and hence it is implied that they represent a uniquely Oklahoman frontier response. But stylistically they did not originate in Oklahoma. They are artifacts based on imported ideas and designed by a European architect. Although they are constructed of red sandstone from the area or brick made from Oklahoma red clay, and thus visually reflect an aspect of the landscape, they are not indigenous expressions. Stylistically they are derived from national and international design ideals. They are a product of the times and reflect concepts of formal expression shared by architects in both Europe and America. Within this region one can find similar buildings in Eureka Springs, Arkansas, or Granbury, Texas. But this origin does not diminish their importance in any way. The buildings of downtown Guthrie represent a remarkable ensemble of structures. They were designed by a very talented and mature architect who had an extraordinary understanding of the elements of design. Collectively, they represent some of the finest Victorian commercial architecture in America. They are valuable artistic and historic artifacts, and we are fortunate to have so many of them.

The original townsite of the city of Guthrie is designated as a National Historic District and has the distinction of being the only intact territorial capital surviving today. Citizens of Guthrie are proud of their community and have engaged in an extensive preservation program. Certainly one dimension of interest in historic preservation, by both people in Guthrie and elsewhere, is related to our aesthetic impulses. Many people simply like the way old buildings look. Theirs is a visual and aesthetic response. They admire the detail, the craftsmanship, and the materials. Irrespective of the revival style, most nineteenth-century buildings have one thing in common: they have a visual hierarchy of scale with a sense of richness and complexity that engages our attention. This dimension of appeal is not a reflex of nostalgia or sentimentality but is, in part, a reaction against the austerity of many modern buildings. Old buildings not only tell us about our past, but the best of them also enrich our eye.

Conclusions

The soddies are gone; all but a few have disappeared. That low-style architecture was simply a reflex of settlement of the rural landscape. It was an important facet of our history and the history of the region. But the sod houses were, after all, only temporary buildings, and to magnify their importance is both to distort and to romanticize the past. But the concept of a low-style/high-style architectural dualism has other meanings. As an agrarian state, Oklahoma has a rich assemblage of vernacular structures, which is particularly apparent when one drives through rural western Oklahoma. For example, the grain elevators, as a vertical element in a flat landscape, serve as powerful magnets, captivating our attention. They are structural metaphors of a culture, a way of life, and they capture the essence of a place's origins, its growth, and its purpose.

Our vernacular architecture also reflects the culture of ethnic groups in Oklahoma. In Hominy a sixteen-sided "round house" continues to function for traditional dances of the Osage tribe. In Hartshorne, Russian and Ukranian immigrants employed in the coal mines built Saints Cyril and Methodius Church in 1916. Constructed of red brick with traditional onion domes, the church served their religious needs and reflected their own cultural heritage.

An irony of Oklahoma is that the same interplay of determinance from both within and outside our culture that produced the rich diversity of architectural styles has also contributed to the popular stereotypes of what Oklahoma is visually and ought to look like architecturally. But the presence of high-style architecture throughout Oklahoma tells us something fundamentally important about our land. From the standpoint of communication of ideas, Oklahoma was *never* an isolated frontier. There are indeed excellent examples of buildings constructed throughout the nineteenth and twentieth centuries that reflect architectural ideals popular and fashionable in other areas of the country. These range from the eclectic tribal council buildings, which mix Italianate and French Second Empire styles, of some of the Five Civilized Tribes to the marvelous Art Deco buildings in Tulsa. And the urban architecture of Guthrie is particularly compelling. It is an expression of form and space that is extraordinarily sophisticated and, for the most part, an architecture created by an exceptionally talented individual.

Our recent architectural history is also rich. Some of our finest buildings were designed by internationally prominent architects. There are three structures in Oklahoma by Frank Lloyd Wright. There are numerous buildings, especially in Tulsa, Norman, and Bartlesville, designed by Bruce Goff; several of them are among his finest works. Two Oklahoma buildings have received the coveted Twenty-Five Year Award of the American Institute of Architects: the Price Tower in Bartlesville by Wright and the Bavinger House in Norman by Goff. Few other states in America can claim this distinction.

This mix of low-style and high-style architecture symbolizes the dual agrarian and urban facets of Oklahoma culture. Our history can be interpreted through our built environment. Certainly our architecture is diverse and reflects the plurality of values of the people of Oklahoma. But this is the case in all good buildings, not only here but also throughout America. This diversity, as manifested in our architecture, is one of the great strengths of our land.

CHAPTER 10

The Passing of Grit: Observations of a Farm Girl, Now a Spectator on the Land

PAT BELLMON

A widespread image of Oklahoma, both among Oklahomans and nationally, is that of romanticized rural, wheat farming, cattle raising, small town life. In this largely autobiographical chapter, Pat Bellmon poetically portrays the far more complex, ambivalence-ridden cultural landscape of rural Oklahoma. She shows both the virtues and the pettinesses of "true grit," grieves its passing even as on her own personal journey she separates from it. Bellmon's chapter attests to the power of art in evoking—never merely describing—culture and of literature's indispensability in truly feeling as well as intellectually understanding Oklahoma or any culture. She poignantly raises questions about the nature of culture change, about what is lost, indeed about what truly was "traditional" in the first place. Other contributors to this volume approach their task and subject more as analytic, if also sympathetic, outsiders. Bellmon, by contrast, paints and sculpts her Oklahoma—heir to the land runs—from within. Her contribution, like that of several others in this volume, raises the disturbing issue about what is actually, as opposed to mythically, unique about Oklahoma.

Popular American culture and that of many Oklahomans both assume a cultural distinctiveness to Oklahoma's rural farming "true grit." In fact, actual cultural content is not unique to Oklahoma but is shared with Kansas and Texas and, in fact, much of the Great Plains as well. The mystique of Oklahomaness and the facts are often at odds, a point many contributors to this volume make.

The promise of owning their *own* land was everything. For Native Americans, who first farmed what would become Oklahoma land, that promise was soon broken. Then came the homesteaders, seeking fulfillment of the promise, newly made.

My paternal grandfather was not far behind. Too young to make the run, he came after the Cherokee Strip opening, bought a relinquishment (homesteaded land relinquished by the homesteader), and lived in a dugout with his young family four years before buying another place and moving into a frame house—this house, the house I live in.

In this house he and my grandmother raised thirteen children. In this house my father and mother raised us three girls, and now my son is growing up here. Although I have returned to the farm, with my generation the family farming chain most surely will be broken. I admit this only with great reluctance. Although I have known that I would not farm, it is only with this writing that I can accept that fact. I have fought that realization mightily—in my heart and as a journalist—defending what I refused to believe was gone. In the admittance, there is sorrow but, at last, serenity—and a little hope.

Although this essay is somewhat personal, it is not merely my story, but also the story of many farm families who have severed their earthy roots and in so doing misplaced their identity. As economic crisis has hit the farm in the decade of the 1980s there has been an increased number of farmer suicides. One hundred sixty farmers killed themselves from 1983 to 1988 (Lee 1989, 1990).

Too, it is part of understanding present-day Oklahoma. Until we realize what the reality of life on the farm was and is and what it was not and is not, we cannot accept what the farm has done—good and bad—to us individually and as a culture. And until we can accept that reality, we cannot go about the healthy and happy task of making it what we want it to be. It is no wonder we have avoided it so long, for it is a wrenching exercise.

My great grandfather moved his family from Kansas to the Beaver River in No Man's Land. His family lived in a dugout and tried to farm but found it more profitable to pick buffalo bones off the prairie, load them into a wagon, and drive them to Kansas to be made into bonemeal. Eventually they moved back to Kansas, leaving my grandfather, then a teen-ager, behind to help round up cattle on the open range so that No Man's Land could be opened for settlement. When the job was over, he returned to Kansas, married, and had a child before he decided to homestead.

To own land was part of the Great American Dream, and the land runs were said to be the last chance for free land. I try to imagine my grandfather's hopes for his own land and wonder what kind of myth he held in his mind. It must have been with a great deal of anxiety and excitement that he returned to the promise of the territories.

It was risky, frightening to look back on. There was the promise of land, but no promise that crops would grow. It took years just to break the sod and plant a few acres to corn (which did not do well) and wheat. Even after the farms were established, there were risky decisions to be made al-most daily.

It was a physically demanding life. Those were the days of subsistence farms, when the family grew everything it needed: vegetables; cattle for butchering, milking, and selling; horses for labor; grain crops; and forage for the animals.

Farming was made more challenging by weather. There were grand meteorological dramas: tornados and droughts and snow storms. That, of course, was before farmers had tractors, much less blades on the fronts of them; four-wheel drive pickup trucks; rotary hoes to break the crust on the dry soil; and other devices to lessen some of the damage.

The farmer had not only the big storms to contend with, but the "normal" weather as well. At certain times, timing is everything. For example, it is preferable to plant when there is moisture in the ground and to harvest wheat when it is ripe and dry. Hard red winter wheat, which is most successful in this region, is planted in fall and harvested in spring or early summer. But May and June are the wet season.

Planting is in the fall, so ground has to be worked in July and August, the dry season, when working the ground into a seed bed is usually a frustrating task. Conditions are seldom right for planting. Usually the weather stays too dry into the fall, then, as it gets cooler, it gets wetter and stays wet, sometimes for weeks.

Equally challenging and more frustrating (since it is man-made instead of natural, and therefore there is the notion that man can do something about it, although the farmer knows he cannot) is the relationship that developed between the farmer and the government. The government controls all aspects of his business: how much he can plant, how much money he can borrow, and how much he gets for the sale of his products.

Contributing, too, to the makeup of the farmer's psyche and the rural mentality is the influence of his culture. Before 1960 there was isolation, but there was also community. In settlement days, neighbors were as close as half a mile away in every direction. They relied on each other, not only to get the work done during threshing time but for socializing as well. Families gathered on a regular basis: weekly baseball games in the pasture, multifamily musical evenings in someone's living room, and social get-togethers at the churches and schoolhouses, which, in those days, were scattered throughout the countryside.

In the Oklahoma Panhandle, where people were farther apart, there was a neighborliness exemplified by the saying, "The latch string's always out," which meant that anyone was welcome to enter even when no one was home, take what they might need, and latch the gate behind them (Calhoun 1987).

Farmers were churchgoers who held fundamental beliefs (that is, a literal interpretation of the Bible). Some even came to the area because other members of their faith had settled here. My father's maternal grandparents chose Oklahoma because they knew other people in Oklahoma who belonged to the Reformed Presbyterian Church (based on genealogy in Pease 1988).

Economically, the farmers were all pretty much in the same boat: they were poor, though by the time of the Depression some had fared better than others because of the discovery of oil on their land. But the division between haves and have-nots was not great.

So these were people who came here to realize the ancestral dream of owning their own land. To do that, they worked hard, despite weather conditions and government controls, and many held to the land—and to religion and each other in a close-knit community.

The myth that emerged was of a rough-hewn, individual-istic people in a quaint yet spare place where the unexpected was expected, doing the noble task of raising food to feed Americans and others as well. Their prize values were con-sidered to be hard work, tenacity, respect for the land, famil-ial closeness, and obedience to God. Farm people were viewed by city-dwellers as good people but parochial, backward, not capable of anything but farming. (It is often considered newsworthy, both locally and nationally, when someone who is creative or bright or enterprising or worldly emerges from the farm environment or is discovered living in a small rural town.)

Now there are fewer farmers—2.16 percent of the Okla-homa population—and the farms are bigger, commercial ones (Lee 1990; *Tulsa World* 1989). In Oklahoma they are still primarily owned and operated by families.

Farming is still a gamble in the long run and on a day-to-day basis. There is a regular series of double binds on the farm. For example, the farmer should wait to bail hay until it is drier so it will roll properly and so the bales will not catch fire in August, but if it is too dry it will lose leaves and, there-fore, protein. And on that same day—say, in early June—the farmer must face the decision not only whether to cut *another* pasture of hay (perhaps it will rain this evening) but also which to do next: cut hay or try to cut the first wheat.

Even after farming twenty or thirty years, many farmers plant wheat based solely on their experience the *previous* year: if they planted early last year and had a bad crop, they plant late this year. If they planted late and had a bad crop, they plant early this year.

Compared to some modern-day jobs, farming is still hard

physical work, largely because of the hours required during the summer and fall months, although it is not as hard when compared to the pioneers' way of doing things. There is still the weather to outmaneuver and the government to cuss and outguess.

These days, there are not so many people in the country, but where people live in the country, they often still live in clusters. Today there is a different kind of isolation. Not only are there fewer people in the country, but also they do not see each other as much, either in the hometowns or in each others' homes. Many farm wives work outside the home. Shopping at home in the small towns where they might see people they know is mostly a quick convenience stop. Shopping in the neighboring larger towns where there is more variety and better prices is not only easier than it used to be, but also now a form of entertainment. Rather than getting together Saturday night on Main Street as their grandparents did, they talk on the telephone and travel to shopping centers.

One exception to the self-imposed isolation is high school athletic events, which still draw the community. Even retired people whose children and grandchildren are long gone still attend basketball and football games.

When there are gatherings in homes they are usually of family members, who visit each other frequently. The people who farm the majority of the land and have been on the farm for generations have extended family nearby. (Indeed, in rural towns there is the joke that everyone is related.) Churches still thrive in rural communities and play a role in socializing, but it is a much diluted role. These days, not everyone in the community feels obligated to attend church.

Now, the division between haves and have-nots is more obvious. Power is more concentrated among the old farming families with money. They run the school and the churches. At the same time, a transient population has grown in recent years. As jobs and money have gotten tighter in urban areas, there has been an influx into rural communities, which are relatively inexpensive places to live—and where there are menial jobs or places from where people can commute.

Something else—something insidious—has happened to

rural communities just since my parents' generation was running things. There is an overt friendliness, even towards outsiders. Visitors comment about how friendly everyone is. But unless you are from the community, have never left it (except for military service), and fit the desired mold, you will never experience more than superficial friendliness. *And* if you challenge the status quo in any way, including innocent suggestions for improvement, you will be defeated without knowing what hit you. This will be done by smiling people who never disagree with you to your face but who take your words and translate them for the people whom they talk to in the coffee shop or local gathering place into "facts" that you would not recognize were you to hear them. You will not hear them, however. No one in the town will betray the rumor mill to those whom the rumors are about. Then frustration and bewilderment build. You begin to recognize little clues that people are avoiding you. You deny this for some time, but it happens more and more. Several "outsiders" who moved to my community with good intentions and innocent actions have eventually left either in bitterness or in total frustration.

It appears that people who have stayed in the rural community are insecure because they have stayed, although their behavior is just the opposite: they exhibit considerable bravura within the community. Anyone who comes from the outside, or has been away and returns, is a threat.

There are people within the small but powerful group who cause other people emotional and physical injury or who otherwise cause others to suffer. If those people are acceptable to the group, it does not matter what they do—they are always acceptable. But those who are not part of the group, who are outside the mold, even if they behave themselves in every other way but in some way do something that is perceived by the group as threatening—such as bringing new ideas—are ostracized, and in many cases there is an organized effort to quiet them, to block their participation in community activities.

The power group not only survives, but also it, its methods, and its attitudes are validated when someone is defeated and leaves; life goes on as before. The only time change is made is when someone within the power group suggests it. Sometimes those suggestions originated with the outsiders, now long gone. By the time the ideas are presented by the group, they are its own.

The farmer and his community generate a complicated set of ambivalences and contradictions that contribute to the state's identity. Don Green, history professor at Central State University, contends that the major factor in the development of Oklahoma culture was a series of tragedies: the Cherokee Indians' Trail of Tears to Indian Territory; the subsequent withdrawal of that promise and that land; the brother-against-brother battles of the Civil War, in which some native American units suffered the largest percentage of loss of life of any political unit; and the deterioration of land and the abandonment of Oklahoma farms in the 1930s. This history of tragedy was exacerbated by the influx of Southerners, who brought values of the South with them. The Southern experience included polite but double-dealing political practices, a history of deep poverty, and religious fundamentalism, which was strongly antiintellectual. Southern farmers were poor because of a lack of education, which was a result of the fact that Southern landowners were an elite group who liked things the way they were, says Green (1990). A prejudice against education still exists.

"The first Oklahomans were populists: the common man, the farmer," says Dave Wemhaner, sociology professor at Tulsa Junior College. (Populists believed in the virtues and wisdom of the common man.) "There are certain things in the Old Testament that indicate God chose to hide things from scholars and that he showed those things to the common man. There are passages in the Bible that say, 'Wise people are fools in the eyes of God.' In some places in Oklahoma you still have to apologize for having a Ph.D." (Wemhaner 1987).

Poor farm people got other messages. "The meek shall inherit the earth," was one Biblical injunction. In other words, if you are poor you are noble. But also, if you are poor, you have a character flaw: you should be able to provide for your family. This may have something to do with the fact that

John Steinbeck's (1939) novel *The Grapes of Wrath* had such a demoralizing effect on Oklahomans. The Okies were the heroes in that book, the Californians the villains. But *Okie* became a bad word here; the book hit too close to home. Oklahoma farmers felt downtrodden, and now the whole world saw them as such; they could not see past that.

The experience of widespread poverty created other enduring characteristics of the Oklahoma psyche. Fatalism, helplessness, and inferiority are innate attitudes of the poor, says Wemhaner. "A fatalistic person doesn't hope too much, so the injury isn't so much. . . . It's a self-fulfilling prophecy" (Wemhaner, in Copeland 1987, 4*b*). Green (1990) writes, "Oklahomans will accept second best in everything—except football." (See the chapter by Tramel in this volume.)

Weather also contributes to the ambiguities by muddying the relationship between God and the farmer. The farmer learns there is only a certain degree to which he is in control of his destiny. When he has done all he can, it is up to weather conditions or to God ("It's up to the Almighty") to make or break the crop. This sets him up. "God, weather, nature and fate are tied up with goodness and badness," says Howard Stein. "If the crop is good, 'I've been good.' If the crop is bad, 'I'm being punished,'" the farmer tells himself (Stein, in Copeland 1987, 4*b*). This concept adds to his fatalism, but an optimism sometimes shines through. In fact at times all farmers seem to exhibit both optimism and pessimism. Depending on the situation, one may say, "I'm never going to get ahead." But then, "There's always next year."

The farmer also has a love-hate relationship with the government. The farmer asks the government to rescue him but also places considerable blame at the feet of Uncle Sam. The irony here is that while the farmer has no control over the weather and not much over the government, and while he is truly reliant on the cooperation of both, he boasts of his independence.

In 1981, when I returned to my hometown wearing my rose-colored glasses, I could see the grit—life appeared wide-open here and these people seemed to have spunk and endurance. I was pleased: that is what I had come home for. And to this day, at first glance, there is something admirably gritty about the place. Maybe it is the fact that keys are still left in the cars on Main Street. Too, life here has a refreshingly slow pace.

And there is the appearance of a sense of individualism: these people *do not* fit a corporate mold. But it is deceiving. They may not fit the corporate mold, but there is definitely a locally required mold. True grit is gone. Independence has become an out-of-date rural myth. Now there is a double message: act like an individualist, but fit the mold.

Within a year, I saw other signs of the passing of grit. For example, I could buy Italian plum tomatoes only forty miles away and the same brand of Italian olive oil—at a cheaper price even than on the East Coast—in Oklahoma City. And I heard of frequent tool and battery thefts from tractors around Billings.

Within five years, I was confused. There was something askew—as if I had misplaced something—but at the same time the horrible feeling that it had never been there. It seemed a mirage, a deception. After three years of trying to cajole and even force improvements, I became discouraged, angry, bitter, defeated, and resigned. Now I see more clearly. This is still, thank goodness, a farming community—a place settled by people like my ancestors who worked hard and died hard fulfilling a democratic ideal of owning their own land. This, in my opinion, is as it must remain.

Predictions are that more and more gentlemen farmers will come to the land—people living here, working elsewhere, tending small patches or none at all—and that farm land will be owned by fewer and fewer people, people who are not farmers. This may or may not be good for the land, for the country (Copeland 1986).

Now I realize that *I* am a spectator on the land, one of the gentlewomen who needs both the country and something more.

Farming is a way of life that is either quickly rejected or that immediately gets into the marrow and stays. As romantic as it sounds, there truly is something comforting about the smell of the earth, something thrilling about nature's drama, something wondrous about watching things grow, something satisfying about hard work, and something noble about owning that land that make some people not only enjoy farming, but also require it to feed their soul.

While I need to live in the country, I did not need to farm. In a way, I wish I did. I love the beauty, the quiet, the solitude of living next to nature. I love the smell of the earth. I love being able to walk for miles, to explore, to see the sunset, to smell the air. I love the rain and the snow and the heat.

I love the farming cycles, the smell of the earth, the excitement of harvest. I love to ride a swather that is cutting hay, despite the heat and the bugs.

I enjoy the simpleness of small-town life. I can get my driver's license and license plates at the lumber yard in five friendly minutes. I can get my mail and see ten people I know.

These are all gifts I received by growing up on a farm.

But it is not the place I thought it was, and I have become one of the ones I dreaded to see come here: someone who loves to live here but who does not make a living farming and who does not fit into or help out in the community.

Like myself, other Oklahomans inherit a mixed-bag legacy from the farms and rural towns. For one thing, pride of our pioneer heritage has spread throughout all of Oklahoma. Some of the attributes of that life are indeed worthy of honor in our society. Tenacity, a willingness to work, and the importance of close family would benefit our culture. (As the number of farmers have dwindled, so have these attributes in the larger society.)

At the same time, we can give up the suffering and sacrifice our pioneer forefathers and foremothers experienced. I am not the only woman of pioneer heritage who, while experiencing frozen and broken water pipes and sick children simultaneously, has suddenly and without warrant felt guilty and weak when someone, to make me feel better, reminds me how my grandmother managed without these "modern conveniences."

The farm has also taught us an obligation to be stewards of

the land and a sense of our own place on the earth. Again, many of those of us who grew up on the farm and left it retain an insatiable love of the land, while at the same time, as the number of farmers has decreased, others have forgotten this responsibility and balance with nature.

In more recent years the rural community has helped promote low self-esteem that manifests itself in a defensive, macho ("nothing bothers me") way that makes life in rural communities sometimes unpleasant and as parochial as city-dwellers believe it to be. It also promotes fundamentalism, antiintellectualism, fatalism, and an increasingly polarized economic system. But in balance, and despite recent trends, life on the farm is desirable. And perhaps the most significant effect the farm has had on Oklahoma in later years is that its effect has diminished so greatly.

I have chosen to stay here, a spectator on the farm, watching the sunsets, tending the garden, driving a wheat truck once in a while. My circle of friends will be small and transient within the community; my real community will be outside this place. It could be the best of both worlds.

CHAPTER 11

The Culture of Oklahoma:
A Group Identity and Its Images

HOWARD F. STEIN AND ROBERT F. HILL

Every culture has an image—multiple images, in fact: that of its members toward it, that of outsiders toward it, and that created by a crucial interplay between the two. How does the third image come to be held in common between insiders and outsiders, and how does its selection take place? This is a crucial question, not only about the culture of Oklahoma, but also about the process of culture formation, continuity, and change everywhere. In this concluding chapter we inquire into the dynamics of Oklahoma's cultural image, an inquiry that might in turn cast some light on understanding any culture. Core cultural elements—many discussed by previous contributors to this volume—are identified, and their symbolic, emotional significance is explored. Again, they are sports, wetness and dryness, cowboys and Indians, flat land, and the psychology of Oklahoma cultural geography. We conclude by asking how a book such as this might contribute to Oklahoma's future development and how the scholarly collaboration exemplified by this book might serve as a model for others who might wish to inquire into their nation, state, ethnic group, religious organization (denomination or local church), corporation, or city, town, or other region.

Using Oklahoma as a case study, this concluding chapter explores the dynamics and meanings of group images and their consequences. Our analysis of the cultural images of Oklahoma builds upon the tradition of studies of national character in anthropology (for example, Mead 1953, Dundes 1984). Moreover, we believe that, as a yet unrecognized service, applied social scientists and humanities professionals in other states might offer their fellow citizens cultural analyses of states (Hill and Stein 1988). The same potential holds, of course, for other group identities such as cities, counties, regions, and towns.

Groups everywhere create and assign images to themselves and to other groups. They likewise contain within their borders places people regard as sacred or profane. Furthermore, they have some sense of boundaries, perhaps not politically formalized (for example, "nations" that are not "nation-states"), that delineate where their group begins and ends. From hunting-gathering peoples such as the Australian aborigines or the Great Basin Shoshones, who traditionally journeyed on an annual round of activities, to nation-states whose people jealously guard their "secure borders," all groups associate their sense of "we-ness" with an imagined membrane in space or time (Stein 1987b). It says, "Here is where we end and where you begin. Inside is what and who we are." Jules Henry, for example, wrote that "Every culture has its own imaginative quality and each historic period, like each culture, is dominated by certain images. Who would deny that the Doric imagination was different from the Hellenistic; that the imagination of the Murngin of Australia is different from that of the Dakota Indians of the United States—or that the American imagination of Tocqueville's day was different from our own?" (1963, 8).

In this chapter, we, applied anthropologists, study Oklahoma as an identity system that serves as a mental map simultaneously within the state, the region, and the nation. In addition to relying upon many years of ethnographic experience, administrative work, and clinical teaching in Oklahoma, we draw upon survey materials and a statistical analysis of the official state magazine, *Oklahoma Today*, gathered by Robert F. Hill. Besides his initial image survey of sixty-seven professional students in pediatrics and public health,

Hill has surveyed an additional 703 Oklahomans (civic leaders, union members, educators, students, and church members from different parts of the state). We shall draw considerably from this last survey below. As well as being a contribution to studying the sense of identity in one state, this chapter, together with the volume it concludes, might also serve as a model for the study of any group identity system and of the consequences of that system for group development.

Surveys of Oklahoma Images

In our first survey, conducted in the fall of 1986, Hill asked sixty-nine graduate students at the University of Oklahoma's Health Sciences Center in Oklahoma City to identify their first image or impression when the words "State of Oklahoma" were mentioned. Their responses focused in mostly oppositional terms on friendly or backward people; cowboys, Indians, or redneck character types; petroleum, farming, or ranching economics; scenic or desolate physical landscapes; and football as a recreational passion. The true Oklahoma, as determined by more objective criteria (predominantly urban; educationally, ethnically, and religiously diverse; and economically dominated by manufacturing, military installations, and institutions of higher education), was totally absent in these responses. We were astonished by their stereotypic narrowness and uniformity.

The image responses from the first survey mirrored almost perfectly the cultural analysis of 149 covers of *Oklahoma Today* between 1956 and 1986. We thematically categorized and distributed these covers in rank order percentages as follows: scenic beauty or landscapes, 36.2 percent; cowboys, horses, and frontier nostalgia, 16.8 percent; Native American people or art forms, 12.8 percent; heroic figures in Oklahoma history, 6.7 percent; sports, 5.4 percent; farming, 4.0 percent; museum displays, 4.0 percent; oil and gas rigs, 2.7 percent; flags, 2.7 percent; and other miscellaneous themes, 8.7 percent (Hill and Stein 1988).

In our second survey, conducted during the fall of 1987

and winter of 1988, we sought to sample a much more diverse group of Oklahomans, first, to confirm or discount our earlier survey results and second, to further pin down those features of Oklahoma's image, both positive and negative, which were most accurate in descriptive terms. Our second survey sample included (1) sixty-one members of Leadership Oklahoma, a statewide organization devoted to developing future leaders in all important sectors of the state; (2) 173 members of the statewide Economic Development Task Force, including union leaders; private business owners; presidents, vice-presidents, and chief executive officers of private corporations; public education administrators; elected officials; clergy; and others assembled in Oklahoma City by the Oklahoma Department of Commerce; (3) eighty-nine members of a Southern Baptist church in Tulsa who attended their regular Wednesday-night prayer service–dinner meeting; (4) forty-two members of a local electrical workers' union in Oklahoma City at the behest of their president (a member of the Economic Development Task Force); (5) 111 members of an upper-division sociology class on the Norman campus of the University of Oklahoma; and (6) sixty-four administrators of the Oklahoma vocational-technical education system who attended a statewide meeting and 163 of their staff employees throughout the state upon the administrators' return home.

In addition to asking respondents an open-ended question to identify their first image or impression of Oklahoma, Hill asked each to pick three features from a list of ten which they felt "best about," and three from another list of ten which they felt "worst about." We derived items on the two lists from common image responses in the first survey and additions by the authors from other ethnographic sources. On the positive or "best" side, these features included (1) friendly people; (2) Christian values; (3) Oklahoma football; (4) Native American art and culture; (5) the farming-ranching way of life; (6) scenic lakes, rivers, plains, and mountains; (7) the oil and gas way of life; (8) industrial diversity; (9) western heritage; and (10) accessible vocational and higher education. Negative items (those felt the "worst" about) included (1) backward people; (2) religious fanaticism; (3) football crazy;

(4) cowboys-and-Indians mentality; (5) violent extreme weather; (6) flat, dry, dull landscape; (7) boom-and-bust mentality; (8) underdeveloped country; (9) Dust Bowl history; and (10) poor-quality, underfunded education.

The findings from our second survey confirmed the findings from our earlier one. Respondents overwhelmingly produced narrow, stereotyped images in response to the open-ended question, irrespective of their varied social backgrounds. The responses differed only in tone; some were more positive, others more negative. They differed little in content. Consider, for example, ten responses, which we have chosen randomly from the Economic Development Task Force group:

> pioneering
> home
> out-of-sync
> oil/agriculture/football
> the state's shape
> the stage play *Oklahoma!*
> my chosen home
> opportunity
> cowboys, Indians, dust
> western

Next consider ten random responses from the Baptist church group:

> mixture of petroleum industry, rural farming, and lakes
> you don't want to know, go to Texas
> progressive cities, backward rural areas
> home—I love it here
> wheat—oil—Indians
> crooked government, rednecks
> a rural state with a strong family image
> backward
> government of the state
> rednecked

Finally, consider twelve responses from the vocational education group:

> technologically behind
> sad

the two universities: OU football, OSU football, wrestling and
   baseball
the musical *Oklahoma!*
the great abundance of oil
oil and money, on the other side high percent illiteracy
slow
I love Oklahoma whether economics are good or bad
oil and gas and farming
I have a strong self-pride for Oklahoma, I think of the prosperous
   times before the recession
home state, something to be proud of
state agencies in Oklahoma and the inefficient way they seem to
   be run

In Fig. 11.1, we present a statistical summary of the "best"
and "worst" features of Oklahoma's image most frequently
chosen by our total sample of 703 respondents. The sequence
of features we present here follows that of the original survey
questionnaire. Although in the questionnaire format there
was much greater separation between the "best" and "worst"
feature lists, we cannot as easily discern here polar oppositions such as "Christian values/religious fanaticism." While
the percentages shown in the figure reflect the choices and
values of the total sample, they do not reflect the significant
subsample variations that were characteristic of fourteen of
the twenty features.[1]

For example, members of Leadership Oklahoma were significantly more likely to choose "friendly people" ($p < .004$)
and "western heritage" ($p < .001$) on the positive axis. Not
surprisingly, members of the Baptist church in Tulsa were
more likely to choose "Christian values" on the positive side,
($p < .001$) and "football crazy" on the negative ($p < .020$),
while undergraduate students at the University of Oklahoma
were more likely to choose "Oklahoma football" ($p < .001$),
"religious fanaticism" ($p < .020$), and "flat, dry, dull landscape" ($p < .001$). Likewise, managers and staff of the Oklahoma vocational-technical education system were more likely
to choose "farming and ranching way of life" ($p < .014$),
"scenic lakes, rivers, and mountains" ($p < .001$), accessible
vocational and higher education" ($p < .001$) "cowboys-and-

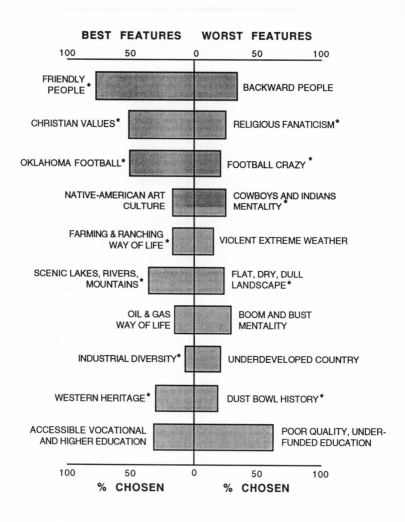

BEST FEATURES WORST FEATURES

100   50   0   50   100

FRIENDLY PEOPLE*   BACKWARD PEOPLE

CHRISTIAN VALUES*   RELIGIOUS FANATICISM*

OKLAHOMA FOOTBALL*   FOOTBALL CRAZY*

NATIVE-AMERICAN ART CULTURE   COWBOYS AND INDIANS MENTALITY*

FARMING & RANCHING WAY OF LIFE*   VIOLENT EXTREME WEATHER

SCENIC LAKES, RIVERS, MOUNTAINS*   FLAT, DRY, DULL LANDSCAPE*

OIL & GAS WAY OF LIFE   BOOM AND BUST MENTALITY

INDUSTRIAL DIVERSITY*   UNDERDEVELOPED COUNTRY

WESTERN HERITAGE*   DUST BOWL HISTORY*

ACCESSIBLE VOCATIONAL AND HIGHER EDUCATION   POOR QUALITY, UNDERFUNDED EDUCATION

100   50   0   50   100
% CHOSEN   % CHOSEN

* Features with significant differences by survey group, Chi square test, ≤ .05 level
**Each respondent was asked to choose 3 of 10 best and 3 of 10 worst features as listed above.

Fig. 11.1. Features of Oklahoma about which respondents feel best and worst. Each respondent was asked to choose three of the ten best and three of the ten worst features listed.

Indians mentality" (p < .015) and "Dust Bowl history" (p < .001). Finally, members of the Economic Development Task Force were significantly more likely to choose "industrial diversity" (p < .055) even though this was the least chosen feature out of twenty by the entire sample. Task force members were also more likely to choose "boom-and-bust mentality" on the negative axis (p < .006), although this was obviously of much less concern to most other survey respondents. Other statistically significant differences in response to the "best" and "worst" features of Oklahoma's image were found in accordance with variation in age, religiosity, sex, nativity, residence, occupation, and political affiliation.[2]

For the remainder of this chapter we discuss in depth several themes of the Oklahoma cultural identity and their relation to Oklahoma's self-image and to the image held about it from without. We refer the reader to earlier interpretive studies by Howard F. Stein (1985, 1987c) which examine the cultural historical and psychological roots of Oklahoma's identity and image: for example, in the late nineteenth century, Oklahoma as a final island of frontier freedom within the continental United States, a kind of America within America (see also Lamar, this volume). Here, settlers who were restless and discontent in their own families and communities of origin could start over again on their own. The themes we shall consider, and which have been addressed from various viewpoints by other contributors to this book (as well as the above survey results), are (1) the Dust Bowl, (2) the cowboy ethos, (3) football, (4) the location or "psychogeography" of Oklahoma, (5) the question of what is "native" (relative to the Euro-American population) and what is "nativist" in the Oklahoma identity system, and (6) the symbolic ambiguity of industry and higher education.

The Dust Bowl

The American state of Oklahoma is haunted by the image of the Dust Bowl of the 1930s. According to Hill's (1987–88) survey, "Dust Bowl history" ranked near the top among ten cultural features which senior Oklahomans "feel the worst about." For those aged twenty-five and under, "Dust Bowl history" ranked last ($p < .002$). There is more to the Dust Bowl than historical memory. Extreme images of desolate dryness and luxuriant wetness, together with their associated excesses and self-privations, transcend yet encompass economic particulars of rain and drought in relation to wheat farming or of the international oil economy that regulates the level of oil and gas exploration and drilling (Hill and Stein 1988). The state and regional boom-and-bust cycle is as much a matter of emotional economy as of political economy (see Nuckolls, this volume). It is as if, in terms of many Oklahomans' inner image of their state, the world must be either/or, an image which recurs throughout religion, politics, and morality alike. Exhilarating lunges toward new heights vacillate with depressive bottoming out. For example, in 1987, at the nadir of one depression, Oklahoma City television channel 4 (KFOR) sought to inspire renewed optimism through the image of a jet plane taking off, accompanied by the exclamation and song, "We're going all out for Oklahoma."

The Dust Bowl image originated during the Great Depression. It was seared into the public consciousness through John Steinbeck's novel (1939) and the subsequent movie (1940, Twentieth Century Fox) *The Grapes of Wrath*, Woody Guthrie's Dust Bowl ballads, and photographer Arthur Rothstein's riveting pictures. It has become a timeless self-image held by Oklahomans of themselves *and* a national image held of Oklahoma. Five decades later, an article on the front page of the business section in the *New York Times* of May 11, 1986, was titled, "Desperation Descends on Oklahoma" (Reinhold 1986, 1; see Fig. 11.2). The article described the four-year energy and agricultural slump and depression and in text and image associated, if not conflated, the difficult present with the past. The photograph beneath the headline pictured three modern Oklahomans—a farm implement dealer, a landholder, and an oil well driller—superimposed over a photograph of a 1935 dust storm.

Desperation Descends on Oklahoma

Dealer. *Sales are down, and the future of Edwin Long's farm implements business is in doubt.*

Landholder. *The money Lavera Mae Reeder got from oil leases is gone, and now her wells are shut off.*

Driller. *Two months ago, Don Hughes was the state's busiest oil well driller. Now he's bankrupt.*

A dust storm in Tyrone, Okla., photographed in 1935.

The New York Times/William E. Sauro

Fig. 11.2. The *New York Times*, Business Section 3, May 11, 1986.

Even when ostensibly forgotten, the Dust Bowl remains a part of the Oklahoma identity, an identity in which being a stalwart survivor is prized above virtually all else. The accursed Dust Bowl image is thus a guardian of that pioneer self-image that contrasts Oklahomans with all outsiders. Yet it is also an image that outsiders attribute to if not externalize onto Oklahoma, mirroring or confirming many Oklahomans' own self-image. Many Oklahomans and outsiders hold this negative image, but many Oklahomans reverse it into a badge of honor and distinctiveness. In the extreme, the Dust Bowl image becomes a cultural prison from which many Oklahomans are loathe to separate and which many outsiders are loathe to disassociate from Oklahoma. On the other hand, when *Oklahoma Today* portray landscapes, the photographs are always in the richest of colors as if to put the dark and parched 1930s forever behind.

Whatever the psychology of the relationship between Dust Bowl folklore and fact in Oklahoma history, the plentifulness of water in today's Oklahoma is an established environmental reality. Numerous lakes were created by public works projects in the 1930s and since. Tulsa is now a port city, joined by a canal to the Mississippi and the Gulf of Mexico. In that, as in many facets of the Oklahoma identity, ecological reality and tenacious ecological myth widely diverge.

Significantly, both the most positive and the most negative nationally shared images of Oklahoma are products of larger American popular culture—that part which anthropologists label "expressive culture." Rodgers and Hammerstein's 1943 musical play and movie *Oklahoma* depicts the positive, optimistic stereotype. Steinbeck's novel—or at least the widespread interpretation of the book—and the movie adapted from it portrays the negative, pessimistic stereotype. Such extremes in emotional climate mirror the boom-or-bust, luxuriant green or parched land, splits in the mental image of the state long held by Oklahomans. Historian William W. Savage, Jr., notes (1989*a*) that the football program at the University of Oklahoma was launched "big-time" specifically in reaction to the negative national and local image of Oklahoma created by *The Grapes of Wrath*—even as football in Oklahoma continued the officially repudiated but nonetheless glorified outlaw image (see also Cross 1977, 7; and Tramel, this volume).

Cowboy

Closely tied, if not tenaciously tethered, to the Dust Bowl image of Oklahoma is that ubiquitous configuration of cowboy, horse, cattle, wide-open spaces, Great Plains, West, newness, opportunity, friendliness, freedom, roughness, wildness, and rurality of which Oklahomans are fiercely proud—and with which selfsame configuration the rest of the nation if not the world associates Oklahoma (see Lamar and Brown, this volume). This interpretation is verified in Hill's survey by the fact that while 27.4 percent of nonnative Oklahomans chose "cowboys-and-Indians mentality" as a negative cultural feature of the state, only 17.9 percent of native Oklahomans felt so ($p < .02$). Further, although within Oklahoma many African Americans and Native Americans wear various accoutrements of the cowboy—wide leather belt with large, decorated buckle; cowboy hat; cowboy boots; bolo tie; and so on—the cultural prototype, popular image, and cynosure is Euro-American, or, in terms of the American racial typology, "white." For comparative purposes, it should be noted that "cowboy" is a local expression of a widespread, if not universal, social type in complex society; the Cossacks of the Ukraine and Russia, the Mongols and early Hungarians from Central Asia, and the gauchos of Argentina are but a few examples of the resolutely unsettled. The question, "Doesn't everyone want to be a cowboy?" takes us to the heart of the free-spirited, unfettered identity, the rebel against being closed in or tied down (Erikson 1963). The virtual antithesis of the image of the sedentary and conservative farmer who seeks security and permanence of place is that of the adventure-seeking cowboy. In his many guises, including modern gas and oil entrepreneurs, roughnecks, and roustabouts, the cowboy is always ready to move to another opportunity without being "fenced in" or "held down." The freedom to pull up stakes and start afresh characterizes the cowboy's outlook.

Although spring azaleas and debutante balls link Oklahoma to the racial caste and poverty-gentility of the Old South—for both of which the cowboy, avatar of social leveling, has only contempt—the Oklahoma cowboy image has also assimilated the rebellious aspect of that same South and has made it into a local mark of pride (an example of which is the ubiquitous Confederate flag as bumper sticker). Lurking beneath the sedentariness and fierce, private familism of Oklahoma wheat farmers and cattle ranchers, and likewise underlying their disdain for "city slickers," is the lore and lure of the cowboy, urban and rural alike, beholden to no one or no tradition. Significantly, the name of the football team of Oklahoma State University is "Cowboys," and their mascot is "Pistol Pete." The cowboy type who reads civilization as the foil against which to define himself or herself feels civilization in all its domesticated guises to be the gravest threat.

The contradiction and ambivalence between the espoused values of independence, individualism, and autonomy and the dependency-fostering groupings of bureaucracy, corporation, and bossism pervade Oklahoma culture and its history. Lurking not far behind the lone cowboy and self-reliant homesteader is the menacing presence of an external control who or which cannot be eluded. Savage pithily writes: "It helps if you think of Oklahoma as a company town. It doesn't matter whose company you're talking about, because if they're big enough, they're all pretty much the same. They act like they own the place. And, in the absence of a diversified economy and independent political leadership, they do. They tell us what they want us to know, and they treat us just as they please. They are concerned solely with profit and how you can help them make it" (1989b,1). Chapters in this book by Howard R. Lamar, Pat Bellmon, Charles W. Nuckolls, and Arn Henderson have illustrated in various ways the cultural conflict between freedom and coercion, diversity and conformism, and how the subtle interplay among personality, values, aesthetics, politics, and economics achieves coercive conformity. As frontiers of self and opportunity close—and close in—Oklahomans tend to vaunt all the more passionately the virtues of the receding frontier (see Fig. 11.3).

The perpetual search for new frontiers to open up and to penetrate—from the settling, homesteading, tilling, fertilizing, planting, and harvesting of the land to the deep drilling into the earth in search of oil and gas—characterizes the psychohistory as well as the economic history of Oklahoma. This quest is an inextricable part of the internal and national image of Oklahoma. Phillip L. Zweig weaves that culture history into his account of the 1982 collapse of the Penn Square Bank:

Fig. 11.3. "The Contemporary Cowboy." (Reprinted with permission of *Oklahoma Today* magazine.)

For the descendants of the pioneers who opened up the Oklahoma Territory for settlement, the Anadarko Basin became a new frontier, one that was, in many ways, more hostile and forbidding than the original. The wildcatters in search of high-pressure gas would find that the earth gave up its riches even more reluctantly than the Indians who once inhabited the Oklahoma plains relinquished their land. Indeed, the search for gas would bring forth individuals whose gambling instincts and opportunistic spirit were bequeathed to them by three generations of Oklahomans who endured Indian raids, dust storms, tornadoes, and oppressive heat. Oklahoma is a state of stark contradictions. . . . Oklahoma is sophisticated Tulsa, with streets named after the prestigious Ivy League colleges of the East. It is also the more boisterous, rough-hewn Oklahoma City, with its broad avenues and unbridled suburban sprawl. . . . Admiration, even reverence, for the opportunist and the risk-taker and, some would say, the white-collar outlaw, survives to this day, side by side with the rigid moral dictates of Bible Belt fundamentalism. (1985, 6–7)

In an essay on Americans' mystique of the West, and of the cowboy who personifies it, Savage writes:

The West, in mythic constructs afforded by American culture, has a good deal to do with nature, or at least with the ways in which Americans perceive nature. . . .
The hero against nature is the cowboy against the Indian, the soldier against the Indian, the trapper against the Indian or the settler against the Indian. That each frontier type also meets the elements and the hostility of the land itself is relevant as well, but the Indian in American fabrications of the West is the first personification of nature. (1980, 302)

Thus, whatever the West is and was—and Oklahoma embodies its essence—the myth of the West is more compelling than the findings of historical fact, and the West elevates the fiction of the cowboy into incontrovertible fact.

Although *cowboy* is intrinsically a masculine term for a male role, its virtues extend to frontierswomen of fact or fantasy. The lore of the region extols the image of the rugged woman, as does the presence of the *Pioneer Woman* statue in Ponca City (see Nuckolls, this volume). Vying with Oklahoma's official Evangelical Protestant–based religious and political pieties and its much-touted friendliness, the value of every-man-for-himself competitiveness and rugged self-reliance likewise attests to Oklahomans' admiration for brazenness and defiance toward "the Law" and a wish to keep civilization's domesticated settledness at arm's length. As we shall now show, the aggressive Oklahoma football image fuses with and condenses into that of the cowboy as a source of fierce state pride.

Football

Any consideration of Oklahoma's image—its self-image, its image to others, and their interplay—requires mention of the vital if not consuming role that collegiate and high school football plays in this state (see Tramel, this volume). The football team of the University of Oklahoma (OU) and only to a slightly lesser extent those of Oklahoma State University (OSU) and Tulsa University (TU) and their fates are a pervasive component and preoccupation of the Oklahoma cultural identity system (see Spicer 1971, Stein and Hill 1977a). "Oklahoma football" ranked near the top among positive cultural features for male respondents to Hill's survey ($p < .05$) and a close second to "Christian values" for respondents who identified themselves as "religious fundamentalists" ($p < .05$). In this largely Evangelical Protestant state (stronghold of Southern Baptist churches, the Church of Christ, and others), in which the very thought and act of violence within one's home and community is severely proscribed (even as it is tacitly practiced in the form of spanking), football is one of the few acceptable occasions and outlets for the discharge of aggression—among fans as well as between players on the field. The night before the annual OU/Texas game is typically one of Saturnalia, saturated with beer, hard liquor, and street fights, all heartily played out on and for the news media. The fierce pride and even haughtiness that are intrinsic to OU football stand in stark cultural contrast to the official religious and moral pieties of humility, modesty, understatement, and conflict avoidance.

One prominent automobile bumper sticker—the popularity of which is an index of its iconic centrality—reads, "It's hard to be humble when you're a Sooner." The multiply layered image of the Sooner reveals much about football and beyond. The OU football team goes by the epithet "Sooner." Historically, the term *Sooner* stems from the pejorative name given to those early settlers to the Oklahoma territories who literally jumped the gun to stake out claims before it was legally time to begin the 1889 Land Run from the Kansas-Oklahoma border. Hiding behind bushes or trees or in prairie grass, these cultural outlaws placed getting there first and having the pick of the land above conformity to "outsiders'" laws, an ethic widespread on the frontier. The tension between law and outlaw values has governed Oklahoma culture from the outset.

To be called a Sooner is to be reprimanded, censured, and derided for stepping beyond life's proprieties. Many Oklahomans feel embarrassed by the image. It means that one has stepped out of line, out of social respectability and conformity. Football, however, is one major cultural institution in which the ordinarily proscribed may be unleashed. In Victor Turner's (1969) term, it is "liminal," that is, outside the bounds of routine decorum. Oklahoma football tacitly encourages if not outright prescribes cultural violations and excesses. Embodying the image of the Sooners, OU football attempts to preserve those frontier values that rebel against the encroachment of civilization, settledness, domestication, and the reign of law and order—virtues extolled in church, school, and legislature. In this view, football plays a familiar role as a "safety valve" to provide a moral holiday from the official virtues.

It plays another important role as well: that of providing a staunchly, if not stridently, positive image of Oklahoma, a bulwark that contrasts with poor self-image and outside images. It is as though through the idiom of collegiate football (and to a lesser extent, other competitive sports) Oklahomans can avenge if not reverse hurts sustained elsewhere in life. Identification with OU team players, with the team itself, and with the long-time former coach Barry Switzer (see

Fig. 11.4) helps patch up self-images in which people feel that something vital is missing or lost from their lives. (See Switzer's best-selling autobiography, *The Bootlegger's Boy* [Switzer and Shrake 1990].) One who feels himself or herself to be a loser in life can by proxy become a winner if OU or OSU has a winning season and can play in a major postseason bowl game. The winning football team becomes a symbol of reversal for unfulfilled ambitions. As long as the football team is alive and well, so too is the idealized frontier spirit of competition, success, and winning preserved.

The devastating turn of events with the OU football team in late 1988 and early 1989 shows what can happen when an emotion-charged identity system is undermined. *Daily Oklahoman* (Oklahoma City) staff writer Kay Morgan wrote of those incidents: "The furor has arisen as one piece of bad news followed another: The entire program was placed on probation by the NCAA; one player was charged with shooting a teammate; three players were charged with raping a woman in the athletic dormitory; a quarterback was charged with selling cocaine" (1989, 1). The cover story in the national magazine *Sports Illustrated*, February 27, 1989, featured the woes of OU football, outraging many in the state. Cartoons in the newspaper comic strip "Tank McNamara" appearing on January 13 and 14, 1989, alluded to the embarrassing onslaught of events. An article by Randy Galloway in the *Dallas Morning News*, dated December 24, 1988, was titled, "That Boom of Laughter: OU Seeing Red." In the news media, several university administrators and athletics chairmen from outside Oklahoma have explicitly made comparisons regarding their hopes for their future by using Oklahoma as a negative image. Much outrage erupted as Oklahoma became, albeit temporarily, a national laughingstock, the object of comparison of what one aspired *not* to be.

The object of fierce local pride had become the object of national derision. In the sense of Oklahoma cultural identity, football (presuming winning seasons and regular trips to the Orange Bowl) was the single source of group self-affirmation in the wake of the statewide economic depression that is nearly a decade long; oil, gas, wheat, cattle, and land all have been

Fig. 11.4. "The Sooners Shooting for No. 1 (Again)," September-October 1986. (Reprinted with permission of *Oklahoma Today* magazine.)

at low ebb. As of this writing in 1991, recovery is slow, more wish and fantasy than reality, held back to some extent by a sluggish national economy.

Every civilization has its discontents. As George A. De Vos writes, no culture is "without cost for the individuals who maintain its continuity" (1978, 256). In Oklahoma culture, football serves as both symbol and symptom: symbol of the effort to shore up a positive identity by relying (indeed, over-relying) on a single cultural element, and symptom of chronic issues of self-esteem that require a preoccupation with shoring up in the first place. If the frontier must, for purposes of identity, remain opened, and if football is a symbolic and ritualized medium through which the idealized virtues of the untamed frontier may be reaffirmed (if not revitalized), then disclosures and humiliations about Oklahoma collegiate football undermine the availability of that positive self-image to provide self-respect, cohesiveness, equanimity, and the management of aggression.

Oklahoma Psychogeography

Psychogeography refers to the fact that people represent and play out their fantasies and conflicts in the physical and social worlds. These perceptions and acts often have their roots in childhood developmental processes (Stein 1987*b*; Stein and Niederland 1989). We often express who we are in terms of where we are. As contributors to this book have repeatedly shown, that sense of whereness is never pure geography but is built from a visual identity and a confluence from the other senses into a whole of what Oklahoma ought to look, sound, taste, and feel like (see especially A. Henderson and Bellmon, this volume).

In the Oklahoma visual identity, several identity maps culturally situate Oklahoma both regionally and nationally. One vital dichotomy is that of center versus periphery, heartland versus coast, local versus cosmopolitan; its moral-religious equivalents of "God's country" versus "the Devil's country" (see Fig. 11.5); and the clash between rural and urban, small-

Fig. 11.5. Jesus and the Devil. (Reprinted with permission of *Oklahoma Today* magazine.)

town and metropolitan. Moreover, the secure, protective flatness of God's country enables one to see "clear to the horizon," to notice and be prepared to fend off any encroachments to one's freedom. To be in the middle is likewise to avoid any extremes (meaning radicalism). It is to be conventional, to not make waves, to not stand out from the crowd. Another psychogeographic point is that while Texas, Kansas, and Oklahoma were all deeply affected by the Dust Bowl, only Oklahoma and Oklahomans bear the stigma of its image.

In relation to other states and regions, Oklahomans speak in terms of "up" to Kansas and Nebraska, "down" to Texas, "back East" (this elastic term denotes shared origins and the past, e.g., east of Oklahoma, east of the Mississippi, Atlantic coast states of the U.S.A.), and "out West" to Arizona and California. In Oklahoma football rivalries, that between OU and Texas is the most vicious and unforgiving. It is in part heir to the image of Texas, the neighbor to the south, as "boastful, big, arrogant," and associated with the Old South, in contrast with Oklahoman virtues of "humility," relative smallness, and "modesty."

The symbolism of the sky, and of its counterpart, the land, plays a central role in Oklahoma psychogeography. To Oklahomans, the sky assumes simultaneously theological or metaphysical, meteorological, and political as well as economic proportions. Oklahomans praise the uninterrupted Oklahoma sky—product of the coincidence of geological formation, geographical location, and weather patternings (see Thompson, this volume)—for its horizon-to-horizon enormity, its visual symbolism of fenceless freedom. They curse the same sky for its crop-, livestock-, property-, and human life–destroying severe spring thunderstorms and tornados and only slightly less for the menace of winter ice storms. For self-made men and women, fatalism and superstition in the face of weather's caprice (or is it God's predestination or judgment?) is an island of resignation in a sea of proud self-control and mastery over nature. If a hail storm devastates or destroys one family's wheat crop but entirely misses a neighbor's fields, the former will see in it a sign of divine anger and punishment and search their conscience for their sin, while the latter will see in it a sign of divine mercy and a mark that they have won divine favor for the way they live. Many Oklahomans do not passively wait for the sky to strike or to pass over them. Rather, the arrival of a tornado or of ice-glazed roads becomes an opportunity for high risk–taking, from trying to outrun a tornado in one's car or pickup truck to driving one's motor vehicle at high speed on ice, daring a stop or curve (or a fellow motorist) to interpose itself upon the human will.

Weather has its many uses for Oklahoma symbol and ritual among Oklahomans and those outside Oklahoma. The driving, usually hot southern wind is an almost animistic presence, a personalized and personified force of nature. It is also a measure of a man's or woman's mettle. If one looks too prettified, too little wind-swept, then one cannot be the genuine-article Oklahoman. When wind and sky and sun are at their best, at peace with the earth, the Oklahoma great dome of the sky is the unsurpassed symbol of freedom for the white man, complementing the red earth, the farmer's beloved dirt; together they confer a sense of home and protectedness to those who measure life by the virtues of frontier isolationism (see Bellmon, this volume). A single symbol never captures the essence of an entire culture, but to fathom the meaning of the sky to Oklahomans—and the meaning that sky has for non-Oklahomans who imagine it to be their American Eden— is to penetrate to the core of the cultural identity system of white Oklahoma.

Nothing better condenses and celebrates the local and the national image of prairie optimism than the lyrics and music of Hammerstein and Rodgers's musical play *Oklahoma!*

Oklahoma! ran on Broadway from its opening in March 1943 through May 29, 1948; the movie version, starring Gordon MacRae and Shirley Jones, was released in October 1955. In both cases, but especially in the context of World War II, the sentiment surrounding *Oklahoma!* rode on the crest of American patriotism if not exuberant nationalism. At that time Oklahomaness reflected and focused the national self-image. Yet, even here, we should not take official images altogether at face value. For the proud, robust aliveness of *Oklahoma!* is also antipodal—one might almost say a cultural antidote—to the dreariness, the deadness, and the shame conjured by the indelible image of the Dust Bowl.

Sky, land, weather, dirt—these are each elements in a vast, encompassing man/nature dichotomy that is not only Oklahoman, but also a dominant characteristic of western civilization and the folklore of the North American West. This dichotomy is a far more self-conscious chasm in Oklahoma culture than elsewhere, where it is more implicit. Pioneer white men and women sought to conquer and domesticate, to dominate nature, not to live subjugated by or in harmony with nature. This ambition to control often flies in the face of constant reminders by nature of how little control human beings in fact do exercise. Seeing themselves ideally as above nature—not only occupationally but religiously as well—they find instead how often they are at nature's mercy. Sky, land, weather, dirt—these implacable presences can foster the quest for freedom, but more often, they oppress instead.

People everywhere conform landscapes—natural ones and those fashioned by human activity—to the imagination. That, in fact, is what psychogeography and ethnogeography are about (Stein 1987*b*, Stein and Niederland 1989). In a passage from *Funny Money,* an account of the 1982 failure of Penn Square Bank in Oklahoma City, Mark Singer (1985) shows a fine flair for the symbolism of oil wells and derricks in the once flourishing Oklahoma City Oil Field:

The entire Oklahoma City Field—comprising about two hundred active wells—currently produces less than twenty-five hundred barrels a day. Surveying the landscape now, you would hardly assume that production had been declining for such a long stretch and had reached such a low level. In the Oklahoma City suburbs, where there are two taco joints for every tree, you see wellheads surrounded by high fences in undeveloped residential zones, you see pumping units in strip-shopping-center parking lots. Four-story derricks straddle the wells on the grounds of the state capitol and the governor's mansion, and it matters very little that so many of the wells are just barely oozing crude—that the derricks' main function is to provide a remembrance of things past. Appearances count. Mythology counts. (1985, 9–10)

Although government agencies rarely use images such as these to "market" the state in official promotional efforts—the pastoral and the western are far more common—the ubiquity of these images in the Oklahoma City and, more widely, state landscape is a testament to the emotional as well as economic importance of that crude "black gold" sought thousands of feet beneath the red, iron-rich Oklahoma dirt. The dialectic of wetness and dryness, of luxuriant boom and spartan bust, whether in the form of water or petroleum (or natural gas), is a recurrent theme in Oklahoma psychogeography (see N. Henderson and Nuckolls, this volume). Irrespective of the material focus, wetness and dryness symbolize the presence or absence of nurturance or sustenance and the never-ending cultural battle between aliveness and deadness, between unbridled hope and the dread of hopelessness.

The Constant Re-creation of Oklahoma Culture

In this section we note the paradoxical process by which a traditional Oklahoma image and identity are created and continuously revised out of contemporary needs and perceptions (see Handler and Linnekin 1984). Although in one respect the cowboy-western image of Oklahoma has been a "timeless" constant since the land runs of 1889, 1891, 1892, 1893, and 1895, in another respect that cowboy image is less purely native and static than the object of an attempt to revitalize an identity that many fear might be lost to urbanization and industrialization. People cannot count upon cowboy and western virtues and images to perpetuate themselves effortlessly. They must, rather, be renewed. They are in fact created out of present needs, not merely passed on from generation to generation. Like the Afro hair style and dashikis among many African Americans in the late 1960s and 1970s, the cowboy image among many Oklahomans can be seen as in part a contemporary nativistic movement whose participants seek to return to a past they are in fact inventing (see Linton 1943; Wallace 1956; La Barre 1972).

In *The Ethnic Imperative* (Stein and Hill 1977a) we distinguished between "behavioral ethnicity" and "ideological ethnicity." The former is a relative unself-conscious being and living in one's culture. The latter is an often painful self-consciousness of who one is in comparison with others who always seem to have a higher status than oneself and one's own group. Ideological ethnicity is the hallmark of groups haunted by constant comparison of themselves with others, what De Vos calls "status anxiety" (1966; see also Stein 1987a). As has been the history of ethnic, religious, and nationalistic movements throughout history and throughout the cross-cultural record (Group for the Advancement of Psychiatry, Committee on International Relations, and Stein 1987), groups recoil from bitter feelings of inferiority by re-creating, reimagining, their own culture into a badge of pride. People elevate symbols of inadequacy into symbols of superiority and potency.

Against a century of minority status, discrimination, segregation, and a struggle for a voice in their own state, Oklahoma African Americans can turn to a far sunnier origin myth: that E. P. McCabe had wanted an all-black state created from Oklahoma Territory and helped to establish over twenty-five all-black towns. Creating and embracing a distinct African-American identity is another way many blacks have dealt with Oklahoman and American status conflict. Native Americans, for their part, often turn to the Trail of Tears for a source of historical grievance and entitlement in the present. Many with even a small percentage of Indian blood attempt to turn minority status and invisibility, if not ostracism from the white mainstream, to economic and political advantage to obtain various social benefits from white society. Groups unable to count on the privileged status of one-upmanship try to trade both consciously and unconsciously in one-downmanship, relying upon the guilt, shame, and perhaps some noblesse oblige in their counterparts. In all cases, Oklahomans of various ethnic and religious and racial constituent groups, and Oklahomans as a group themselves, constantly experience status anxiety and constantly renegotiate their cultural selves. They redefine them over time, using ideology as a way of attempting to correct painful discrepancy between social status they wish or expect and their perception of what and who they are.

For all human groups, historian Leopold von Ranke's objectivist sense of history (*wie es eigentlich gewesen* ["as it exactly happened"], a factuality difficult if not impossible to determine) blurs into historical perception based on psychological uses in the present. Much of what we call history serves a mythological or ideological function of creating a usable past which we experience as having created us. Just as land openings play an important role in the ongoing white and far more national sense of Oklahomaness, likewise, forced migration of the Five Civilized Tribes (Cherokee, Creek [Muskogee], Choctaw, Chickasaw, and Seminole) plays an important role in the continuously re-created sense of place not only for Native Americans but for all other Oklahomans as well. Just as the dichotomy wet/dry conspicuously pervades Oklahomaness, the upbeat imagery of the land openings have as their counterpart the defeat and ignominy of the Trail of Tears. While superficially each of these belongs to a different group (white or Indian), the group sense of Oklahomaness brings them into anxious association. We can put this in something of a formula: the Run of '89 is to the Trail of Tears as wet is to dry, as lush green landscapes are to the Dust Bowl. If this formula is a century old, it is also continuously revalidated, updated, and revised as part of the contemporary drama of status and identity.

The western cowboy image of Oklahoma (fused with the football image of ruggedness and aggressiveness) is frequently more a mark of cultural discontinuity (in its nativistic aspect) than it is one of cultural continuity (in its century-old cultural aspect) (see Sisk 1987). The current image is an amalgam of the old cowboy and the new cowboy. The horse has been supplemented if not supplanted by the ubiquitous pickup truck, a vehicle which many people now value at least as much for its statement of style and identity as for its instrumental functions. As an independent, rebellious cultural type, Henry Fonda in the 1940 film *The Grapes of Wrath* wore a fulsome "duck bill hat." Oklahoma farmers of the Dust Bowl era wore mostly weather-beaten rimmed hats and duck bills, distinctive from today's baseball caps. Boots of that era, too, were functional rather than emblematic. The currently fashionable western look of cowboy hat, snakeskin hatband, leather belt with large decorative buckle, and often exotic-skinned cowboy boots dates from three decades later. The era of the election and two-term presidency of Ronald Reagan was one in which cowboy virtues were nationally embodied and extolled by the leader. Far from being backward Okies (a term, sometimes derisive, at which many Oklahomans wince), Oklahomans could now proudly claim to be at the vanguard of the national ethos of individualism, nationalism, militarism, and the restoration of manliness.

Still, Oklahomans continued to be hounded by reminders of their ascribed status of intrinsic inferiority. For example, when in the early 1980s Stein attended a medical conference in New York City, several physicians greeted him with virtually the same question: "Are you still in Oklahoma?" Others wondered and asked him why he would want to be in or stay in Oklahoma. At those moments he felt the emotions that many native-born Oklahomans (he was born in western Pennsylvania) have felt, as if there was something intrinsically wrong with himself (with being Oklahoman), that whatever he achieved, he was still held suspect because of his association with Oklahoma. The stigmatized ascribed status influenced not only what could be achieved, but also the perception and evaluation of the achievement itself (that is, if it is Oklahoman, it cannot be very good). As the *New York Times* story discussed earlier (Reinhold 1986) attests, in the national group fantasy Oklahoma's economic woes of the 1980s merge with the Dust Bowl of the 1930s. If Oklahomans are stuck in their psychohistory, one large part of it is that many in the national cultural system continue to impose that frozenness in time upon Oklahoma.

Many Oklahomans today speak of the state having an "inferiority complex," one that is at least partly cultivated by comparisons Oklahomans make with others, a self-image that interacts with outsiders' evaluations of Oklahoma. The cowboy image, together with such expressions as advertisement of vacations on dude ranches, and the enlargement of Native American displays and festivals (such as the annual Red Earth in Oklahoma City), constitute an intensification and elaboration of the western cowboy aspects of Oklahoma culture. In effect, Oklahomans dramatically change the core of that ethos and then retrospectively say that Oklahoma has been changelessly cowboy all along.

In Hill's survey, members of the Economic Development Task Force chose "western heritage" as the cultural feature which they "feel the best about" more than twice as often (46.3 percent) as did educators (21.5 percent) or church members (20.2 percent; $p < .002$). "Cowboy" (together with its associated images) now becomes an Oklahoman ideological statement of superiority over those with whom Oklahomans have compared themselves and felt inferior. The sense of alienation from mainstream culture, together with a fear of mainstream culture, precipitated an identity crisis which found resolution in Oklahoman nativism. The western cowboy ethos is at once an ideological solution to internal Oklahoman problems and to national group dynamics in which Oklahoma occupies a role, fantasy, and identity in the life of the nation. Such constriction of identity suggests a narrow future in which the state's own image and identity coincide with and internalize the outside image and identity to which it is, in a grim sense, condemned. Consider, for example, the meteoric rise to success of country-and-western singer Garth Brooks, an Oklahoman from Yukon, whose *Ropin' the Wind* is, at the time of this writing, the top-selling album in the nation. Applied social scientists and humanists alike would do well to consider how the intergroup reciprocity of images which we have identified in this chapter leads to a role rigidity difficult to alter or to transcend.

The Symbolic Ambiguity and Marginality of Industry and Higher Education

Ironically, as much as gas and oil contribute to Oklahoma's economy, they are rarely featured as components of Oklahoma's image. It is as if there has long been a disparity between the economic and social realities of Oklahoma and the official self-portrait that agencies offer. *Oklahoma Today*, for example, has for years featured vivid cover pictures with cover stories on Native Americans, verdant landscapes, Southern-heritage azaleas, traditional cowboys, and modern football, yet only four covers on oil and gas have appeared in thirty years. The industrial image is treated as a blatant affront to the idyllic view. Modern industry, it would appear, has no place in what many people insist Oklahoma ought to be and how it ought to be kept.

There is something reassuringly predictable, cyclical, and eternal about the annual round of cattle and wheat. The world of gas and oil and other industries, on the other hand, seems dramatically disruptive and unsettling. Consequently, many planners and image makers consider it unthinkable, and in poor taste, in Oklahoma culture to feature a General Motors automobile assembly plant or a U.S. Air Force base on the cover of *Oklahoma Today*. These facilities provide thousands of jobs, but Oklahomans turn to other images to represent their identity as a state. The situation is the same with higher education. Oklahoma is blessed with more than forty colleges and universities that provide opportunities and jobs for thousands, yet Oklahomans do not think of the various campuses as visual trademarks. Seats of higher learning do not occupy the core of Oklahomaness to merit being portrayed to the world. Education, like the gas and oil industry, no doubt means change. It threatens the comforting sameness of Oklahoma's traditional images. Although "poor, underfunded education" was the most frequently chosen feature of the state which Oklahomans feel "worst" about (see Fig. 11.1, above), adequate funding, long recommended reforms, and a more progressive approach to the distribution of education resources seem as difficult to accomplish now as ever. This remains true despite recent state legislation that provides increased funding for common (public) schools.

The Future?

In every society, disparity exists between what people actually do and what they say they do, between their espoused ideals or beliefs and those that govern much behavior (Devereux 1967; Spiegel 1971). This observation applies to a group's collective identity as much as to other dimensions of culture. Oklahomans are not different from other groups. Problems arise when a group, out of fear, clings to old images and makes adaptation to change difficult. Oklahomans may, for example, wish to uphold and perpetuate a pastoral self-image at all costs. Even today, when confronted with the fact that considerable economic diversity already exists (see Fig. 11.6), many Oklahomans still insist that Oklahoma is mostly, and ought to remain, a rural cattle and wheat state (Troy 1989). Nonetheless, a cultural denial of reality not only distorts reality but also can ultimately undermine it in a self-fulfilling prophecy.

What kind of image might best fit Oklahoma's state identity in the future? What might that image mean and how might it feel? Mere opportunistic image-making will not do. The question is deeper than one of finding the best ad agency and marketing a new logo. Genuine renewal comes from the inner spaces. Oklahoma needs a sense of being at home at the core, which is not equivalent to receiving a coat of glossy veneer that may quickly wear away and leave Oklahomans vulnerable to exploitation (boom and bust once again). An identity that bridges the past and integrates it with the present and future would help Oklahomans feel more confident and whole. Aviation is one promising candidate.

An identity that is secure is one that is not in constant need of shoring up against its opposite. Oklahomaness has been plagued for a century by "either/or" dualities (wet/dry, rural/urban, boom/bust). Oklahomans have alternately tried to live down the degrading Okie stereotype or have raised it into a badge of honor. Dare Oklahomans, and outsiders as well, imagine an integration and celebration of "both-and" rather than perpetuate their cherished compartmentalizations? Might not Oklahomans freely choose for their identity positively valued features of their culture rather than make cultural choices out of reaction against being haunted by more negative features or out of a sense of being condemned to be Oklahoman? Can Oklahomans let go of and mourn the past—the Depression, the Dust Bowl—rather than obligate each next generation in the name of family and group loyalty to enshrine and perpetuate myth as compelling reality? Can Oklahomans bear the guilt of separating from this past and then in turn relinquish the shackling guilt as well (see Modell 1984)?

Further, people often try to obtain everything in their identity from a single type of group or category, say, ethnic, re-

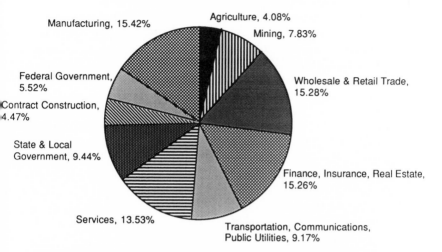

Fig. 11.6. Oklahoma Gross State Product by Sector, 1989. (Source: Oklahoma Department of Commerce, September 1989 [see Troy 1989].)

ligious, or occupational or a group based on sex or age or the like. "Oklahomaness," too, can be a straitjacket of identity. Perhaps that is why many Oklahomans place such high stakes on keeping Oklahoma's identity from changing. Any identity becomes a kind of indomitable fortress when its members have narrowed their range of group affiliations and meanings so much. Oklahomaness could become more expansive, more inclusive, the more people identify with several, if not multiple, cultural systems. Finally, the more familiar people become with the forces that shaped their own childhoods and early families of origin, the better they will understand, and attain a degree of liberation from, the powerful sources of meaning and feeling invested in Oklahoma symbolism. With that increased awareness will also come the greater freedom to choose their cultural future. One cannot transcend an identity one does not first profoundly know.

In seeking to know more about his own identity as Oklahoman, for example, one of the authors (Hill) learned that both his grandfathers were pioneer immigrants to Oklahoma from Kansas. Both were farmers, attracted no doubt by the mythos of free land described so well in the chapter by Lamar. Neither grandfather got free land, of course. Myth is not the same as reality. But by the early 1900s both the families of Fred Hill and Fred Zipse had established homesteads in Oklahoma several years before it became a state. In Fig. 11.7, Hill's grandfather Zipse is shown in the upper right hand corner, surrounded by all his valued worldly possessions: farmhouse, four children, wagon, five horses, two mules, and a cow. In Fig. 11.8, the same family is shown fifteen years later, shortly after oil was discovered on their farm. The children now number seven. They are shown in the foreground left and left center flanking their pioneer mother and father. The two mules, brought from Kansas almost twenty years earlier, were still an important, if somewhat symbolic, part of the new material configuration.

Already accorded a place of honor within Oklahomans' repertory, the image of the pioneer may still have some life to it. A pioneer pursues ideas and opportunity yet is never a mere opportunist. In the past a pioneer might have traveled long distances over difficult terrain. Today, a pioneer moves less across the prairie geographically, but creatively encompasses great spans of mental space. A genuine pioneer is at once both exuberant and practical, idealist and realist. He or she never loses sight of inner goals and thus keeps working diligently towards their realization. Finally, a pioneer reveres certain aspects of the past and learns from the past, but is not shackled to it. Undaunted, he or she is able to leave the past to embrace an unknown future created together with contemporaries. The crucial issue is whether Oklahomans can resolve and transcend their cultural contradictions and ambivalences identified throughout these chapters or whether the future will be sealed to repeat the past and the pioneer will remain a lofty, unreachable, forbidden ideal.

Cultural images are never merely images. They carry the emotional and cognitive freight of identity, of obligation, of destiny. The issue of how Oklahomans think of themselves, of how others think of Oklahoma, and of the interplay between

Fig. 11.7. The Zipse family on their leased farm near Walters in southwestern Oklahoma, 1906. (Family-purchased photograph; frontier photographer unknown.)

Fig. 11.8. The Zipse family on their deeded farm near Walters in southwestern Oklahoma, March 10, 1919. (Family-purchased photograph; frontier photographer unknown.)

these is neither idle nor academic. It affects who and what Oklahomans are and become. It is our hope, as authors of this concluding chapter and as editors of this volume, that this book will help Oklahomans and non-Oklahomans to become more consciously aware of the tugs and currents of symbols that affect the state's image.

A single book cannot address everything present in a culture. It is a widely shared illusion that a lifelong study of any culture could result in a complete ethnographic account, for alas, cultures—which are, after all, people—change. On the other hand, a good cultural account identifies key themes and patterns that subsume the bottomless well of cultural data. This book, for example, does not have an individual chapter devoted exclusively to religion in Oklahoma. Yet the reader can easily discern how religion pervades Oklahomaness. Similarly, Native American history and race (black, white, and red) are interwoven throughout this book as well as being featured in chapters by Hill and colleagues and by Smallwood and Phillips.

The proof of Oklahomaness, in fact, lies in how scholars and writers of widely diverse backgrounds and interests independently state and reiterate overlapping cultural nodal points throughout this book. Precisely because religion, Indians, and race loom so large culturally, no matter where an account might start, it *must* end up encompassing them. These topics, or other cultural focal points, do not require separate chapters in order to be acknowledged as vital. At the same time, other facets of Native American life have long been hidden from the Oklahoma self-image and deserve to be more closely explored, and the process of Native Americans' exclusion and anonymity needs to be better understood.

Donald N. Brown's contribution has illustrated the range of ethnic or national diversity in Oklahoma (see *Newcomers to a New Land* 1980). The future holds great promise for the study of the interplay between ethnonational or religious groups in Oklahoma and Oklahomaness which these groups have in fact helped to create. Many colleagues, some Oklahomans, have noted to us that there are in fact "states within the state of Oklahoma." For example, Little Dixie in the southeastern corner, the Short-grass Country of the southwest, the Wheat Belt in the northwest, the Urban Corridor from Tulsa through Oklahoma City, and so forth. Certainly the rural/ urban distinction, together with the increased absorption of rural areas by cities, is an essential feature of the cultural map of Oklahoma. Future studies will reveal the complex cultural counterpoint between these sometimes overlapping, sometimes competing, sometimes compartmentalized identities within the state of Oklahoma.

We hope that this book will spawn a revitalization in studies of cultures as identity systems. Such studies should consist not only of tribes, ethnic groups, and nation-states—the traditional units of sociologists, historians and anthropologists—but of other states within the United States and of more regional and local cultural systems within other nations as well. Oklahomans, after all, are a variant on the theme of being human. If the model offered by this book is valid for the study of Oklahoma, it holds the promise of being generalizable to the study of cultural identity systems anywhere.

Notes

1. Those features not shown had a mean selection percentage total (x) which was equal to or less than one-fifth of the total sample. Probability $(p <)$ values shown under each feature in the figures represent the mathematical likelihood that the observed values occurred by chance. Thus, in the first feature of Fig. 11.1, "friendly people," it can be seen that 90.2 percent of the Leadership Oklahoma group chose this feature, compared to 71.2 percent of the student group. The p value $< .004$ means that if other members of these same two groups were surveyed under like conditions, the likelihood of different percentages resulting is less than four in a thousand. A p value of .050 or less is often chosen for designation as statistically significant.

2. Summarizing additional differences: Young respondents (under age twenty-five) were significantly less likely than those over twenty-five, to choose among their best features "Christian values," "scenic lakes and rivers," and "accessible education." They were significantly more likely to choose "religious fanaticism," and "flat, dry, dull landscape" for their worst features. Religious fundamentalists on the other hand, were much more likely than their counterparts to choose "Christian values," "Oklahoma football," and "football crazy" and much less likely to choose "reli-

gious fanaticism" and "western heritage" on both the positive and negative dimensions. Similarly, males were significantly more likely than females to choose "Oklahoma football," "flat, dry, dull land," "boom-and-bust mentality," and "underdeveloped country"; they were less likely than females to choose "football crazy," or "accessible education." Furthermore, Oklahoma natives were significantly more likely than nonnatives to choose "friendly people," "accessible education," "scenic lakes . . . ," and "cowboys-and-Indians mentality" and less likely to choose "western heritage," "Native-American art and culture," "flat, dry, dull land," and "violent extreme weather." Full-time employees were much more likely than others to choose "scenic lakes," "accessible education," "boom-and-bust mentality," and "Dust Bowl history" and much less likely to choose "Christian values," "Oklahoma football," "football crazy," or "flat, dry, dull land." Finally, Republicans were significantly more likely than Democrats or Independents to choose "Christian values," and less likely than Democrats or Independents to choose "accessible education."

Contributors

PAT BELLMON, a free-lance writer, graduated from Oklahoma State University in 1970 and worked for eleven years as a reporter and feature writer for the *Washington Star*. She is the daughter of former governor and U.S. senator Henry Bellmon. In 1981 she returned to her hometown of Billings, a wheat and cattle farming community in north central Oklahoma, and has remained on the family farm. Her current book about the day-to-day life of three farm families is under review for publication. Her five-part series about the contemporary condition of the family farm and its future appeared in the *Tulsa Tribune* in December 1986. In April 1987 she wrote an extensive article for the *Tulsa Tribune* on Oklahoma's psyche.

DONALD NELSON BROWN is professor of anthropology in the Department of Sociology at Oklahoma State University in Stillwater. He completed his bachelor's degree at Harvard and graduate degrees at the University of Arizona. Two of the principal themes which characterize his distinguished academic career, through publication and applied projects, are Native American ethnomusicology and ethnic groups in Oklahoma. He has recently coproduced three television programs for public television which reflect these interests. All first-person quotes in this chapter are from tape-recorded interviews by the author that were collected during the Crossroads Oklahoma Project in 1980–81.

J. DENNIS FORTENBERRY, a behavioral epidemiologist, is a physician with specialty board certification in internal medicine. He graduated from high school in Yukon, Oklahoma, and from the University of Oklahoma he earned degrees in medicine and public health. He is currently an associate professor of pediatrics and medicine at the University of Oklahoma Health Sciences Center and the head of the Adolescent Medicine Program at Children's Hospital of Oklahoma in Oklahoma City. He has written numerous published articles on a variety of adolescent medicine topics and was recently awarded a five-year Physician-Scientist Research Award from the National Institutes of Health, Washington, D.C.

FRED R. HARRIS is a former U.S. Senator and a widely published author and has been a distinguished member of the political science faculty at the University of New Mexico since 1976. Designated an "Eminent Scholar" by the New Mexico Commission on Higher Education, Harris has produced thirteen books, including *The New Populism*. In 1988 he cochaired (with Roger W. Wilkins) the 1988 Commission on the Cities and is coeditor with Wilkins of *Quiet Riots: Race and Poverty in the United States*.

A Phi Beta Kappa graduate in political science of the University of Oklahoma, Harris holds a J.D. degree "with distinction" from the same institution. He has been a Fulbright Scholar for research and study in Mexico (1981) and a Distinguished Fulbright Lecturer in Uruguay (1989). In 1986 he taught in a London Semester Program and lectured at Oxford University.

Harris was a member of the U.S. Senate from Oklahoma (D., 1964–73); a member of the President's National Advisory Commission on Civil Disorders, the Kerner Commission (1967–68); chair of the Democratic National Committee (1969–70); cochair (with John V. Lindsay) of the National Urban Coalition's Commission on the Cities in the 1970s; and an unsuccessful 1976 candidate for his party's presidential nomination. As a result of a recently completed study of the U.S. Senate for the Twentieth Century Fund, his new book, *The Nationalization of the United States Senate*, will be published soon by Oxford University Press.

ARN HENDERSON, professor of architecture at the University of Oklahoma, is a native Oklahoman. He did his undergraduate work at the University of Oklahoma and completed his graduate studies at Columbia University. During the past decade he has worked extensively in historic preservation and the history of Oklahoma architecture. Most recently his research has focused on folk and vernacular buildings in the rural landscape of the southern plains. Professor Henderson also maintains an architectural practice and has received design awards from the Oklahoma Chapter of the American Institute of Architects. In 1992 he received the Shirk Memorial Award for historic preservation from the Oklahoma Historical Society.

J. NEIL HENDERSON is assistant professor in psychiatry at the University of South Florida Health Sciences Center; project coordinator of the U.S.F. Geriatric Education Center, which is funded by the Bureau of Health Professions; and coordinator for the Division of Education and Training at the U.S.F. Suncoast Gerontology Center since 1982. Dr. Henderson, who is a native Oklahoman, earned his Ph.D. at the University of Florida in 1979 in the field of medical anthropology. Dr. Henderson became a member of the faculty at East Central Oklahoma State University for four years. He has conducted research and published on issues related to aging and long-term care, Alzheimer's disease, institutionalization, dementia-specific care units in nursing homes, and Alzheimer's disease support groups in ethnic populations.

ROBERT F. HILL is associate professor of pediatrics, College of Medicine, University of Oklahoma Health Sciences Center, and former administrative director of the Adolescent Medicine Program for the Department of Pediatrics and the Children's Hospital of Oklahoma. He currently teaches in the University of Oklahoma's Liberal Studies, Child Abuse Prevention, and Public Health programs. Since completing his doctoral studies in anthropology at the University of Pittsburgh in 1972, and subsequently taking a faculty position at the University of Oklahoma, Dr. Hill has written two books and more than thirty scholarly articles on a variety of topics in social science and medicine. He has also been the recipient of numerous national and local awards and grants.

HOWARD ROBERTS LAMAR, Sterling Professor of History at Yale University, has long specialized in the history of the American West and in comparative frontier history. Former chairman of the Department of History and dean of Yale College, Professor Lamar has written numerous papers and books and has edited many volumes on the West, among them *The Far Southwest, 1846–1912* (1966), *The Reader's Encyclopedia of the American West* (1977), and *The Frontier in History: North America and Southern Africa Compared* (1981), with Leonard Thompson, coeditor.

CHARLES W. NUCKOLLS, a cultural anthropologist, is currently assistant professor in the Department of Anthropology at Emory University in Atlanta, Georgia. He received his Ph.D. in 1987 from the University of Chicago. Author of articles on South Asia and ethnopsychiatric systems, he was a recipient of the 1989 Stirling Award for Contributions to Psychological Anthropology.

CRISPIN A. PHILLIPS, a native of Massachusetts, an honor roll student, received his B.A. degree, with a double major in history and political science, from Dillard University in New Orleans.

JAMES M. SMALLWOOD, professor of history at Oklahoma State University, was born and raised in Terrell, Texas. He received his Ph.D. in 1974 from Texas Tech University in Lubbock, having major fields in Southern and black history; at Oklahoma State he has also developed offerings in Oklahoma history. Author of nine books and approximately forty journal articles, Smallwood won the Texas State Historical Association's 1982 Coral H. Tullis Award for best book of the year on Texas history: *Time of Hope, Time of Despair: Black Texans during Reconstruction* (1981). His books on Oklahoma history, all published by the University of Oklahoma Press, include *And Gladly Teach: Reminiscences of Teachers from Frontier Dugout to Modern Module* (1976); *Urban Builder: The Life and Times of Stanley Draper* (1977); and *An Oklahoma Adventure: Of Banks and Bankers* (1979). In the late 1970s and early 1980s he edited ten books on Oklahoma's "favorite son," Will Rogers.

GLENN W. SOLOMON, a public health specialist, recently completed his doctorate in public health and human ecology from the University of Oklahoma. He was most recently the American Indian affairs counselor for the university's College of Allied Health. He is a member of the Cherokee Nation of Oklahoma. His family allotment in the tribal town of Ochelata, Oklahoma, dates back to the Dawes Commission. He has worked in local, tribal, and national American Indian organizations for more than twenty years and has spent most of his professional life in Indian education at the college and university level. He is currently nearing completion of a scholarly biographical study of Carlos Montezuma, the first American Indian physician.

HOWARD F. STEIN, professor of family medicine at the University of Oklahoma Health Sciences Center in Oklahoma City, is a medical anthropologist, psychoanalytic anthropologist, and psychohistorian. Dr. Stein directs behavioral science teaching at the Enid Family Medicine Clinic, a community-based residency program in northwest Oklahoma. He received his Ph.D. from the University of Pittsburgh in 1972. From 1980 to 1988 he edited *The Journal of Psychoanalytic Anthropology.* Author of 150 scholarly and clinical papers, his twelve books include: *Developmental Time, Cultural Space* (1987) and *Maps from the Mind* (1989, coedited with William G. Niederland), published by the University of Oklahoma Press. He is 1992 recipient of the Donald J. Blair Friend of Medicine Award from the Oklahoma State Medical Association.

GARY L. THOMPSON, associate professor in the Department of Geography at the University of Oklahoma, has maintained an interest in the human geography of the southern plains for many years. His work on this region includes articles on the wheat harvest, patterns of rural poverty, the economic structure of small towns, and transportation systems. He has most recently coedited a monograph entitled *Oklahoma Resource Book* which is presently under review for publication. Another monograph, *Law and Geography*, is in final stages of manuscript preparation.

JANE K. TIGER is a special instructor with the Oklahoma University College of Public Health and the associate director of the Graduate Program in Public Health for American Indians. She attended high school at Chilaco Indian School in Chilaco, Oklahoma, and completed her B.S. degree at Northeastern State University in Tahlequah, Oklahoma, in 1985 and her master of public health in health education degree at the University of Oklahoma in 1988. Her American Indian ancestry is Cheyenne and Arapaho.

BERRY WAYNE TRAMEL, assistant sports editor of the *Norman Transcript* since 1978, was born and reared in Norman, Oklahoma. He has reported on all the major sporting events in Oklahoma, including those at the University of Oklahoma. He is currently a student of English and history at the University of Oklahoma.

References

Abel, Annie H. 1915. *The American Indian as Slaveholder and Secessionist.* Cleveland, Ohio: Arthur H. Clark.

Aldrich, Gene. 1973. *Black Heritage of Oklahoma.* Edmond, Okla.: Thompson Book & Supply Co.

American Academy of Pediatrics. 1988. "Position Statement: The Impact of Rock Lyrics and Music Videos on Children and Youth." *AAP News,* November: 5.

Andriot, J. L., ed. 1983. *Population Abstract of the United States,* vol. 1. McLean, Va.: Andriot Associates.

Aro, S., and J. Hasan. 1987. "Occupational Class, Psychosocial Stress and Morbidity." *Annals of Clinical Research* 19:62–68.

Barnard, Evan G. 1936. *A Rider of the Cherokee Strip.* Boston: Houghton Mifflin.

Barnes, Grace M., and John W. Welte. 1986. "Patterns and Predictors of Alcohol Use among 7–12th Grade Students in New York State." *Journal of Studies on Alcohol* 47(1):53–62.

Baum, Laura E. 1940. "Agriculture and the Five Civilized Tribes." M.A. thesis, University of Oklahoma, Norman.

Baumrind, Diana. 1987. "A Developmental Perspective on Adolescent Risk Taking in Contemporary America." In C. Irwin, ed., *Adolescent Social Behavior and Health,* pp. 93–125. San Francisco, Calif.: Jossey-Bass.

Bellah, Robert N., et al. 1985. *Habits of the Heart: Individualism and Commitment in American Life.* Berkeley: University of California Press.

Berger, Peter, and Thomas Luckmann. 1966. *The Social Construc-*

tion of Reality: A Treatise in the Sociology of Knowledge. New York: Doubleday.

Bibb, Tollie Marion. 1985. "A Study of the Presidential Role in University Athletics of the Big Eight Athletic Conference." M.S. thesis, University of Oklahoma, Norman.

Bittle, William, and Gilbert Geis. 1964. *The Longest Way Home: Chief Alfred Sam's Back-to-Africa Movement.* Detroit: Wayne State University Press.

Black Dispatch (Oklahoma City). 1938. December 17.

———. 1960. January 27, August 5, October 21, and November 18.

———. 1963. July 5.

———. 1964. July 17 and November 6 and 20.

———. 1970*a*. April 2 and 16.

———. 1970*b*. July 16.

Blake, William. 1979. Quoted in *The Oxford Dictionary of Quotations,* 3rd ed., p. 86. New York: Oxford University Press.

Boeger, Palmer H. 1987. *Oklahoma Oasis: From Platt National Park to Chickasaw National Recreation Area.* Muskogee, Okla.: Western Heritage Books.

Bolton, Herbert E. 1921. *The Spanish Borderlands: A Chronicle of Old Florida and the Southwest.* New Haven: Yale University Press.

Boulton, Scot W. 1980. "Desegregation of the Oklahoma City School System." *Chronicles of Oklahoma* 57:192–220.

Brown, Donald N. 1981. *The Vietnamese-American Experience in Oklahoma.* Stillwater, Okla.: Crossroads Oklahoma Project.

Brown, Loren N. 1937. "The Work of the Dawes Commission among Choctaw and Chickasaw Indians." Ph.D. diss. University of Oklahoma, Norman.

Buchanan, James S., and Edward E. Dale. 1924. *A History of Oklahoma.* Evanston, Ill.: Row Peterson.

Burns, A. 1978. "Cargo Cult in a Western Town: A Cultural Approach to Episodic Change." *Rural Sociology* 43(2):164–77.

Burright, Orrin U. 1973. *The Sun Rides High.* Ed. Ora B. Burright. Wichita Falls and Quanah, Tex.: Nortex Publications. Excerpts in *Cimarron Valley Historical Society Journal* 1 (January 1973).

Calhoun, Ed. 1987. Interview by Pat Lewis Copeland, Beaver, Okla., April 17.

Cavendish, Richard. 1978. *King Arthur and the Grail: The Arthurian Legends and Their Meaning.* London: Weidenfeld and Nicholson.

Chapman, Berlin B. 1948. "Freedmen and the Oklahoma Lands." *Southwestern Social Science Quarterly* 39:150–54.

Cherokee Outlet Papers. Western History Collections, University of Oklahoma Library.

Copeland, Pat Lewis. 1986. "Rural America: Will It Survive?" *Tulsa Tribune*, December 15: 1A, 4A.

———. 1987. "Oklahoma's Image." *Tulsa Tribune*, April 15: 1B, 4B.

Crockett, Norman L. 1979. *The Black Towns*. Lawrence, Kans.: Regents Press of Kansas.

Cronon, William. 1989. "Where Nature and History Meet." Paper presented at conference, the Future of the Western Past. Yale University, New Haven, Conn., April 26.

———, George Miles, and Jay Gitlin, eds. 1992. *Under an Open Sky: Rethinking America's Western Past*. New York: W.W. Norton.

Cross, George Lynn. 1975. *Blacks in White Colleges: Oklahoma's Landmark Cases*. Norman: University of Oklahoma Press.

———. 1977. *Presidents Can't Punt: The OU Football Tradition*. Norman: University of Oklahoma Press.

———. 1989. Interviewed by Berry Wayne Tramel, Norman, Okla., July 6.

Daily Oklahoman (Oklahoma City). 1908. January 1 and 10.

———. 1961*a*. March 19 and July 7.

———. 1961*b*. November 19.

———. 1963. July 30 and August 30.

———. 1965. April 9.

———. 1990. January 24.

Dale, Edward E., and Morris Wandell. 1950. *History of Oklahoma*. New York: Prentice-Hall.

Debo, Angie. 1940. *And Still the Waters Run*. Princeton: Princeton University Press.

———. 1985. *Prairie City: The Story of an American Community*. Tulsa: Council Oak Books.

DeFrange, Ann. 1989. "Grapes of Wrath Still Remembered after 50 Years." *Sunday Oklahoman*, September 3: A20.

deMause, Lloyd. 1982. *Foundations of Psychohistory*. New York: Creative Roots.

Devereux, George. 1967. *From Anxiety to Method in the Behavioral Sciences*. The Hague, Netherlands: Mouton.

———. 1975. "Ethnic Identity: Its Logical Functions and Its Dysfunctions." In G. De Vos and L. Romanucci-Ross, eds., *Ethnic*

Identity: Cultural Continuities and Change, pp. 42–70. Palo Alto, Calif.: Mayfield Publishing Co.

De Vos, George A. 1966. "Toward a Cross-Cultural Psychology of Caste Behavior." In G. A. De Vos and H. Wagatsuma, eds., *Japan's Invisible Race*, pp. 377ff. Berkeley and Los Angeles: University of California Press.

————. 1978. "The Japanese Adapt to Change." In G. Spindler, ed., *The Making of Psychological Anthropology*, pp. 219–57. Berkeley and Los Angeles: University of California Press.

Diffendaffer, Lee M. 1929. "Administrative Practices and Objectives of Interscholastic Athletics in the High Schools of Oklahoma." M.S. thesis, University of Oklahoma, Norman.

Dreyfoos, Joy G. 1990. *Adolescents at Risk*. New York: Oxford University Press.

Drummond, L. 1986. "The Story of Bond." In H. Verenne, ed., *Symbolizing America*. Lincoln: University of Nebraska Press.

Du Bois, W. E. B. 1903. *The Souls of Black Folk*. New York: Bantam, 1989.

Dundes, Alan. 1984. *Life is Like a Chicken Coop Ladder: A Portrait of German Culture through Folklore*. New York: Columbia University Press.

Durkheim, Emile. 1912. *The Elementary Forms of the Religious Life*. New York: Collier Books, 1961.

Earls, Felton, et al. 1989. "Comprehensive Health Care for High-Risk Adolescents: An Evaluation Study." *American Journal of Public Health* 79:999.

Ebel, Henry. 1989. Personal correspondence with H. F. Stein, June 7.

Edgely, Chuck. 1990. Interviewed by Berry Wayne Tramel, Stillwater, Okla., January 7.

El Reno News. 1896. September 25.

Erikson, Erik H. 1963. "Reflections on the American Identity." In *Childhood and Society*, 2d ed., pp. 285–325. New York: W. W. Norton (1st ed., 1950).

————. 1968. *Identity, Youth, and Crisis*. New York: W. W. Norton.

————. 1974. *Dimensions of a New Identity*. New York: W. W. Norton.

Fletcher, Ben C. 1988. "Occupation, Marriage, and Disease-Specific Mortality Concordance." *Social Science and Medicine* 27:615–22.

Flora, Snowden D. 1953. *Tornadoes of the United States*. Norman: University of Oklahoma Press.

Foreman, Grant. 1932. *Indian Removal: The Emigration of the Five Civilized Tribes of Indians*. Norman: University of Oklahoma Press.

————. 1948. *The Five Civilized Tribes: Brief History and Century of Progress.* Norman: University of Oklahoma Press.

Franklin, Jimmie Lewis. 1980. *The Blacks in Oklahoma.* Norman: University of Oklahoma Press.

Friedman, Lawrence S., Brenda Johnson, and Allan S. Brett. 1990. "Evaluation of Substance-Abusing Adolescents by Primary Care Physicians." *Journal of Adolescent Health Care* 11:227–30.

Fujita, T. Theodore. 1987. *U.S. Tornadoes: Part 1, 70-Year Statistics.* Chicago: Satellite and Mesometeorology Research Project, Department of Geophysical Sciences, University of Chicago.

Galloway, Randy. 1988. "That Boom of Laughter: OU Seeing Red." *Dallas Morning News*, December 24.

Gautt, Prentice. 1989. Telephone Interview in Kansas City, Missouri, by Berry Wayne Tramel, Norman, Okla., October 11.

Geer, Lois, and Michael Resnick. 1988. *The Minnesota Adolescent Health Survey.* Minneapolis, Minn.: School of Public Health and Minnesota Department of Health.

Gibson, Arrell M. 1973. *The Chickasaws.* Norman: University of Oklahoma Press.

————. 1981. *Oklahoma: A History of Five Centuries.* Norman: University of Oklahoma Press (orig. pub. 1965, Harlow Publishing Co.).

Glasscock, Carl B. 1937. *Then Came Oil: The Story of the Last Frontier.* Indianapolis: Bobbs-Merrill.

Goble, Danny. 1980. *Progressive Oklahoma: The Making of a New Kind of State.* Norman: University of Oklahoma Press.

Green, Don. 1990. Interview by Pat Lewis Copeland, Central State University, Edmond, Okla., January.

Green, H. J. 1989. Interviewed by Berry Wayne Tramel, Oklahoma City, Okla., July 17.

Group for the Advancement of Psychiatry, Committee on International Relations, and Howard F. Stein. 1987. *Us and Them: The Psychology of Ethnonationalism.* GAP Report No. 123. New York: Brunner/Mazel.

Hale, Douglas. 1975. "European Immigrants in Oklahoma: A Survey." *The Chronicles of Oklahoma* 53:179–203.

Hall, Roberta L., and Don Dexter. 1988. "Smokeless Tobacco Use and Attitudes toward Smokeless Tobacco among Native Americans and Other Adolescents in the Northwest." *American Journal of Public Health* 78(12):1586–88.

Halliburton, Rudi. 1975. *The Tulsa Race War of 1921.* San Francisco: R&E Research Associates.

———. 1977. *Red over Black*. Westport, Conn.: Greenwood Press.

Handler, Richard, and Jocelyn Linnekin. 1984. "Tradition, Genuine or Spurious." *Journal of American Folklore* 97(385):273–90.

Harlow, R. 1928. *Oklahoma Leaders*. Oklahoma City: Harlow Publishing Co.

Harris, Otis R. 1929. "The Dawes Commission to the Five Civilized Tribes." M.A. thesis, University of Oklahoma, Norman.

Hartsell-Brown, Opal. 1977. *Murray County Oklahoma: In the Heart of Eden*. Wichita Falls, Tex.: Nortex Press.

———, and R. Garrity. 1981. *City of Many Faces*. Oklahoma City: Western Heritage Books.

Hawgood, John A. 1967. *America's Western Frontiers: The Exploration and Settlement of the Trans-Mississippi West*. New York: Knopf.

Henderson, Arn. 1974. *Document for an Anonymous Indian*. Norman, Okla.: Point Riders Press.

———. 1980. "Joseph Foucart, Territorial Architect." In H. Meredith and M. Meredith, eds. *Of the Earth: Oklahoma Architectural History*. Oklahoma City: Oklahoma Historical Society.

Henry, Jules. 1963. *Culture against Man*. New York: Random House.

Hill, Harry. 1889. "Settlement of Oklahoma. The Rush of the 'Boomers' Founding a Territory in the 'Beautiful Land.'" *New York Herald Tribune*, Library of *Tribune* Extras, No. 1, New York, July.

Hill, Robert F., and J. Dennis Fortenberry. 1990. "Adolescence as a Culture-Bound Syndrome." *Social Science and Medicine* 35(1): 73–80.

———, J. Dennis Fortenberry, and Howard F. Stein. 1990. "The Role of Culture in Clinical Medicine." *Southern Medical Journal* 83(9):1071–83.

———, and Howard F. Stein. 1988. "Oklahoma's Image." *High Plains Applied Anthropologist* 8(2):29–43.

Hine, Robert V. 1980. *Community on the American Frontier: Separate but Not Alone*. Norman: University of Oklahoma Press.

Hodge, Frederick W., ed. 1907. *Spanish Explorers in the Southern United States, 1528–1543*. New York: C. Scribner's Sons.

Holmgren, Charles, B. J. Fitzgerald, and Roderick S. Carman. 1983. "Alienation and Alcohol Use by American Indian and Caucasian High School Students." *Journal of Social Psychology* 120:139–40.

Horwitz, Allan V., and Helene R. White. 1987. "Gender Role Orientations and Styles of Pathology among Adolescents." *Journal of Health and Social Behavior* 28:158–70.

Hughes, Thomas. 1857. *Tom Brown's School Days*. Reprint, New York: Penguin Books, 1984.

Indian Chieftain (Vinita, Oklahoma). 1896. September 24.

Jarvis, George K., and Herbert C. Northcott. 1987. "Religion and Differences in Morbidity and Mortality." *Social Science and Medicine* 25:813–24.

Jeltz, Wyatt F. 1948. "The Relations of Negroes and Choctaw and Chickasaw Indians." *Journal of Negro History* 33:31–32.

Jessor, Richard, and Shirley Jessor. 1977. *Problem Behavior and Psychosocial Development: A Longitudinal Study of Youth*. New York: Academic Press.

Johnston, J. H. 1929. "Documentary Evidence of the Relations of Negroes and Indians." *Journal of Negro History* 14:34–35.

Jones, Stephen. 1972. *Atlas of Oklahoma Political Maps, 1907 through 1970*. Enid, Okla.: Stephen Jones.

Jones-Saumty, Debra, et al. 1983. "Psychological Factors of Familial Alcoholism in American Indians and Caucasians." *Journal of Clinical Psychology* 39(5):783–90.

Keith, Harold. 1989. Interviewed by Berry Wayne Tramel, Norman, Okla., November 8.

Kessler, Edwin, and Gilbert F. White. 1983. "Thunderstorms in a Social Context." In E. Kessler, and G. F. White, eds., *Thunderstorms: A Social, Scientific and Technological Documentary*, 2d ed., rev. Norman: University of Oklahoma Press.

King, Duane H., and E. Raymond Evans, eds. 1978. "The Trail of Tears: Primary Documents of the Cherokee Removal." *Journal of Cherokee Studies*, Special Issue, 3: 131–90.

King, Paul. 1988. "Heavy Metal Music and Drug Abuse in Adolescence." *Postgraduate Medicine* 83(5):295–304.

Kingfisher Free Press. 1896. September 24.

Kingfisher Weekly Star and Free Press. 1908. January 2.

Kipling, Rudyard. 1945. "The Ballad of East and West." In *Rudyard Kipling's Verse: Definitive Edition*. pp. 233–36. Garden City, New York: Doubleday, Doran and Co.

Kroeber, Alfred L. 1957. *Style and Civilizations*. Ithaca, N.Y.: Cornell University Press.

La Barre, Weston. 1972. *The Ghost Dance: The Origins of Religion*. New York: Dell (orig. 1970).

———. 1980. *Culture and Context*. Chicago: University of Chicago Press.

Lamar, Howard R. 1989. "The Most American Frontier: The Oklahoma Land Rushes, 1889–1893." *Humanities Interviews* 7(1): 4–9.

Lee, Mark. 1989. Figures from joint study by the *Tulsa World* and Oklahoma State University. *Tulsa World,* September 12:A1.

———. 1990. Interview by Pat Lewis Copeland, April.

Legislative Journal of Oklahoma Territory, 1890. 1890. Guthrie: Oklahoma Territorial Legislature.

Lenkoff, S. E., et al. 1988. "Illness Behavior in the Aged: Implications for Clinicians." *Journal of the American Geriatric Society* 36:622–29.

Lewis, Anne. 1924. "La Harpe's First Expedition in Oklahoma, 1718–1719." *Chronicles of Oklahoma* 2(1924):253–68.

Linton, R. 1943. "Nativistic Movements." *American Anthropologist* 45:230–40.

Littlefield, Daniel. 1977. *Africans and Seminoles: From Emancipation to American Citizenship.* Westport, Conn.: Greenwood Press.

———. 1978. *The Cherokee Freedmen: From Emancipation to American Citizenship.* Westport, Conn.: Greenwood Press.

Luper, Clara. 1979. *Behold the Walls.* Oklahoma City: Jim Wire.

Mangum Weekly Star. 1915. June 24.

Maron, David, et al. 1986. "Correlates of Seatbelt Use by Adolescents: Implications for Health Promotion." *Preventive Medicine* 15:614.

Mathews, J. J. 1951. *Life and Death of an Oilman: The Career of E. W. Marland.* Norman: University of Oklahoma Press.

May, Philip. 1982. "Substance Abuse and American Indians: Prevalence and Susceptibility." *International Journal of the Addictions* 17(7):1185–1209.

McBride, Jack E. 1965. "The History and Development of Faculty Controls of OU Athletics." M.A. thesis, University of Oklahoma, Norman.

McReynolds, Edwin C. 1964. *Oklahoma: A History of the Sooner State.* Norman: University of Oklahoma Press.

Mead, Margaret. 1953. "National Character." In Alfred L. Kroeber, ed., *Anthropology Today: An Encyclopedic Inventory,* pp. 642–67. Chicago: University of Chicago Press.

Miles, George A. 1989. "Directions for Native American History." Paper presented at conference, the Future of the Western Past. Yale University, New Haven, Conn., April 27.

Miller, Robert Worth. 1987. *Oklahoma Populism: A History of the Peoples' Party in the Oklahoma Territory.* Norman: University of Oklahoma Press.

Mills, Roger, Roger Dunham, and Geoffrey Alpert. 1988. Working with High-Risk Youth in Prevention and Early Intervention Programs. *Adolescence* 23:643.

Modell, Arnold H. 1984. *Psychoanalysis in a New Context.* Madison, Conn.: International Universities Press.

Moore, David. 1990. "Drinking: The Construction of Ethnic and Social Process in a Western Australian Youth Subculture." *British Journal of Addiction* 85:1265–78.

Morgan, Anne Hodges, and H. Wayne Morgan. 1982. "Preface." In A. H. Morgan and H. W. Morgan, eds. *Oklahoma: New Views of the Forty-Sixth State*, pp. ix–x. Norman: University of Oklahoma Press.

———, and Rennard Strickland, eds. 1981. *Oklahoma Memories.* Norman: University of Oklahoma Press.

Morgan, Kay. 1989. "OU Fans Feel Real Pain, Experts Say." *Daily Oklahoman*, February 23: A1–2.

Morris, John W., Charles R. Goins, and Edwin C. McReynolds. 1986. *Historical Atlas of Oklahoma*, 3rd ed. Norman: University of Oklahoma Press.

Murray, David M., et al. 1987. "Seventh-Grade Cigarette, Alcohol and Marijuana Use: Distribution in a North Central U.S. Metropolitan Population." *The International Journal of the Addictions* 22(4):357–76.

Muskogee Cimeter. 1905. May 18.

Needle, Richard, et al. 1983. "Reliability and Validity of Adolescent Self-Reported Drug Use in a Family-Based Study: A Methodological Report." *International Journal of the Addictions* 18(7):901–12.

Newcomers to a New Land. 1980. 10 vols. Norman: University of Oklahoma Press.

New York Times. 1921. June 2.

———. 1923. July 1 and August 19.

———. 1947. "'Oklahoma!' Wins Hearts of London," May 1: 35.

———. 1963. July 12.

Norman Transcript (Norman, Okla.). 1890. March 8.

———. 1895. November 9 and December 7.

O'Dea, Thomas F. 1957. *The Mormons.* Chicago: University of Chicago Press.

Oetting, E. R., Fred Beauvais, and Ruth Edwards. 1988. "Alcohol and Indian Youth: Social and Psychological Correlates and Prevention." *Journal of Drug Issues* 18(1):87–101.

O'Hare, William P., et al. 1991. *Population Bulletin: African Americans in the 1990s.* Washington, D.C.: Population Reference Bureau.

Oklahoma. 1907. *The Constitution of Oklahoma.* Oklahoma City: *Daily Oklahoman.*

———. 1908. *Session Laws of 1907–1908.* Guthrie, Okla.: Oklahoma Printing Co.

———. 1910. *Session Laws of 1910.* Guthrie, Okla.: State Capital Co.

Oklahoma Board of Agriculture. 1959. *Forest Trees of Oklahoma.*

Oklahoma City Times. 1960. January 16–17 and August 5.

———. 1971. December 29.

———. 1972. February 1.

Oklahoma Daily (University of Oklahoma). 1990. January 16.

Oklahoma Eagle (Oklahoma City). 1893. December 29.

Oklahoma Guide (Guthrie). 1900. August 31.

———. 1901. October 2.

Patterson, Zella J. 1979. *Langston University: A History.* Norman: University of Oklahoma Press.

Patton, Hal. 1989. Interviewed by Berry Wayne Tramel, Moore, Okla., August 16.

Pease, Edith. 1988. *The John and Ann Dunn Caskey Family.* Fort Morgan, Colo.: Morgan Printers.

Peterson, Jacqueline, and Jennifer S. H. Brown, eds. 1985. *The New Peoples: Being and Becoming Métis in North America.* Lincoln: University of Nebraska Press.

Porter, Pleasant. 1900. "Chief P. Porter's Message Delivered to the Creek Council, October 2, 1900." Muskogee, I.T., 1900. Copy in Yale Western Americana Collection, Beinecke Library.

Prucha, Francis Paul. 1979. "The Board of Indian Commissioners and the Delegates of the Five Tribes." *Chronicles of Oklahoma* 56:247–64.

Purcell Register. 1907. December 26.

Quint, Howard H., Milton Cantor, and Dean Albertson, eds. 1972. *Main Problems in American History.* Belmont, Calif.: Wadsworth Publishing Co., 1988.

Ramsey, Christian N., Troy D. Abell, and Lisa C. Baker. 1986. "The Relationship between Family Functioning, Life Events, Family Structure, and the Outcome of Pregnancy." *Journal of Family Practice* 22:521–27.

Rawick, George. 1972. *The American Slave: A Composite Auto-biography.* Westport, Conn.: Greenwood Press.

————, ed. 1973. *Oklahoma: Ex-Slave Narratives.* Westport, Conn.: Greenwood Press.

Reinhold, Robert. 1986. "Desperation Descends on Oklahoma." *New York Times,* May 11, sect. 3: 1, 8, 9.

Rentzel, Lance. 1972. *When All the Laughter Died in Sorrow.* New York: Saturday Review Press.

Reps, John W. 1965. *The Making of Urban America: A History of City Planning.* Princeton: Princeton University Press.

Rister, Carl C. 1942. *Land Hunger: David L. Payne and the Oklahoma Boomers.* Norman: University of Oklahoma Press.

Rock, Marion T. 1890. *Illustrated History of Oklahoma.* Topeka, Kans.: C. B. Hamilton and Son, Printers.

Rohrer, John H., and Munro S. Edmonson, eds. 1964. *The Eighth Generation Grows Up.* New York: Harper Torchbooks.

Rohrs, Richard C. 1980. *The Germans in Oklahoma.* Norman: University of Oklahoma Press.

————. 1981. *The German-American Experience in Oklahoma.* Stillwater, Okla.: Crossroads Oklahoma Project.

Rooney, John F. 1974. *A Geography of American Sport.* Reading, Mass.: Addison-Wesley.

————. 1986. "The Pigskin Cult and Other Sunbelt Sports." *American Demographics,* September 1986.

————. 1990. Interviewed by Berry Wayne Tramel, Stillwater, Okla., January 16.

Roosens, Eugene E. 1989. *Creating Ethnicity: The Process of Ethnogenesis.* Newberry Park, Calif.: Sage Publications.

Sandweiss, Martha A. 1989. "Views and Reviews: Western Art and Western History." Paper presented at conference, the Future of the Western Past. Yale University, New Haven, Conn., April 28.

Satz, Ronald M. 1985. *Tennessee's Indian Peoples.* Knoxville: University of Tennessee Press.

Savage, William W., Jr. 1980. "What You'd Like the World to Be: The West and the American Mind." *Journal of American Culture* 3(2):302–10.

————. 1989a. Personal communication with Howard F. Stein, 12 June.

————. 1989b. "Remembering Karen Silkwood." *Oklahoma Gazette,* November 8: 1–3.

Scales, James R., and Danny Goble. 1982. *Oklahoma Politics: A History.* Norman: The University of Oklahoma Press.

Scott, Clarissa S. 1974. "Health and Healing Practices among Five Ethnic Groups in Miami, Florida." *Public Health Reports* 83: 524–32.

Singer, Mark. 1985. *Funny Money.* New York: Knopf.

Sisk, John P. 1987. "Cowboy." *The American Scholar,* Summer: 400–406.

Smith, Michael M. 1980. *The Mexicans in Oklahoma.* Norman: University of Oklahoma Press.

———. 1981. *The Mexican-American Experience in Oklahoma.* Stillwater, Okla.: Crossroads Oklahoma Project.

Snow, Loudell. 1974. "Folk Medical Beliefs and Their Implications for the Care of Patients." *Annals of Internal Medicine* 81: 82–96.

Socolofsky, Homer E., and Huber Self. 1988. *Historical Atlas of Kansas,* 2d ed. Norman: University of Oklahoma Press.

Spicer, Edward H. 1971. "Persistent Cultural Systems." *Science* 174 (November 19): 795–800.

Spiegel, John. 1971. *Transactions: The Interplay between Individual, Family, and Society.* New York: Science House.

Stein, Howard F. 1977. "Identity and Transcendence." *University of Chicago School Review* 85(3):349–75.

———. 1980. "Culture and Ethnicity as Group Fantasies: A Psychohistoric Paradigm of Group Identity." *Journal of Psychohistory* 8(1):21–51.

———. 1984. "Sittin' Tight and Bustin' Loose: Contradiction and Conflict in Midwestern Masculinity and the Psychohistory of America." *Journal of Psychohistory* 11:501–12.

———. 1985. *The Psychoanthropology of American Culture.* New York: The Psychohistory Press.

———. 1987a. "Adversary Symbiosis and Complementary Group Dissociation: An Analysis of the U.S./USSR Conflict." In H. F. Stein and M. Apprey, eds., *From Metaphor to Meaning: Papers in Psychoanalytic Anthropology,* pp. 272–301. Monograph Vol. 2. Charlottesville: University Press of Virginia.

———. 1987b. *Developmental Time, Cultural Space: Studies in Psychogeography.* Norman: University of Oklahoma Press.

———. 1987c. "Farmer and Cowboy: The Duality of the Midwestern Male Ethos—A Study in Ethnicity, Regionalism, and National Identity. In H. F. Stein, and M. Apprey, coauthors, *From Metaphor to Meaning: Papers in Psychoanalytic Anthropology,* pp. 178–227. Monograph Vol. 2, Series in Ethnicity,

Medicine, and Psychoanalysis. Charlottesville: University Press of Virginia.

————. 1990. "The Internal and Group Milieux of Ethnicity: Identifying Generic Group Psychodynamic Issues." *Canadian Review of Studies in Nationalism* 17(1–2):1–24.

————, and Robert F. Hill. 1977a. *The Ethnic Imperative: Examining the New White Ethnic Movement.* University Park, Pa.: Pennsylvania State University Press.

————, and ————. 1977b. "The Limits of Ethnicity." *American Scholar* 46(2):181–89.

————, and ————. 1988. "The Dogma of Technology." In L. Bryce Boyer, and Simon Grolnick, eds., *The Psychoanalytic Study of Society* 13: 149–179. Hillsdale, N.J.: The Analytic Press.

————, and William G. Niederland, eds. 1989. *Maps from the Mind: Readings in Psychogeography.* Norman: University of Oklahoma Press.

Steinbeck, John. 1939. *The Grapes of Wrath.* New York: Viking Press, 1958.

Sulphur, Oklahoma. 1913. Reprint, Sulphur: Arbuckle Historical Society, 1984.

Swain, Ruth E. 1978. *Ada Lois: The Sipuel Story.* New York: Harper & Row.

Swanton, John R. 1979. *The Indians of the Southeastern United States.* Washington, D.C.: Smithsonian Institute Press.

Switzer, Barry, and B. Shrake. 1990. *The Bootlegger's Boy: My Story.* New York: William Morrow & Co.

Teall, Kaye M., ed. 1971. *Black History in Oklahoma: A Resource Book.* Oklahoma City: Oklahoma City Public Schools.

Telander, Rick. 1989. *The Hundred Yard Lie: The Corruption of College Football and What We Can Do to Stop It.* New York: Simon & Schuster.

Thompson, Gary L. 1972. The Spatial Convergence of Environmental and Demographic Variables in Poverty Landscapes. In *The Southeastern Geographer* 12(1):14–22.

Thompson, John. 1986. *Closing the Frontier: Radical Response in Oklahoma, 1889–1923.* Norman: University of Oklahoma Press.

The Times (London). 1947. "Oklahoma!" May 1: 6.

Tolson, Arthur L. 1972. *The Black Oklahomans: A History, 1541–1972.* New Orleans: Edwards Printing Co.

Troy, Frosty. 1989. "Raising Oklahoma." *Oklahoma Observer* 21 (17):1.

Tulsa World. 1989. Figures from U.S. Census and 1987 Agriculture Census by the U.S. Census Bureau, September 16:1C.

Turner, Frederick Jackson. 1893. "The Significance of the Frontier in American History." *American Historical Association Annual Report*. Washington, D.C.: The Association, 1894.

Turner, Victor. 1969. *The Ritual Process*. Chicago: Aldine.

United States Statutes at Large. 1889. 25:757, 1004.

U.S. Department of Commerce Bureau of the Census. 1892. *Compendium of the Eleventh Census, 1890: Population*. Part 1. Washington, D.C.: Government Printing Office.

———. 1864. *Eighth Census of the United States, 1860: Population*. Washington, D.C.: Government Printing Office.

———. 1902. *Twelfth Census of the United States, 1900: Population*. Part 1. Washington, D.C.: Government Printing Office.

———. 1920. *Fourteenth Census of the United States Taken in the Year 1920*, vol. 5, *Agriculture, General Report and Analytical Tables*. Washington, D.C.: Government Printing Office, 1922: 34–35.

———. 1987a. *Census of Agriculture*, vol. 1, *Geographic Area Series*. Part 16, *Kansas, State and County Data*. Part 36, *Oklahoma, State and County Data*, table 13. Washington, D.C.: Government Printing Office, 1990: 253–56.

———. 1987b. *Census of Agriculture*, vol. 1, *Geographic Area Series*. Part 51, *United States Summary and State Data*, table 1. Washington, D.C.: Government Printing Office, 1990: 144–50.

———. 1990. *1990 Census, Summary of Population and Housing Characteristics*. Washington, D.C.: Government Printing Office.

U.S. News and World Report. 1991. July 22.

Van Kirk, Sylvia. 1980. *Many Tender Ties: Women in Fur Trade Society, 1670–1870*. Norman: University of Oklahoma Press.

Wallace, Anthony F. C. 1956. "Revitalization Movements." *American Anthropologist* 58:264–81.

Washington, Nathaniel J. 1948. *Historical Development of the Negro in Oklahoma*. Tulsa: Dexter Publishing Co.

Waters, Mary C. 1990. *Ethnic Options: Choosing Identities in America*. Berkeley and Los Angeles: University of California Press.

Weber, Marianne. 1988. *Max Weber: A Biography*. New Brunswick, N.J.: Transaction Books.

Weissman, A. 1990. "Race-ethnicity: A Dubious Scientific Concept." *Public Health Reports* 105(1):102.

Welte, John W., and Grace M. Barnes. 1987. "Alcohol Use among

Adolescent Minority Groups." *Journal of Studies on Alcohol* 48(4):329–36.

Wemhaner, Dave. 1987. Interview by Pat Lewis Copeland, Tulsa Junior College, Tulsa, Okla., February.

Whitehead, Alfred North. 1925. *Science and the Modern World.* New York: Macmillan.

Wiedman, Dennis. 1990. "Big and Little Moon Peyotism as Health Care Delivery Systems." *Medical Anthropology* 12(4):371–88.

Wilkins, Thurman. 1986. *Cherokee Tragedy: The Ridge Family and the Decimation of a People.* Norman: University of Oklahoma Press.

Winfree, L. Thomas, and Curt T. Griffiths. 1983. "Youth at Risk: Marijuana Use among Native American and Caucasian Youths." *International Journal of the Addictions* 18(1):53–70.

Woodward, Grace Steele. 1963. *The Cherokees.* Norman: University of Oklahoma Press.

Worsley, Peter. 1959. "Cargo Cults." *Scientific American* 200: 117–28.

Wright, Muriel H. 1974. "Foreword." In *Oklahoma Place Names,* 2d ed., revised and enlarged, pp. vii–viii. Norman: University of Oklahoma Press.

Zelinsky, Wilbur. 1973. *The Cultural Geography of the United States.* Foundations of Cultural Geography Series. Englewood Cliffs, N.J.: Prentice-Hall.

Zweig, Phillip L. 1985. *Belly Up: The Collapse of the Penn Square Bank.* New York: Fawcett Columbine.

Index

DATE DUE

CGL NOV 2 1 2003			
	UCL/R NOV 1 9 2003		
GAYLORD			PRINTED IN U.S.A.